THE RACIAL RAILROAD

nation – whiteness, class...
(class collaboration)

deportation/border: rail→air
    southwards border – Sabel, Summit of
        the Amricas
    UK Rwanda policy

LNG & Friederly-trains

The Racial Railroad

Julia H. Lee

NEW YORK UNIVERSITY PRESS
New York

NEW YORK UNIVERSITY PRESS
New York
www.nyupress.org

References to Internet websites (URLs) were accurate at the time of writing. Neither the author nor New York University Press is responsible for URLs that may have expired or changed since the manuscript was prepared.

Library of Congress Cataloging-in-Publication Data
Names: Lee, Julia H., author.
Title: The racial railroad / Julia H. Lee.
Description: New York : New York University Press, [2022] | Includes bibliographical references and index.
Identifiers: LCCN 2021037352 | ISBN 9781479812752 (hardback ; alk. paper) | ISBN 9781479812776 (paperback ; alk. paper) | ISBN 9781479812813 (ebook) | ISBN 9781479812783 (ebook other)
Subjects: LCSH: Railroads—Social aspects—United States—History. | Racism—United States—History. | Minorities—United States—History. | United States—Symbolic representation. | United States—Race relations.
Classification: LCC HE1041 .L44 2022 | DDC 385.0973—dc23
LC record available at https://lccn.loc.gov/2021037352

New York University Press books are printed on acid-free paper, and their binding materials are chosen for strength and durability. We strive to use environmentally responsible suppliers and materials to the greatest extent possible in publishing our books.

Manufactured in the United States of America

10 9 8 7 6 5 4 3 2 1

Also available as an ebook

To my parents

Kee Chin Lee and Joung Hwan Lee

CONTENTS

Introduction

What are the places that come to mind when one thinks of the history of race relations in America? Such a question might seem irrelevant; after all, does where an event happened matter as much as what happened or who the actors were? The central premise of *The Racial Railroad* is that the where does matter and that it can have a decisive and even formative impact on how we comprehend the meaning of race. This book examines the intertwining of race and railroad in literary works, films, visual media, and songs from a variety of cultural traditions to highlight the surprisingly central role that the railroad has played—and continues to play—in the formation and perception of racial identity and difference in the United States. For many reasons, several of which this book explores, the train is one of the exemplary spaces through which American cultural works explore questions of racial subjectivity, community, and conflict.

Since the mid-1800s, Americans have with astonishing regularity situated narratives relating to racial identity and interracial relations on the train. How can we explain that? We might chalk up the frequent appearances of the railroad in so many mid-nineteenth century cultural productions to its relative novelty as a technology at that time. The train's omnipresence in early twentieth-century American works is no doubt a function of its axiomatic role in American life. The numbers from this time period, often called the golden age of rail travel, are staggering. In 1920, which was a record year for US rail ridership, 1.27 billion passengers rode over 474 million miles of track.[1] The advent of the automobile caused a precipitous decline in these numbers starting in the mid-twentieth century. Given this downturn in popularity and ridership, one would expect the train to gradually disappear from American cultural narratives starting in the 1950s or 1960s. After all, how many people these days ride a train as a regular—or even irregular—part of their lives?[2] And yet, despite the fact that most people have nothing to do with the railroad in their everyday routines, trains continually pop up in our cultural landscape. They are everywhere: in literary fiction, poetry, films, television, advertisements, paintings, and photographs. Popular film and television series continually set stories of havoc, romance, and murder on the train. Children still play with train sets, and parents still run a railroad track under the tree every Christmas. Library and bookstore shelves groan under the weight of histories about the train, and museums and galleries are filled with photographs, landscapes, and art depicting the railroad. The train's continuing popularity in American culture—especially in the last fifty years—cannot then be ascribed to its ubiquity in modern life. Its simultaneous absence in our daily lives and omnipresence representationally suggests that it serves a purpose that goes beyond transportation. Its importance lies not in its convenience or its physical pervasiveness but in its status as an ideal and its ability to tell a story. It is this aspect of the railroad that this book explores.

The Racial Railroad argues that the train has been a persistent and crucial site for racial meaning-making in American culture for the past 150 years. Unlike other sites that are associated with race or racial conflict (such as ethnic urban enclaves, the back of a bus, the National Mall in Washington, DC, or a raft on the Mississippi River), the railroad operates across multiple scales of experience and meaning, as both an invocation of and a depository for all kinds of social, historical, and political narratives, great and small. Its ability to signify across registers is evident in the words that we use to describe it: *train* implies a mobile space in and through which bodies move and interact, whereas *railroad* names a system for organizing spaces and bodies. My discussion of the railroad will reflect the different registers across which the train operates. As a symbol of Manifest Destiny and of the nation's unity, ingenuity, and vastness, the train exemplifies US exceptionalism. As an instrument for dislocating Native populations and "opening" the West, the Pacific, and Asia to Anglo-American settlement or trade, the train carries (and carries out) the nation's settler and imperial ambitions. As a technological feat that standardized time, produced wealth, and enabled the rapid movement of goods, capital, and people, it serves as a proxy for private industry and the state. As a place that is an overlooked part of our built environment, it typifies the quotidian and the material. As a space in which people from all walks of life must interact with each other in confined quarters, it is intersectional and dynamic. Because it simultaneously blurs and solidifies the oppositions that are foundational to our understanding of identity, community, and modernity, the train can reveal how racial interactions, formations, and conflicts are constituted in significant and contradictory ways by the spaces in which they occur.

Trains and the railroad have played a central role in controlling the movement and settlement of communities of color throughout US history. Just as powerfully, the railroad has also been used to justify and reinforce racist hierarchies and narratives of exclusion and extermination. Native Americans were displaced by the railroad, and the technological modernity that the train ostensibly embodied served as a justification for that removal. The train was also one of the instruments for American empire, built to facilitate trade with Asia at the expense of Native Americans and Californios with the goal of extending US influence and domination across the continent and then the Pacific. During the mid- to late nineteenth century, Chinese and Mexicans workers were recruited to lay down track in the American Southwest and West, and trains have long been a part of the implementation of imprisonment and deportation in this country. The train car was the setting for *Plessy v. Ferguson*, the US Supreme Court case that made segregation the law of the land in 1896, and it was on the very cars that they could not ride as passengers that thousands of African American men and women worked as porters, maids, and waitstaff. Trains, often imagined as the symbol of American freedom and equality, were segregated not just racially but also by gender (ladies' cars) and by class (from third class, sometimes called "emigrant" cars if the train was traveling west, to first class, with Pullman cars being considered the height of luxury train travel). As a technological achievement, the train was a sign of the nation's exceptionalism and its modernity, traits that could never be applied to or claimed by other, "inferior" races. The intersection of race, class, and gender on the train car manifests itself in contradictory ways: an African American woman traveling as a maid with her white employer, for example, would be able to board a first-class, whites-only car as a passenger, yet the same woman might be denied entry into the same car if she were traveling alone, even if she had bought and paid for a first-class ticket.[3]

Clearly, then, the train has been an instrument of disenfranchisement and violence, used to extract labor or to control, marginalize, and terrorize racialized individuals and communities. Nevertheless, the train is also deeply embedded in the psyches, histories, and cultures of racialized communities. Slaves in the antebellum South associated the railroad with physical freedom (as evidenced by the use of terms like the Underground Railroad). A generation later, it was the railroad that took African American families and laborers north to Chicago and New York during the Great Migration of the early twentieth century. The expansion of railroad lines in the American South in the years following the Civil War created the social conditions that enabled the emergence of various forms of musical and cultural expression. Black musicians and composers made the train a central trope in the blues. Asian North American writers and historians have looked to the labor of Chinese workers on the Transcontinental Railroad to imagine their place within nations that have viewed them as intrinsically foreign. In contemporary and popular culture, African American, Asian American, Native American, and Latinx artists turn to the railroad to launch their critiques of nation, capital, and globalization. Writers and artists of color have reappropriated the railroad's meaning and set their stories on the train as a way of exploring relationships between subject, state, and space. The train, in other words, is a particularly compelling and congenial space for dramatizing stories about race because it holds many layers of meaning, the interpretation of which depends on who is looking at it, who is building it, who is riding it, or who is working on it. It is precisely because the train operates across so many diverse discourses—historical, material, cultural, symbolic, spatial—that it occupies such a central place in American cultural imaginings about race and identity. Its portability as a technology and as a symbol across geographies, communities, and histories has made and will continue to make the railroad an effective emblem of political resistance. A multitude of texts from a variety of ethnic cultural traditions choose the train to spatialize their narratives of racial formation; they use the railroad to legitimate or challenge their stories of race or racism. This project calls attention to the train as a unique space and technology in and through which subjects form, perceive, and narrate their racial identity and difference.

As should be clear by now, this book is not a history of the railroad in a traditional sense. *The Racial Railroad* is not interested in cataloging the types or amount of goods that were transported on railroad cars either in the past or currently. It does not detail the advances in railroad technology or locomotion or the dips and rises in passenger travel. It does not provide analysis of shifts in carrier law, nor does it comb through the articles of incorporation for railroad companies. Although I am interested in how the experiences of railroad laborers—the Chinese who constructed the Transcontinental, the African American men who served as porters—are represented, I am indifferent to the lives of the executives, speculators, engineers, politicians, and military officials who had a hand in the development of the railroad. To the railroad historian, this book's approach to the subject of the train may seem highly idiosyncratic or obscure. All these things I acknowledge because I believe that the train's significance encompasses more than technical specifications measured by tonnage or distance traversed or passenger miles. Those aspects of the train are the least helpful in figuring out the train's cultural appeal. Many historians of the railroad in the United States participate in what Manu Karuka accurately calls the "gaseous political oratory" of national exceptionalism that echoes the rhetoric and practices of the men who built the train in the first place.[4] While there are several exceptions to this discourse, history's breathless cataloging of the railroad as an incredible technological accomplishment or a solution to the nation's problems generally relies and builds on the ideologies that made it an ideal vehicle for genocide, exploitation, and ecological ruin in the first place.

Finally, this book is not an archival project in the traditional sense. In *In the Wake* (2016), Christina Sharpe explores the problem of studying slavery and/in the archive. The archive that is available to Black studies scholars is one that presupposes and depends on the annihilation of Black experience. The archive that Sharpe wishes to enter is one that tracks how African Americans "resist, rupture, and disrupt . . . aesthetically and materially" the "immanence and imminence" of Black death.[5] This is not the kind of archive that one can find at a research library, a government depository, or in the special collections of a museum or university. Railroad archives are filled with the absences of racialized bodies, whether those folks were riders, passengers, porters, or builders, erasures that can be noted but cannot be represented. Rather than plumbing the depths of such repositories, hoping to find some piece of evidence that will then explain the experiences of those who have been excised from history; rather than affirming the legitimacy of these archives by turning to them in the hope that if we only look deep enough or hard enough, we will find whatever it is we seek, I turn to the creative workings of artists who are no less invested in these questions and whose imaginings on the subject may tell us something just as vital, namely, the signification of the railroad in their communities.

The Racial Railroad looks at the train as a technology, a symbol, a space, and a memory, all of which produced this country's sense of itself as a nation, enabled it to provide an alibi for its imperial and settler power, and divided those within its borders into citizen, foreigner, and other. The underlying assumption of *The Racial Railroad* is that the railroad reflected and contributed to a political system that depended on the exploitation of the environment and the exclusion of various communities while at the same time acting as a powerful expression and representation of resistance and disruption. The contradiction that I allude to at this book's start, which can be summarized by the statement that the railroad is everywhere even though it is nowhere, is the launching point for an examination of the role of the train in the imagination of the American mind.[6]

The thread that links these chapters and my readings together, then, is the train's role throughout the years as a site of and for racial meaning-making in the nation. In other words, rather than thinking of the train as simply a screen against which stories about race are played out, these texts illustrate how the train forms the stories we tell about race in the first place. How the works discussed in this book conceive of or represent race depends in large measure on how they conceive of or represent the train—as a technology for establishing state domination, as a reclamation project for memorializing certain narratives or counternarratives, as a symbol of both freedom and tyranny, as a carrier/mover of people, goods, and capital, as a workplace for those who built it and labored on it, as a space that passengers occupied and moved through, as an everyday experience that was shared by millions. As much as we tell stories about the railroad, the railroad tells us stories about race.

In keeping with the omnifarious role of the railroad in narratives of race, the works under consideration in *The Racial Railroad* draw from several cultural traditions, traverse a relatively large span of American history (from the nineteenth century to the present day), and encompass a number of forms and genres: the textual, the musical/performative, the visual, and the cinematic. In the following chapters, I examine long-form literary fiction such as James Weldon Johnson's *The Autobiography of an Ex-Colored Man* (1912), Maxine Hong Kingston's *China Men* (1980), and Colson Whitehead's *The Underground Railroad* (2016); short stories by Willa Cather, Frank Chin, and Ralph Ellison; and essays by W. E. B. Du Bois and John Edgar Wideman. I contrast the role of the train in early twentieth century African American literary texts with early twentieth-century blues and folk music. I contextualize the use of the train in visual works such as John Gast's *American Progress* (1872), Frances Flora Bond Palmer's *Across the Continent: Westward the Course of Empire Takes Its Way* (1868), and Jerry Bruckheimer Films production logo (2013); in popular advertisements for the Northern Pacific Railroad's North Coast Limited route and the Atchison, Topeka and Santa Fe Railroad's flagship passenger train the Chief; and in the graffiti art of Native American artist Jaque Fragua. The train is an enduringly popular trope in the plots of countless films, popping up in a wide variety of video and film genres, from Hollywood blockbusters such as Gore Verbinski's *The Lone Ranger* (2013) to music videos like "Immigrants (We Get the Job Done)" (from the phenomenally popular *Hamilton Mixtape)* to contemporary arthouse films like Bong Joon-ho's *Snowpiercer* (2013). By putting such a wide range of works that are not bound by historical period, genre, or movement in conversation, this book provides a sense of the various ways that the train has been deployed in American culture to explore racial conflict and formation. My own disciplinary roots are in English, and in the initial stages of plotting out this book, my focus was almost exclusively on literary texts by American authors. However, it quickly became impossible for me to ignore how pervasive the railroad was in every aspect of American culture and that the claim I was envisioning for the book was not necessarily bound by medium or time period, a fact that is reflected in the organization of the book, which takes a thematic (rather than chronological or medium-specific) approach.

Earlier, I briefly noted that the train lends itself to stories about race because of its heterogeneous signification across multiple discursive formations. In the following pages, I would like to explore in more detail why this is the case. Why is it that when artists, photographers, writers, directors, and other cultural producers depict the railroad, they so often make the link between the train and race? My argument for why the railroad emerged as a site for racial exploration and why it continues to fulfill this function despite its gradual obsolescence in the lives of most Americans, rests on the notion that both race and the railroad operate under similar systems of conceptual possibilities that govern their logic and signification. In other words, many of the discursive formations that manage the way we think about race are used in thinking about the railroad as well. In the following pages, I will briefly discuss four key aspects of the railroad and railroad discourse that are also central to the formation of race and racial identity: the train's particular narratological qualities, the railroad's role in myths of American exceptionalism, the railroad as a sign of Western modernity, and the train car as an apportionment of space that requires a compulsory sociability.

Trains as Narratives

My first proposition is that there is an affinity between narrative and the train. Here, I reiterate the claim I made above: the train is never merely the setting for stories, nor does it merely act as an inspiration for storytelling. Instead, the train itself is constitutive of the story. The qualities that we associate with narrative—that it has a start, a middle, and an end; that it is enjoyable; that it "give[s] experience a form and a meaning"—are also characteristic of the train.[7] The seeming structural or operational kinship between stories and trains makes clear not only why so many cultural narratives of the past, present, and speculative future include trains and railroads, it also makes clear why race—which is, after all, another type of national storytelling—is so often present in narratives on and around the railroad. There is something about riding, building, and working on the railroad that is intrinsically narratological; these experiences of being on or around the train reinforce, undermine, and completely alter the story of race and national identity that the nation and its surrogates are attempting to tell.

Consider, for example, the curiously invisible presence of the train in Jhumpa Lahiri's novel *The Namesake* (2003). The novel is in many ways a classic immigrant narrative, focusing in its first third on the experiences of Ashoke and Ashima Ganguli as they migrate from India to the United States in the late 1960s before chronicling the bildungsroman of their son Gogol as he attempts to understand what role if any his parents' ethnic and cultural identity have on his own life as a well-educated, professional young man. Despite the fact that the novel is set squarely within an era of extensive jet travel—indeed, all the main characters travel back and forth between India and the United States with relative ease—it is not the airplane that drives the narrative, it is the train. Indeed, the memory of a horrific train accident in India opens the novel. The memory belongs to Ashoke, who has just arrived in the United States and is waiting in a Boston hospital for his wife, Ashima, to give birth to their first child, who will eventually be named Gogol. As Ashoke paces in the maternity ward, he remembers the train derailment that nearly killed him seven years previously on October 20, 1961.[8] This extensive narrative flashback—placed just a few pages into the novel—describes Ashoke's experience riding on the Ranchi express from Calcutta to Jamshedpur to visit his retired grandfather. Ashoke spends most of the train ride prior to the derailment reading his favorite book, a collection of short stories by the Ukrainian-Russian writer Nikolai Gogol, the namesake of the novel's second-generation protagonist. The novel describes the intensity with which Ashoke identifies with Gogol's characters, particularly Akaky Akakyevich, the antihero of "The Overcoat," Gogol's most famous story and Ashoke's favorite. Ashoke's response to the story is in sync with his body's physical response to the train. As he reads, Ashoke feels the

> steam engine puff[ing] reassuringly, powerfully. Deep in his chest he felt the rough jostle of the wheels. Sparks from the smokestack passed by his window. A fine layer of sticky soot dotted one side of his face, his eyelid, his arm, his neck; his grandmother would insist that he scrub himself with a cake of Margo soap as soon as he arrived. Immersed in the sartorial plight of Akaky Akakyevich, lost in the wide, snow-white, windy avenues of St. Petersburg, *unaware that one day he was to dwell in a snowy place himself*, Ashoke was still reading at two-thirty in the morning, one of the few passengers on the train who was awake, when the locomotive engine and seven bogies derailed from the broad-gauge line [emphasis added].[9]

The book ends up saving Ashoke's life; as rescuers overturn the flaming rubble looking for survivors, one of them catches a glimpse of a page from "The Overcoat" falling from Ashoke's clenched hand. The derailment causes Ashoke lifelong trauma, what we might today call post-traumatic stress disorder. For the rest of his life, he has nightmares about waiting to be rescued, experiences anxiety attacks if he finds himself in confined spaces, and habitually reaches for his rib cage (a gesture that his children will witness repeatedly but not understand) to "make sure they are solid."[10]

Although this train ride and the derailment are clearly important plot developments in the novel, my claim about the narratological qualities of the train rests on more than plot. Just as his mind is one with the life of Akaky Akakyevich, so too is Ashoke's body at one with the powerful humming of the locomotive engine. Ashoke's bodily reaction to riding the train recalls Nicholas Daly's argument regarding the importance of the train to nineteenth-century subjects. Daly claims that as train travel became more widespread, subjects looked for ways to "register and accommodate the newly speeded up world of the railway age."[11] The "novel of sensation" emerged in response to that demand; reading it was "thought to conjure up a corporeal rather than a cerebral response in the reader."[12] The purpose of these novels was to ease subjects into the disorienting world of speed. Based on Daly's argument, one might argue that the train ushers Ashoke into a newly modern world of speed, anxiety, and disorientation. The only problem with this is that Daly's argument specifically pertains to the Victorian era and the literature of the late nineteenth century, while Lahiri's *The Namesake* was published in the early years of the twenty-first century. Presumably, Ashoke and the other characters, comfortable as they are with modern life and travel, are accustomed to life at speed. So what function is the railroad—associated as it is with anxiety, bodily trauma, and migration—serving in this novel set in the jet age?

It is certainly true that the depth of Ashoke's identification with Akaky Akakyevich's story emblematizes literature's ability to "transport" the reader to different and foreign worlds. The narrative is also an on-the-nose illustration of another humanistic bromide—that literature can save lives. Indeed, Ashoke comes to subscribe to this axiom; even though he is totally irreligious, he takes it as gospel that Nikolai Gogol—and in particular, Gogol's "The Overcoat"—saved his life and brought about a kind of rebirth, one that encouraged him to leave India for the

United States. What is noteworthy about this passage for my purposes is that the novel presents this familiar defense of the humanistic value of storytelling as inseparable from the experience of riding the train itself. Ashoke's physical experience of riding the train—his bodily reactions and the eventual trauma—cannot be disentangled from the story he is reading and that he eventually passes on to his son. This story of the train ride that changed everything serves as the keystone of the family's entire immigrant experience. The novel's awkward use of a future-in-the-past tense in the passage quoted above (Ashoke is "unaware that one day he was to dwell in a snowy place himself") marks Ashoke's past and ongoing relationship to narrative, a narrative that originates on the train. The narratological qualities of Ashoke's life as an immigrant is inseparable from his experience on the train. In other words, Ashoke's train ride cannot be disentangled from the story he is reading, and this in turn cannot be disentangled from his own life's story. Even Ashoke's premature death of a massive heart attack in the middle of the novel does not end the association between the train and the family's immigrant story, for now it is his son Gogol's turn to consider the story of his father's train ride. Gogol himself rides the train frequently between Boston and New York. In scenes that are meant to evoke his father's experience, Gogol takes the train to visit his parents or various girlfriends, and he frequently falls asleep on these rides (covered by his overcoat). It is on the train that he discovers his wife's infidelity. The train accident wasn't just an incident that occurred prior to Ashoke's arrival in the United States, it is constitutive of Ashoke's migration story in the first place.

In making this claim about the train as a kind of narrative, I rely and build upon the work of critics like Michel de Certeau, who in *The Practice of Everyday Life* (1980) emphasizes the train's ability to elicit stories. The link between narrative and movement through space is best exemplified by the *metaphorai*, the vehicles for mass transit in modern-day Athens. De Certeau writes, "To go to work or come home, one takes a 'metaphor,' a bus or a train. Stories could also take this noble name: everyday they traverse and organize places; they select and link them together; they make sentences and itineraries out of them. They are spatial trajectories."[13] The English word *metaphor*, which shares the same root as *metaphorai*, is derived from the ancient Greek for "transfer" or "carrying over" (from *meta*, meaning "over, across" and *pherein*, meaning "to carry, bear"). De Certeau's point in making these connections is to highlight how stories and movement are mutually defined by each other. To have a story to tell, something must be carried over or across a span of space or time; to move from one place to another, one must be able to recount a story about it. This explains de Certeau's fascination with trains as a kind of narrative and as a spatial trajectory because it is in the ordinary act of riding the train that a passenger can reappropriate the rituals that institutions seek to impose. Even amid the well-regulated incarceration that is train travel, in which passengers are "pigeonholed, numbered, and regulated," in which control and food are "move[d] from pigeonhole to pigeonhole," de Certeau recognizes that there are spaces of escape: "Only the restrooms offer an escape from the closed system. They are a lovers' phantasm, a way out for the ill, an escapade for children ('Wee-wee!')—a little space of irrationality."[14] "Stories thus carry out a labor that constantly transforms places into spaces or spaces into places," and it is this transformational quality that may explain why the train is so associated with stories of racial identity and interracial relations: the train accentuates the multi-directionality and fluidity of these types of narratives. If "every story is a spatial practice," as de Certeau claims, then the train is the space where stories about race are practiced.[15]

The shared structure of the train and narrative can perhaps best be seen in an early genre of cinema known as the phantom ride. Phantom rides are single tracking shots "that show the landscape through which the train travels, without showing the train—hence [its] name."[16] A camera was strapped to the cowcatcher and positioned at such an angle that the viewer could see the tracks in front as well as the landscape ahead. Phantom rides as a stand-alone genre of film were hugely popular with audiences through the 1890s and into the early years of the twentieth century, prior to the advent of what we would recognize now as narrative cinema. I will be discussing this genre of filmmaking again later in the book, but for now, I want to highlight how the phantom ride reveals the link between the train and storytelling. In asking the viewer to identify with the train as if it were a narrator, the phantom ride reveals a correspondence between the train and the narrative itself. At a time when film's ability to suggest movement to stationary viewers was still an awe-inspiring novelty, the phantom ride provided a narrative structure to the images that flashed before the spectators' eyes. Nanna Verhoeff's description of the phantom ride evocatively hints at this very identification: "What more significant and beautiful image of linear perspective as the visual imagining of endpoint and endlessness, than the two parallel lines of a receding railway track that approach each other but never touch?"[17] Verhoeff's description of the phantom ride suggests what makes the train so appealing. It contains multiple oppositions that are fundamental to mythographies of the nation, particular in relation to the West. It has an endpoint and is at the same time endless, and it follows a track that dictates a passenger's path but that cannot be seen past the horizon. Verhoeff's characterization of the train is equally applicable to the act of narrative itself. The promise of storytelling, of course, is manifold. Aristotle teaches us that humans enjoy mimesis for two reasons: because it is soothingly orderly and rhythmic and because it is pedagogical—stories teach us something. The train tracks that run ahead of us but that we know never resolve into a single line are not unlike narratives, which fundamentally, in the words of J. Hillis Miller, "do not satisfy." For Miller, every story, no matter how epic, elaborate, or brief,

> leaves some uncertainty or contains some loose end unraveling its effect, according to an implacable law that is not so much psychological or social as linguistic. This necessary incompletion means that no story fulfills perfectly, once and for all, its functions of ordering and confirming.[18]

Miller's description of narrative's inability to resolve itself and our attempts to impose closure on signs that slide in signification has a resonance when we think about it in relation to the railroad, which is often thought of as the very "image of determinism."[19] What the phantom ride reveals is the exact opposite: that the "image of determinism" is a fantasy. Our determination to see the train as following a set path reflects a desire for an "ordering" that is otherwise impossible. This is as true today as it was in the early twentieth century, for despite the relative brevity of its heyday, the genre of the phantom ride lives on in many ways in our present moment. Anyone who has ridden a simulator attraction at an amusement park or watched videos of "free-flying wing-suiters, mountain climbers, bike riders, and skateboarders" with "tiny

GoPro cameras [strapped] to helmets, feet, and handlebars" is seeking the same kind of visual and bodily thrill as his or her early twentieth-century counterpart.[20] Verhoeff's account of the railroad emphasizes an analogous tension. Visually, the track represents a predetermined path forward, but the passenger's position on the train, which precludes him or her from seeing the entirety of the train's preset journey, suggests the possibility that arrival or closure will never be achieved, even though it seems enticingly on the verge of doing so. The railroad is a story that promises but cannot achieve any kind of closure.

Railroad Exceptionalism

Although the concept of American exceptionalism can be traced as far back as the seventeenth century with John Winthrop's sermon "A Model of Christian Charity" (1630) and its famous invocation of the "city on the hill," exceptionalist rhetoric plays a huge part in railroad discourse, from the magnates and industrialists who enriched themselves building it, to the politicians who subsidized it, to the scholars and historians who have glorified it. American exceptionalism trumpets the nation's unique and exemplary position vis-à-vis other nations, particularly those of the Old World as represented by Europe.[21] Along with this insistence that the US differs politically and morally from the old European powers, American exceptionalism insists that the US is uniquely—even divinely—positioned to lead the world and that its political power is such that it will never decline in influence as other great powers have in the past.[22] Manifest Destiny, which I will discuss in my next chapter, is a form of American exceptionalism, but one that has a settler colonial focus on the acquisition and incorporation of land at the expense of Indigenous inhabitants. Disentangling these two nationalist discourses can be difficult, but for now I just want to emphasize that both are often presented as race-neutral projects, even as they have been used to justify the extermination of Native peoples and the exclusion of racialized individuals.

American exceptionalism has no greater enthusiast in American literature than Walt Whitman. Unlike his fellow writers and thinkers of the nineteenth-century who viewed the railroad with trepidation if not downright hostility (Henry David Thoreau famously lamented in

Walden that "we do not ride on the railroad, it rides upon us"), Whitman enthusiastically believed in the potential of the train to express and convey American individuality and freedom.[23] In his poem "A Passage to India" (originally published in 1870), Whitman called the "mighty railroad" one of the "modern wonders" of the "New World." His effusive description of the experience of riding across the continent on the railroad is worth quoting extensively here:

> I cross the Laramie plains, I note the rocks in grotesque shapes, the
> buttes,
> I see the plentiful larkspur and wild onions, the barren, colorless,
> sage-deserts,
> I see in glimpses afar or towering immediately above me the great
> mountains,
> I see the Wind river and the Wahsatch mountains,
> I see the Monument mountain and the Eagle's Nest, I pass the
> Promontory, I ascend the Nevadas,
> I scan the noble Elk mountain and wind around its base,
> I see the Humboldt range, I thread the valley and cross the river,
> I see the clear waters of lake Tahoe, I see forests of majestic pines,
> Or crossing the great desert, the alkaline plains, I behold enchanting
> mirages of waters and
> meadows,
> Marking through these and after all, in duplicate slender lines,
> Bridging the three or four thousand miles of land travel,
> Tying the Eastern to the Western sea,
> The road between Europe and Asia.[24]

Characteristic of Whitman's poetry, the poetic "I" inhabits the bodies of others; it declares at the start of "Song of Myself" that "what I assume you shall assume." Kevin Wilwhite calls Whitman's persona to be a kind of "poetic totalitarianism, an effort by the poet to colonize the reader in an unceasing struggle for domination."[25] As this stanza from "Passage to India" indicates, the ever-expanding nature of Whitman's poetic self is not limited to the human body or perspective; in this case, it encompasses the train itself. At the stanza's start, there is a distinction drawn between speaker and the train, but by about halfway through the stanza

("I pass the Promontory, I ascend the Nevadas, / I scan the noble Elk and wind around its base . . . I thread the valley and cross the river"), that line has blurred until the two become indistinguishable. The poetic "I" and the locomotive are a united force; the man is the embodiment of the engine, and the train becomes an explorer and adventurer. The train and the poet traverse a continent that has been emptied of its Native populations, rendered majestic precisely because it has been conquered by the twinned power of the word and the locomotive. And as suggested by its title, "Passage to India" does not end at land's end; instead, the train "ties" East to West, serving as the "road between Europe and Asia." According to Henry Nash Smith, this was a natural stage in the "glorious rise of America" as the nation "ushers in a millennium of some sort that is vaguely associated with the contact between America and Asia across the Pacific."[26] The train runs parallel with the "course of empire" and the "cult of Manifest Destiny," further enabling and cementing these ideologies.[27]

Whitman's blending of his poetic persona with the train transforms the latter into the ultimate expression of an American ideal of discovery and achievement; it also transforms the train into the ultimate expression and instrument of the American imperium. The railroad in Whitman's telling is not just traversing the United States, it is—as much as the valleys, the mountains, and the plains that make up the nation's geography—a manifestation of the nation's unprecedented ascendance. If American exceptionalism is defined as the idea that "American values, politics, and history are unique and worthy of universal admiration," and that the United States is "destined and entitled to play a distinct and positive role on the world stage"; if the United States is an "empire of liberty," "a shining city on a hill," "the last best hope of Earth," "the indispensable nation"[28]—then in Whitman's telling, the railroad is the foundation for and expression of that logic. If the rhetoric of American exceptionalism is one that pervades American politics, then so too does the rhetoric of what I would call railroad exceptionalism—if America represents the apotheosis of political possibility, then the railroad is its most visible expression.

Railroad exceptionalism often reaches its zenith in narratives surrounding the construction of the First Transcontinental Railroad. Manu Karuka notes that the dominant historical take on the railroad relishes the drama of "railroad corporations racing to cover as much ground as possible before meeting each other."[29] This particular narrative, which he calls the "Race to Promontory Point," and others like it fill histories and archives of the railroad, relying on a highly "linear trajectory" that portrays "capitalism as a coherent and discrete system" and the US nation-state and US capitalism as "fixed end-points whose preeminence is both obvious and permanent. Indigenous nations and Chinese workers appear, if at all, as contextual backdrop, colorful diversions from the main story."[30] Characterizing the construction of the Transcontinental Railroad as a self-contained "race" reduces it to an easily digestible and thrilling narrative of worthy opponents outdoing each other to achieve a feat with no historical precedent. The exceptionalism of this type of race narrative depends on seeing the railroad in linear terms (Who can get from point A to point B in the shortest amount of time?), a move that, as Karuka points out, obscures the exploitation of labor and resources.

The exceptionalist rhetoric used by Whitman and historians to talk about the railroad was by no means unusual; as Richard White wryly notes, the "kind of hyperbole recently lavished on the Internet was once the mark of railroad talk."[31] In the case of Whitman's "To the Locomotive in Winter" (1876), that ecstatic possibility is represented in highly sexualized terms. The poem exhorts the "gyrating," "metrical," "swelling," "protruding," "rumbling," and "rousing" locomotive to "roll through" the land and "launch o'er the prairies wide," "unpent, and glad, and strong."[32] The transformation of the train into a phallus that is set loose on a passive and fertile land domesticates the relationship between rail and soil and imposes a hierarchy that renders in heteronormative terms the train's destructive invasion into the continent's interior. Whitman's imagining of the train as a phallus that would ecstatically link man, machine, and nature might seem excessive, but that impulse to imagine the train as a part of the anatomy of the nation's body, as intrinsic and fundamental to the functioning of its economy, culture, and social life, is one in which many artists, politicians, and other public figures have engaged. This notion that the health of the nation is dependent on the health of the railroad network was by no means limited to Whitman. For a much less sexy example, look no further than Woodrow Wilson, who like Whitman constructs the train in biological terms: "To the men who run the railways of the country, whether they be managers or operative employees, let me say that the railways are the arteries of the nation's life, and that upon them rests the immense responsibility of seeing to it that these arteries suffer no obstruction of any kind, no inefficiency or slackened power."[33] As James Ward notes, images of health, unity, and kinship were often used in describing the railroad networks and their impact on the nation—what was the good for the railroad, it was often thought, was good for the country.[34]

Thomas Wolfe echoed these comments when he wrote that "in America, the train gives one a feeling of wild and lonely joy, a sense of the savage, unfenced, and illimitable wilderness of the country through which the train is rushing, a wordless and unutterable hope as one thinks of the enchanted city toward which he is speeding, the unknown and fabulous promise of the life he is to find there."[35] This quotation captures the fundamental contradiction at the heart of railroad exceptionalism, which is the idea that railroads singularly enable one to appreciate the unique wildness of the American landscape. It relies on the notion that the train provides the lens through which the passenger-citizen can truly see the land that surrounds him as wilderness. Wilderness is only appreciable if it is crossed on a conveyance whose existence depends on the grading of the land and the destruction of native habitat, as well as the shattering of the rhythms and sounds of non-human life. It is only by riding the train that one can have an authentic relationship with that wilderness. I discuss these ideas in greater detail in chapter 1, but for now, I will just note that the notion that wilderness is illimitable is the trick at the heart of imperial logic, for wilderness can only exist in distinction from civilization, and that dyad imposes a limit on the wilderness's supposed illimitability. Heightening this distinction between nature and civilization is the fact that this appreciation of the "savage, unfenced, and illimitable wilderness" occurs as the passenger is on his way to "the enchanted city" that is the train's ultimate destination.

While much of the writing on the railroad tends to uncritically repeat this notion of the railroad as the ultimate symbol of the nation's attitude toward its own status as modern and emerging global power, there are historians and scholars of the railroad who resist this easy narrative. I consider my own work to be built from the work of several scholars who highlight or interrogate the role of the train in disciplining bodies, enabling the accrual of wealth by a small percentage of elite, and cor-

Du
Bois

poratization. Richard White's *Railroaded: The Transcontinentals and the Making of Modern America* (2011) is one example of a history about the railroad that goes against the grain and cuts through exceptionalist discourse. White argues that the Transcontinental Railroad was a failure on every level—economically, socially, and politically. White's point is that the rhetoric of modernity, individual freedom, and exceptionalism that surrounded the railroad masked its complete reliance on governmental financing and bailouts, a process that enriched a few while saddling the nation with the cost of the railroad's construction and then upkeep. The railroad decimated the Native peoples who had lived on the land that it traversed and brought financial ruin to the arrivistes who moved to the "frontier" and "produced crops, cattle, and minerals beyond what markets could profitably absorb."[36] The railroad also wrought environmental disaster as workers blasted mountains and clear-cut forests to lay down track, while its reach across the country enabled the extraction and production of materials in a way that "yielded great environmental and social harm."[37] White's point that the Transcontinental Railroad was a multiscalar boondoggle that did irreparable social, political, and environmental harm exposes the often ignored costs of the railroad, overlooked in the rhetoric of equality and freedom.

The rhetoric and imagery employed in the name of American exceptionalism make "Passage to India" and other works like it a manifestation of what Manu Karuka has perceptively called "railroad colonialism," which constructs and views trains as "infrastructures of reaction [and] as attempts to control the future."[38] This notion of the railroad as part of the apparatus of colonialism is borne out by the argument that the railroad was a unifying force in the era after the American Civil War. The standard historiographical line about the railroad's significance in the postbellum era was that it "promoted national reunification" in the aftermath of sectarian division.[39] But as Sarah Gordon points out, "A program of internal improvements"—meaning improved transportation to the interior of the country—"had since the early days of the republic been seen as a remedy for the nation's perceived 'fragility.'"[40] Even prior to the Civil War, the railroad was promoted repeatedly as a way for the nation to achieve "national unity based on commerce."[41] Gordon's intervention into this rhetoric of national healing highlights the decidedly *un*exceptional sense of fragility that permeated the nation's sense of itself since the early years of the republic. Even prior to the Civil War, commerce was a part of the state's plan to counter that fragility. Not only did the railroad bring together "the nation's trading interests *and* the political goals of the government," it enabled the nation to paper over its defensiveness about its exceptionalist status.[42]

Railroad Modernity

When Peter Osborne suggests that "modernity is a culture of time," he is talking about a conception of time that began to emerge in the fifteenth century as the West moved from Christian temporality that emphasized "eternity and eschatology" toward a secular temporality that was "measurable, rational, and progressive" and based on capitalist notions of "productivity."[43] Based on this notion of modernity, it is clear that temporality offers a powerful instrument and justification for "divid[ing] ostensibly 'advanced' or 'up-to-date' societies from 'backward' ones."[44] The imbrication between modernity and race is so strong that Zygmunt Bauman goes so far as to argue that

> racism is unthinkable without the advancement of modern science, modern technology and modern forms of state power. As such, racism is strictly a modern product. Modernity made racism possible. It also created a demand for racism . . . Racism, in short, is a thoroughly modern weapon used in the conduct of premodern, or at least not exclusively modern, struggles.[45]

According to Bauman's argument, modernity is not just operational but is foundational to the current political, socioeconomic, and discursive structures of racism. In reviewing the links between racism and modernity, Devin Vartija similarly claims that "European imperialism in the Americas and the growth of the transatlantic slave trade and race-based slavery are fundamentally constitutive of modernity."[46] And while definitions of modernity vary and shift, Anthony Giddens's is particularly relevant when thinking about the railroad. Giddens defines modernity as possessing "the separation of time and space," "the development of disembedding mechanisms" in which the social can be "lifted out" of local contexts, and "the reflexive appropriation of knowledge" in which "systematic knowledge about social life becomes integral to system reproduction."[47] Rather than a carefully controlled political or social project, modernity as characterized by Giddens is a "careering juggernaut," one in which the ordered rationality that is the railroad's seeming hallmark is constantly undermined by the "irrational rhythms" of what Susan Sontag has called the "imagination of disaster."[48]

This notion of the train as an impending disaster is important for several reasons. The train disrupts the body's experience of time and space, making railroad travel a somatic experience, which brings it squarely within the realm of the racialized. The nineteenth century's obsession with railroad accidents is one manifestation of that anxiety. Legal historian Barbara Welke argues that it was the fear of train derailments—and the unprecedented casualty tolls that they could cause—that was instrumental in transforming the conditions of individual liberty in the nineteenth century, moving from an "era of steadfast commitment to American ingenuity and independence" to one that was defined by "ordered liberty, [or] liberty assured through restraint."[49] In other words, the introduction of the railroad brought about a hardening of state determinations as to who was eligible for protection from harm. A growing awareness of the dangers of railroad travel and compilation of statistics regarding fatalities and injuries meant that the nation looked increasingly to the state and its regulatory power to safeguard against injury, trauma, and death. But Welke argues that the extension of state regulatory power to safeguard passengers depended on making certain categories of individuals more worthy of governmental care than others. Anxieties about the possibility of railroad catastrophes thus smoothed the way for the increasing legal codification of modernity's racialist categories.

The railroad's intensification of modernity's racialization also plays out in cultural terms as well as legal. Nicholas Daly, in his study of the subgenre of railway novels, argues that "the railway journey is described as a constant assault on the fragile nervous system of the traveler."[50] Reading the newly emerging genre of sensation novels "trained . . . readers to deal with the temporality of the railway age."[51] Wolfgang Schivelbusch notes that while the "normal functioning [of a train] was . . . experienced as a natural and safe process," any kind of disruption of that function would "immediately reawaken the memory of forgotten danger and potential violence"; riding the train feels ordinary until the moment something seems to go wrong, at which point the passenger is reminded of everything that could possibly go wrong.[52] It is for this reason that many critics of the late nineteenth and early twentieth century have argued that cultural obsession with the railroad is due in part to the fact that the railroad *trained* people for life at speed, or what David Harvey has called "time-space compression."[53] Riding the rails prepared passengers to confront time-space compression in other areas of their lives. Lynne Kirby argues, for example, that the reason the railroad is so deeply embedded in the early days of film (so much so that the train was a favorite subject for early filmmakers and that much of the vocabulary of filmmaking— for example, tracking shot—is borrowed from the railroad) is because riding the train was itself a "protocinematic experience."[54]

As the nation's courts moved to protect railroad companies and carriers from liability in cases of accidents and derailments, their rationale for doing so was rooted in the logics and progressive ideas of modernity. In her book *Shifting the Blame: Literature, Law and the Theory of Accidents in Nineteenth-Century America* (1998), Nan Goodman highlights the curious case of a Mrs. Palsgraf, who was injured in what can only be called a freak accident while waiting on a platform for her train. Another passenger was running for his train, which was departing, when he was given a helpful push by a railroad employee. In being so pushed, this passenger lost control of a package he was carrying, which contained fireworks. The fireworks then ignited, and the resulting blast caused some scales at the other end of the platform to fall onto the unsuspecting head of Mrs. Palsgraf. Mrs. Palsgraf sued the railroad company for damages. After a series of victories for the plaintiff, the case was ultimately adjudicated by the New York Appellate Court in favor of the railroad company. For Goodman, this case points to the moment

> when causation lost its salience in determining the nature of human responsibility within the accident context. Indeed, the story of individual responsibility and blame at the turn of the century and throughout the first quarter of the twentieth century is shaped by this paradox: as technology improved, especially the technology of signaling which was designed to protect passengers and personnel on the railroad, the causal

trajectory of accidents became in many ways more certain, and yet the nature of the human role or what was often called the human equation was lost.[55]

The Palsgraf case called into question the very nature of "cause" and "effect" (what Goodman calls the "hypothetically endless chain of causality") at about the same moment that scientists like Werner Heisenberg were theorizing that the "position and velocity of subatomic particles could only be known in relation to each other." Although the appellate court does not explicitly mention Heisenberg's uncertainty principle or Einstein's general theory of relativity to justify its ruling, Goodman argues that the emerging principles of relationality that underlie modern quantum mechanics nevertheless find legalistic expression here.[56]

Modernity's reordering of racialized bodies at the very moment that the railroad accelerated the movement of those bodies is the foundation for Schivelbusch's argument that the railroad indicted subjects into modernity by shocking them physically, socially, and visually. The management of that shock and the isolation and alienation that it engenders make the experience of riding the train emblematic of industrial modernity. For Schivelbusch, "the idea that the railroad annihilated space and time must be seen as the reaction of perceptive powers that, formed by a certain transport technology [e.g., the horse], find suddenly that technology has been replaced by an entirely new one."[57] Schivelbusch elaborates that the "annihilation of space and time was the topos that the early nineteenth century uses to describe the new situation into which the railroad placed natural space after depriving it of its hitherto absolute powers. Motion was no longer dependent on the conditions of natural space, but on a mechanical power that created its own new spatiality."[58] With its ability to reorganize (or "annihilate" to use Schivelbusch's term) space and time "based on the speed that the new means of transport was able to achieve," the train became a site for contesting conventions associated with gender, race, and class.[59] It solidified the nation's sense of itself as a modern and modernizing global power. It accelerated the movement of goods and people, standardized time, created a leisure and travel industry based on the commodification of the land, and initiated people—whether as riders or laborers—into new systems of space, time, and seeing. The train, according to Lynne Kirby, is a "technology that profoundly influenced the ways in which we perceive and use the modern world. . . . It is the perceptual paradigm for modern life."[60]

It is for all these reasons that Marian Aguiar argues that "modernity [is] deeply embedded within colonial and neocolonial projects" like the railroad.[61] The railroad has long been touted as modernity's sign and exemplar. The railroad represents a certain kind of relationship to modernity that is profoundly racial in its construction. Whether or not one considers racism to be the exclusive product of modernity's "institutional, rationalizing, and centralizing forces," there is no question that the technology and standardization that the railroad required, created, and symbolized intensified racist ideologies.[62] The train is the paradigm through which Americans understood modernity and their own relationship to that modernity; as a particular ordering of space and time around technology, it was foundational to the emergence of the US into nationhood and accelerated its imperial projects, first against Native American populations but eventually into other parts of North America and across the Pacific to Asia. The train's transformative reordering of space and time renders it particularly hospitable for articulating the contours of racial difference and identity precisely because our notions of "otherness" are founded upon and articulated by spatiality and temporality. As I noted earlier in this chapter, despite the rhetoric of equality and individualism that has long attached itself to the railroad, the train has often been associated with the segregation and categorization of individuals based on race, class, and gender. It is not that modernity's disciplinary and hierarchizing reach only applies to some bodies and not others, it is that modernity does not exist without the existence of bodies that are racialized and excluded.

Spatial Railroad

Finally, the railroad highlights the relationship between race and space. According to Schivelbusch, the train ended the traveler's ability to experience "space as a living entity." Pre-technological experiences of space were "organically embedded in nature"; the railroad's rise created a contradiction in terms of subjective experiences of space: "On the one hand, the railroad opened up new spaces that were not as easily accessible before; on the other, it did so by destroying space, namely the space between points."[63] Travelers could experience locations that were once impossible to access because of the slow speed of and dangers associated with transport, but this seeming "creation" of spaces that had been hitherto unknown or unknowable caused a simultaneous erasure of the between spaces that had once been traversed by foot or by horse. We hear traces of this in contemporary usage when we refer to the American Midwest as consisting of "flyover" states, locations that are only identifiable or significant because they are not places that one actually visits.

Schivelbusch's claim that the train both creates and destroys space suggests that movement does not always translate into freedom or progress. Critics such as Henri Lefebvre and David Harvey argue that spaces that are highly regimented, planned, and scheduled (like the train car) produce and perpetuate capitalist systems of production. Railroads are part of a system of "abstract space" that discipline subjects/riders via technology, social conventions, and laws. De Certeau elaborates on this notion when he argues that the train is a "bubble of panoptic and classifying power" that produces docile subjects who are "pigeonholed, numbered, and regulated in the grid of the railway car."[64] Mobility studies scholars are particularly interested in how mobility informs the constitution of spaces like the train car, which are ostensibly public in their nature but also rely on a tenuous notion of privacy or domesticity in order to appeal. A mobility-studies paradigm for studying the railroad recognizes the centrality of physical movement in constituting power, identity, and modernity. Scholars such as John Urry are interested in how the railroad enacts contradictory spatial processes; on the one hand, the railroad collapsed space by bringing places closer together; on the other hand, it expanded space by connecting places that would have never been otherwise connected to each other.

While the railroad is presented in highly spatialized terms by de Certeau, it is important to note that race is constituted both within space and across time. Mikhail Bakhtin's definition of the chronotope is instructive here, as it speaks to the "intrinsic connectedness of temporal and spatial relationships." Riding the train enables time to "thicken" or "take on flesh."[65] As Elizabeth Grosz points out, "The kinds of world we inhabit, and our understanding of our places in these worlds are to some extent an effect of the ways in which we understand space and time."[66]

Grosz cites Kant's argument regarding the connection between space and time to better elucidate the terms of that relationship: "While space and time are *a priori* categories we impose on the world, space is the mode of apprehension of exterior objects, and time a mode of apprehension of the subject's own interior."[67] The connectivity between space and time in the formulation of bodies (through space) and subjectivities (across time) is important to the experience of riding the train for racialized individuals. Bakhtin argues that the chronotope is constitutive of literature broadly, but the railroad, with its space-destroying and time-altering properties, clearly intensifies that time-space connection. This is visible in narratives by authors of color, who experience the despatialization that racism enables in both spatial and temporal terms. We will see, particularly in the works of African American authors, that the experience of riding a segregated train car disrupts time-space so that the "flesh" of racial identity can manifest.

The disjunctive temporalities that these writers chronicle is also a result of the horizontal sociality that is compulsory for the train's occupants. Even passengers who are divided by race, gender, and class into their respective compartments or cars must interact with individuals from other spaces, whether that is in the corridor, in a restaurant car, or in the station. Compulsory social spaces such as the train afford subjects an alibi for being in close proximity with excluded, marginalized, or otherwise contaminated bodies. In these spaces and moments of ritual encounter, racial identities can be reestablished, hierarchies can be recommitted to memory (as if they were ever forgotten in the first place), and the ebb and flow of power can be channeled. The railway car is a place and space where ideologies of race and nation collide with anxieties about the alienating effects of modernity on the individual. The train is key precisely because it is both a social space and a motile space, a faithful rendering of social strata and political hierarchies that are imagined to be stable *and* a fluid space defined by its mobility and intersectionality.

The railroad initiates its subjects into a racial order because it paradoxically brings into close proximity people whom society otherwise strives to keep apart and because it reveals how racialization is a process that depends on a temporality that is foundational to narratives of descent. The railroad's unique merging of space, time, and politics enables us to see how racial identities emerge horizontally (interracially or con-textually, based on those who occupy the space around an individual) as well as vertically (genealogically, based on what is passed down over time to an individual from previous generations). Focusing on the rail-road thus enables us to pay attention to representational processes and to decipher what Colleen Lye has called the "power of racialization's ef-fects" across space and through time.[68]

Chapter Summaries

The structure of this book requires some explanation. Its organization attempts to capture the complexity of the railroad in relation to the nation and to race. Although my work is grounded in particular histori-cal spans of the nation and its constituent ethnic communities, it is not chronological in its approach, nor is it meant to present a sustained, con-tinuous cultural history of the railroad. Rachel Lee's notion of "lateral" reading in arguing that Asian America is a "multispecies assemblage" is not unlike what I am attempting here.[69] Lee defines this kind of reading as one that "abjur[es] [a] vertical buildup toward a singular message or outcome."[70] Each chapter contains reflections on the train's role within the context of a particular historical moment, racialized community, or theme. It is my hope, however, that there is space in each reading for convergences to emerge between and across chapters. Chapter 1, "Tracks across the Land: Visualizing the Railroad in Settler Colonialism," exam-ines an eclectic array of visual works from the mid-nineteenth through the twenty-first centuries that imagine the train as a tool of settler colo-nialism. I argue that nineteenth-century landscape paintings by John Gast and Frances Flora Bond Palmer, the early twentieth-century travel advertisements for the Atchison, Topeka and Santa Fe Railroads, and the twenty-first century production reel for Jerry Bruckheimer Films make the railroad the centerpiece of a visual logic that I call railroad creationism, which was designed to erase the influence and presence of Native Americans on the lands of the "frontier" (in the case of the landscape paintings) or commodify the Indian by conflating the figure with the land and the train itself (in the case of railroad advertisements). Bong Joon-ho's film *Snowpiercer* and Jaque Fragua's "Graffiti on a Train" public art projects resist the spatializing and settler-colonial logics that the railroad imposes. *Snowpiercer*'s depiction of the train makes use of mobile framing techniques that counter the relentless westward drive of Manifest Destiny. Fragua's "Graffiti on Train" series, which involves spray-painting the side of working freight cars, transforms the railroad yet again, from instrument to medium, reversing a settler-colonial dynamic that portrays the Native American as the ground on which the nation's commerce runs.

Chapter 2, "The Chinaman's Crime," explores the relationship between race and railroad from a distinctly anti-Chinese perspective: that of Willa Cather. In Willa Cather's short story "The Affair at Grover Station" (1900), the railroad is the lens that both explains and obscures Chinese racial difference. Cather's "Chinese fiction" stories express a particular strain of Sinophobia that emphasizes the unnatural ancientness of the Chinese both individually and culturally. In the case of "The Affair at Grover Station," this is complicated by the fact that Freymark, the half-Chinese cattle magnate who is the story's villain, possesses a seeming uncanny ability to navigate masterfully the modernity that the US imagined itself to embody and that was supposed to be antithetical to the Chinese.

In "The Affair at Grover Station," the Chinese, even when they disappear as Freymark does, haunt the nation via the railroad, destabilizing Cather's insistent belief in the country's resourcefulness. The ghostly presence of the Chinese on the railroad also preoccupies Chinese American writers, although for very different reasons than Cather. "Chapter 3, "Telling Stories: The Transcontinental Railroad as Chinese American Narrative," examines how Chinese American authors David Henry Hwang, Frank Chin, and Maxine Hong Kingston construct the train as a form of textual narrative, one they can read or narrate to make visible the erasure of Chinese American life and experience in the United States. Their works offer the railroad not only as a key for understanding Chinese American subject formation but also a strategy for narrating Chinese American experiences in the face of marginalization and expunction from the nation's history. Like the relationship between signifier and signified, the train functions as a vehicle for figuring Chinese workers and conceptualizing an absent Chinese American past.

Chapter 4 delves further into the imagined relationship between Chinese Americans and the railroad. "Remembrance and Reenactment at

Promontory Summit," explores memory from the perspective of Chinese American artists, who are cut off from the experiences of Chinese American railroaders by the archival silence that shrouds their lives in the nineteenth and early twentieth centuries. This chapter focuses on Chinese American textual and artistic reenactments of the famed golden spike (the moment the final spike was driven into the final rail signaling the completion of the Transcontinental Railroad) or the "champagne photo" (the photograph taken at the railroad's completion in which no Chinese are included). These artistic reenactments of these historical moments reveal that these seeming moments of authentic origin—whether it involves the putative completion of the Transcontinental Railroad or the founding of the nation—are always fictions, reiterations, and/or performances repackaged as legitimate and legitimating.

From Chinese American attempts to imagine a past for themselves via the labor of Chinese railroad workers, the next two chapters shift to a consideration of African American experiences as passengers on the railroad in the segregated South. Chapter 5, "The Jim Crow Train in African American Literature," examines the signification of the train in the era of Jim Crow in African American literary texts. It specifically focuses on literary representations of African American passengers riding Jim Crow and how the spatialization of the train car contributes to constructions of Black identity. Most of these texts explored in this chapter—including Ralph Ellison's "Boy on a Train" (written ca. 1937, published 1996); James Weldon Johnson's novel *The Autobiography of an Ex-Colored Man* (1912); W. E. B. Du Bois's essay "The Superior Race" (1923); and Anna Julia Cooper's *A Voice from the South* (1892)—are set in the era of Jim Crow, but the chapter also explores narratives of Jim Crow in slave narratives by Frederick Douglass and George and Ellen Craft. Perhaps more than any other system of social categorization, Jim Crow reveals how ideas about race are inextricably linked to and informed by ideas about space. All these works narrate how the experience of riding Jim Crow profoundly despatializes the Black subject, a process that requires the Black passengers to negotiate how his or her body moves in or through that space. These moments of racial encounter reveal how space and temporality—the positioning of bodies in relation to each other and to the environment—are constitutive of racial identity. As such, riding the rails calls into question the relationship not just between subjects and their communities but also how the subject situates his or her identity within and across space and time.

Chapter 6, "Riding the Blind," contrasts African American literary culture's view of the train with the representation of the train in Black folk music and blues of the early twentieth century. Whereas African American literature of the early twentieth century tends to treat the experience of riding the Jim Crow railcar as a profoundly alienating spatial experience, blues and folk songs form this time period associate the train with movement that is unmoored from white sociality. If riding the Jim Crow train further encloses Black subjects into a space that constructs them as invisible, then singing about the train in blues and folk songs seems to indicate a disarticulation from white spatial logics.

Black mobility and spatiality serve as the segue into chapter 7. "Speculative Trains: Colson Whitehead's *The Underground Railroad*" considers the impact of Whitehead's move to literalize and materialize the Underground Railroad, the putative network of individuals and safe houses that aided escaped slaves fleeing north in antebellum America. In addition to figuring Black movement across the nation, Whitehead also expresses Black mobility through a trope of depth. Instead of the railroad running *on* land, in Whitehead's world, the train runs *underneath* it. This notion of the Black subterranean and superterranean is echoed in the protagonist Cora's occupancy of an attic crawl space in the middle of the novel, a move that is directly inspired by Harriet Jacobs's *Incidents in the Life of a Slave Girl* (1861). By literalizing the Underground Railroad, Whitehead disrupts notions of slave mobility and focuses on the possibilities that Black spatiality may offer.

Chapter 8, "Fugitive Trains," takes up the supposed divide between mobility and carcerality. This chapter focuses on how the train makes the interplay between mobility and carcerality more visible, particularly as it relates to migrant bodies, in the music video for "Immigrants (We Get the Job Done)" (2017), directed by Tomás Whitmore. "Immigrants (We Get the Job Done)" illustrates how the fundamental condition of the migrant is a carceral mobility, which is mobility that is controlled or disciplined without the need for physical imprisonment. Although this interplay between the carceral and the mobile can be seen in the lyrics for "Immigrants (We Get the Job Done)" and in the embodied performances of the four rappers, K'naan, Snow tha Product, Riz MC, and Residente, the key to understanding the song and video's critique of carceral mobility is the "mobile framing" the video employs.

As I hope these summaries have indicated, *The Racial Railroad* is an excavation of how railroad and race were linked from the mid-nineteenth century to the present. It uncovers how race has governed talk and thought about the railroad and how the railroad is a vehicle that enables the consolidation of and resistance to state power. My argument is premised on the notion that the railroad is everywhere. Alas, I cannot account for that omnipresence within the confines of an academic book. Among the things this book does not cover are Native American or Chicanx literary representations of the railroad, even though the train plays significant roles in the works of writers such as Zitkála-Šá, Leslie Marmon Silko, and María Ruiz de Burton. *The Racial Railroad* is also silent on the use of trains in the evacuation and internment of Japanese Americans during World War II, nor does it address the Bracero program that brought Mexican laborers into the US during World War II to build railroads, or the hiring of Navajo men as trackmen by the Atchison, Topeka and Santa Fe Railroad (ATSF) starting in the nineteenth century. Hoboing, which was an important part of twentieth-century labor history and which appears in texts like Carlos Bulosan's *America Is in the Heart* (1946) and Ralph Ellison's "I Did Not Learn Their Names" (published in 1996), is also relatively untouched. Although I cover the meaning of the train in African American folk songs of the early twentieth century, I do not discuss important folk figures like John Henry or historical events like the unjust arrest and imprisonment of the Scottsboro Nine. My reading of "Immigrants (We Get the Job Done)" would have no doubt been enriched and complicated by an analysis of Cary Joji Fukunaga's film *Sin Nombre* (2009), which depicts the journey of a Honduran girl and a Mexican gang member on La Bestia. I have had to lay aside discussing a number of Hollywood films featuring interracial male leads that incorporate the train into their plots, from M. Night Shyamalan's superhero film *Unbreakable* (2000; features a train crash), to Tony Scott's action film *Unstoppable* (2010; revolves around a runaway train), to Barry Sonnenfeld's western comedy *Wild Wild West* (1999; incorporates the golden spike into its plot). Television series like AMC's *Hell on Wheels* (2011–2016), which is about the construction of the Transcontinental Railroad and features several Chinese American actors, and WGN's *Underground* (2016–17), which is about the Underground Railroad in Georgia, did not make the cut.

I am sure there are dozens more examples that I am not thinking of or have never heard of; at any rate, the list of works that could have been included in this book goes on and on. And that's an important point. Anyone with even the most elementary knowledge or grasp of American culture will be able to identify works that should have been included because that is how pervasive narratives of race and railroad are. I can ask only that the reader take up the gaps in this book to consider the broader argument I am making: how writers and artists of color must often use the very same instruments that have oppressed them to resist systems that despatializes them, erase their presence from history, and insist on portraying them as criminal or out of control.

1

Tracks across the Land

Visualizing the Railroad in Settler Colonialism

In 1868, one year before the completion of the First Transcontinental Railroad, General William Jackson Palmer—Civil War veteran,
decorated Union officer, engineer, and executive of the Union Pacific
Railroad Eastern Division (UPRED)—penned a report titled *Report of
Surveys across the Continent in 1867–1868*.[1] This obscure volume was
written with one purpose in mind: to convince the federal government
to provide financial support for an UPRED extension from Kansas
to the Pacific. In a section titled "Why the Government Should Aid,"
Palmer points to the precedent of federal support for the Central Pacific
and Union Pacific Railroads. But the heart of his argument has nothing
to do with demanding that the government provide the same benefits to
UPRED as it did to its competitors. Instead, Palmer's plea rests on two
points. First, the UPRED extension would pacify the Indian populations
that had for the past "200 years [waged] a relentless war against all white
men and . . . have harried our miners, and those who go to supply their
wants, until steady industry has become almost impossible."[2] Palmer
suggests that railroads are the most effective and economical method
of "protecting the hundreds of frontiersmen who are dying because of
Indian aggression every year in the American West." Railroads are more
practical than army garrisons, the construction and manning of which
"cost more than a foreign war" and do nothing in terms of deterrence.
To prove his point, Palmer cites a previously published report by then
secretary of war Ulysses S. Grant that chillingly opined that "the completion of the railroads to the Pacific will go far toward a permanent
settlement of our Indian difficulties." The railroad, in other words, was
a more effective Indian killer than any bullet.

The second point is related to the first, and it has to do with Palmer's
frustration at the glacial pace of settlement and development in the West

broadly. As a staunch unionist, Palmer believes that the railroad will cement the nation's presence in the frontier, which he fears is in constant
danger of fading away. In his report, he writes that

> in a few years, there will not remain as many traces of American existence
> in the whole country as are now to be found of Aztec civilization within
> a few miles along the valleys of the Little Colorado or Verde. Just as the
> Mexicans have diminished, from 120,000 to 80,000 in Sonora since the
> 'Gadsden Purchase,' are gradually receding toward the coast, in conse-
> quence of the incursions of the Gila Apaches, so our hardy pioneers must
> utterly give way in New Mexico, Arizona, and Colorado, unless some
> plan, founded on reason and experience, be adopted for their relief and
> for the encouragement of emigration.[3]

Somewhat surprisingly, in justifying the railroad's necessity, Palmer
does not necessarily present American dominion over the land as being
more powerful or genuine than that of the Aztecs or the Mexicans in
the region. Instead, Palmer portrays the nation's domain over these
lands as being under constant threat, suggesting that the relationship
between the state and the land it claims is not as inevitable or powerful
as the myth of Manifest Destiny might suggest. Palmer's concern that
America's "hardy pioneers" might suffer the same fate as the Aztecs
or the Mexicans and gradually be erased from the land indicates an
underlying fear that as long as the land is under the control of the
Apaches, it will be incapable of holding settlement and civilization.
Indeed, Indian control of the land means that the "risks to property
[are] so great as to forbid enterprise or accumulation."[4] Palmer is
suggesting here that Native tribes and the lands that are under their
control are inimical to projects of capitalist enterprise and empire
building. The land itself is intractable, an anarchic, shapeless void that
refuses to be imprinted by the usual tools of empire: settlers, capital
economies, and extraction industries. The UPRED extension, then, is
not just about the subsidizing of US corporations or the facilitation of
trade and travel; in its fate lies the fate of the nation. In light of this
existential threat, Palmer's statement that "unless this country be pen-
etrated by a railroad, it must be practically abandoned" isn't dramatic.
It is cold hard fact.[5]

Palmer's report betrays a deep-seated but deeply denied "fear of disorder in the landscape."[6] That fear, which manifests itself in a multiplicity of ways, explains why so many in the nineteenth century pinned their hopes regarding Manifest Destiny and US primacy on the railroad. The railroad was necessary because it was seen as transformational, eliminating Native Americans and making the land legible for incorporation into the nation. In making this claim, I build on scholarship by a number of scholars, including Manu Karuka and Iyko Day, that characterizes the railroad as a powerful tool of colonial power and settler expansion. The railroad, like the camera, offered a way for Native Americans to be "controlled, catalogued, and owned."[7] David Nye has argued that white settlers "constructed stories of self-creation in which the mastery of particular technologies played a central role"; these settlers "construct[ed] stories that emphasized self-conscious movement into a new space."[8] According to this master narrative, technologies wielded by white settlers, including the railroad, "reshape the land," transforming it into something productive and valuable.[9] The nation has long espoused a belief in the transformative power of technology to solve its perceived problems and as a means of demonstrating American ingenuity and superiority. Palmer's narrative expands the role of the railroad. It also reflects a tension within settler colonial discourse, one strain of which insists on portraying the land as empty and passive as it awaits civilization, the other of which (like Palmer's report) expresses frustration with the land's perceived recalcitrance and resistance to settlement. The railroad in these reports fulfills a slightly different but much more outsized role: it has the power to cement the relationship between settler and land, physically and discursively disconnecting Native Americans from the land in question. Within the logic of US settler colonialism, the train transforms the disturbing unproductivity of the land prior to settler migration and settlement into a *place* in the de Certeauvian sense—one that is ordered, gridded, and proper.

As Palmer's report makes clear, in nineteenth-century America, the train was not just a carrier of space, it was also perceived as *creating* national space. This notion that the train creates space is not new to this book. I have already discussed in the introduction how Schivelbusch identified the central contradiction of train travel in the nineteenth century, namely, that "on the one hand, the railroad open[ed] up new spaces that were not accessible before it; on the other hand it [did] so by destroy-ing space, viz., the space in-between."[10] The advent of the railroad shrank the distances between cities, annihilating the "the space between points," bringing together places that had once been distinct "into each other's immediate vicinity." Schivelbusch's critique is inclusive of both space and time; the railroad disrupted the "mimetic relationship" between time and the space traversed, a unit of subjective experience that Schivelbusch calls "the durée." The annihilation of space that I am discussing here is of a different sort, however. The railroads in the American West were perceived as not just creating a new conception of *durée* for the individ-ual passenger-citizen of the train; they were meant to create a new type of space altogether, one that responded to the demands of the nation, empire, and capital. What is being destroyed by the train in the West is not the organic relationship between time and space as in Schivelbusch's conception but the relationship between Native and land that is seen as being resistant to habits of nation, empire, and capital building. Literary historian Hsuan Hsu notes that various events of the nineteenth century (the Louisiana Purchase, the Mexican American War, the annexation of Hawai'i, the War of 1898)—not to mention the numerous treaties made between tribes and the US government—had the effect of making Ameri-cans feel "that they were literally witnessing the emergence of new spaces, the gradual manifestation of their nation's geographical destiny."[11] Mobil-ity in this instance meant progress and destiny.

This chapter examines how visual artists from the nineteenth through the twenty-first centuries use the train to settle and spatialize the nation. My readings are organized into two clusters, the first of which broadly addresses the shifting relationship between railroad, land, and the "In-dian." The visual texts at the heart of this first cluster are nineteenth-century landscape paintings (John Gast's *American Progress* [lithograph, 1872], Frances Flora Bond Palmer's *Across the Continent: Westward the Course of Empire Takes Its Way* [lithograph, 1868], and *Through to the Pacific* [lithograph, 1870]); the production reel for Jerry Bruckheimer Films (2013); and Bong Joon-ho's dystopian film *Snowpiercer* (2013). The landscape images that I cite above are some of the most famous representations of Manifest Destiny in American visual arts; in fact, Roger Aikin calls these types of landscapes "the paintings of Manifest Destiny" because they depict the "belief that Americans were destined by Divine Providence to expand their national domain to the Pacific Ocean."[12] While I agree with Aikin's broad categorization of these types of paintings, I want to focus on a subset that specifically depict the train. I call the conceptual and visual paradigm that these works espouse "railroad creationism," which specifically credits the train with transforming a land perceived at times as featureless or resistant to civilizing forces into a landscape that can be part of the national narrative. These images represent the train as transforming chaotic, featureless, or unformed land that is occupied by Indigenous peoples into a landscape that can support "civilization." My use of the religiously inflected term *creationism* is deliberate; it is meant to invoke a viewpoint that presents itself as "natural," "moral," and the "truth" but that masks the ideological and intellectual labor that goes into maintaining such fictions. My reading of these works expands W. J. T. Mitchell's persuasive and important argument that the landscape represents the "dreamwork of imperialism" by arguing that the railroad drives that very work.[13] The railroad enables us to see how landscape can be transformed "from a noun to a verb," to borrow Mitchell's formulation.[14] The railroad drives the transformation from what has been a static genre in art history to an action driven by national and imperial ambitions.

My inclusion of contemporary works like the production reel for Jerry Bruckheimer's films and Bong Joon-ho's film *Snowpiercer* in this discussion of nineteenth-century landscape painting might seem quixotic, violating standards of period and genre, but I would argue that these more recent cultural products reveal the extent to which the mythologized relationship between land and nation is embedded in our culture's psyche. *Snowpiercer* in particular is highly aware of the iconography of railroad creationism as it launches its critique against global capital. I base this claim on Roger Aikin's observation that the paintings of Manifest Destiny all exhibit a strong "left-moving composition"; in other words, the westward progress depicted in these images is echoed in the painting's directional composition leftward.[15] Aikin argues that this suggests that the paintings were meant "to be read as maps . . . literally pointing the way west to California and Oregon." The action of *Snowpiercer* also has a strong directional orientation; in the case of the film, it is rightward (or eastward), a striking counterpoint to the leftward/westward composition of the paintings of railroad creationism. *Snowpiercer*'s strong eastward orientation visually dismantles the links settler ideology make between land, train, and Indigeneity. *Snowpiercer* makes conspicuous use of the spatial particularities of the train to launch a critique of settler spatiality that directly challenges the representations of the train as a sign of spatial incorporation, instead resisting and critiquing the projects of settler colonialism and racial capital by its highly disciplined reimagination of mobile framing techniques.

The second cluster of readings in this chapter is anchored by another group of visual works: the early twentieth century railroad advertisements commissioned by the Northern Pacific Railroad and the Atchison, Topeka and Santa Fe Railway (ATSF) and the multimedia art of Jemez Pueblo artist Jaque Fragua, particularly his installation pieces *Stop Coal, Untitled 2012*, and *Untitled 2015* (which I collectively call his "Graffiti on a Train" series). Unlike the first cluster, which focuses on railroad creationism as a way of despatializing Native spaces into national ones, this cluster examines how railroad companies transformed the figure of the Indian into one that is highly aestheticized and interchangeable with the landscape in order to reap greater commercial benefits. As Native Americans became disembedded from land that the United States was eager to incorporate into the nation, they became increasingly associated with landscape. This shift in association explains why Indians appear extensively in the art that was commissioned by the railroads to advertise leisure travel through the West and Southwest. Indian tours were such an integral part of the ATSF's business that its flagship all-Pullman luxury passenger train was called the Chief.[16] I argue that these railroad advertisements reveal how the demands of capitalism transformed Native Americans from anachronistic threats whose presence might destroy the land to anachronistic and romantic embodiments of the land itself. Fragua's "Graffiti on a Train" series responds directly to discourses that render the Indian as commensurate with touristic landscape. Like Bong, Fragua uses the train as the ground to launch his critique of settler notions of space and land. In *Stop Coal, Untitled 2012,* and *Untitled 2015*, Fragua graffities freight cars with images and text to resist the erasure of Native Americans from the land. By inscribing text onto the freight car, Fragua makes space for Native histories and bodies that the train has been used in a multitude of ways to eradicate. In other words, Fragua uses a space-centered epistemology to assert a different kind of relationship between Native and land, one that is not aestheticized or commercialized but that nevertheless recognizes the long-lasting impact of settler incursions upon the land. Fragua's move is an indicator of how "Indigenous geographies persist within and confront the US settler colonial nation."[17]

Manifest Destiny and Railroad Creationism

Manifest destiny is often characterized as being "predicated upon two myths . . . that the land was unoccupied and that it was ecologically pristine."[18] For example, Mary Pat Brady argues that to recruit the necessary Anglo settlers to the West, the land needed to be transformed from terra incognita "into something recognizably 'American': a region that did not resist Anglo incursions, a region where all 'foreignness' had been eradicated, where threats to Anglo hegemony were minimized."[19] Brady's focus is on American writers who "repeatedly characterized the land in a manner that would privilege an Anglo sense of superiority in the face of daunting difficulties."[20] Brady goes on to argue that the "doubled narrative of terra incognita at once justified the imperial project in a well-wrought discourse of adventure, discovery, and conquest, and it foreclosed the extensive and carefully developed knowledge of the region produced in other tongues."[21] US discourses and incursions "remapp[ed] occupied territory as virgin soil ready for occupation."[22]

But this description does not tell the whole story. The version of Manifest Destiny that we observe in paintings of railroad creationism acknowledges the presence of Native Americans (although not Mexicans). To put it another way, the paintings that engage in railroad creationism do not necessarily portray the land as terra incognita. While the land is devoid of markers of civilization, it is not empty or unknown. Rather, the paintings portray the land as terra nullius, land that is undeveloped, chaotic, or unproductive, land that is occupied by but not owned by Indigenous peoples. If we think of Manifest Destiny as an explicitly settler project (rather than a strictly nationalist one), then that distinction between versions of Manifest Destiny becomes clear. As Kelly Lytle Hernández writes, the whole purpose of settler colonial projects is to

seek land. On that land, colonialists envision building a new, permanent, reproductive, and racially exclusive society. To be clear, settlers harbor no intentions of merging with, submitting to, or even permanently lording over the Indigenous societies already established within the targeted land base. Nor do settlers plan to leave or to return home someday. Rather, settlers invade in order to stay and reproduce while working in order to remove, dominate, and, ultimately, replace the Indigenous populations. In the words of historian Patrick Wolfe, settler societies are premised on the "elimination of the native."[23]

In settler colonialism, the Native's presence can be acknowledged before it is eliminated. However, the process of eliminating the Native is not as easy as simply imagining that he or she isn't there. It requires time and effort, what Hi'ilei Julia Hobart calls a "*process* of deanimation" (emphasis mine) in which "discourses of absence have systematically produced [Native lands] as a place without humans, spirituality, nation, or even atmosphere."[24] Deanimation usefully names a laborious and time-spanning process of Indian removal that was meant to be seen as natural and instantaneous. What's more, deanimation is not a process consigned to the past. We catch a glimpse of this every time reference is made to the nation's myth of its own origins, which frequently paints the "new" world as a pristine landscape, studiously ignoring all archaeological and geological evidence that suggests that Indigenous peoples had altered the land to suit their needs long before Europeans had ventured across the Atlantic.[25]

Landscape images filled a powerfully symbolic role in the nation's construction of its history, its present, and its future. Within the context of nineteenth-century visual culture, art historians have traditionally "focused on landscape painting as the preeminent pictorial locus for disseminating the widespread belief in the country's Manifest Destiny to settle and develop the continent."[26] Manifest destiny is not just about acquiring land for its own sake; it is also about the development or transformation of that land. John O'Sullivan, who first used the phrase in 1845 to describe the significance of the US government's annexation of Texas, called it the nation's fate to "overspread the continent allotted by Providence for the free development of our yearly multiplying millions."[27] Because landscape represents an aestheticized and therefore mediated view of land, it is generally aligned with projects of nation and empire. Matthew Johnston makes the case that landscape painting has a visual rhetoric that implies a kind of "control or mastery over . . . history on the part of the viewer."[28] Leo Marx famously noted that "the function of the landscape" is to be "a master image embodying American hopes."[29] W. J. T. Mitchell highlights the ideological role of landscape in nation and empire building when he notes that "the discourse of landscape is a crucial means for enlisting 'Nature' in the legitimation of modernity."[30] Landscape paintings feed into American exceptionalist rhetoric, as they suggest that the nation's modernity—"superior to everything that preceded us, free of superstition and convention, masters of a unified, natural language"—can be found in the land itself.[31]

Paintings and lithographs produced by artists in the late nineteenth century reflect in visual terms the rhetoric of Manifest Destiny. The landscape in these visual images and others worked "to ground Manifest Destiny in the immanence of nature." Just one look was enough to convince (or more likely, affirm to) the viewer that there was something special and eminently American about this land. These landscapes fulfilled the nation's need for a "cultural sublimity commensurate with the geopolitical power of a fast-industrializing nation."[32] Angela Miller writes of the "invention" of the US national landscape between 1840 and 1875 as a means of establishing the nation's position at "vanguard of history."[33] Landscape paintings "signaled a "collective identity that was both unmistakably American and fit to be the heir of the ages."[34] These paintings did more than try to capture the American past; they were meant to project the nobility and inevitability of the nation's founding into the future.

Ironically, given the emphasis on "naturalness" that pervades landscape paintings, the relationship between landscape as an aesthetic, the geographical features of the continent, and the ideological imperative of the settler nation was not an easy one to forge. As many art historians note, problems existed on a multitude of levels. On a technical level, landscape's "long-standing association in modern art history with the pictorial, with formal composition, and with the aesthetic" presented a unique technical problem for US landscape artists who were confronted with the relative flatness and the lack of dramatic geographical features in the middle of the country. These topographical "problems" required artists to experiment with different and new techniques to represent what Aikin calls seemingly "empty, directionless land."[35] Additionally,

Miller points out that landscape's signification presented a problem for American landscape artists, who were "[c]ommitted to an identifiably New World image yet were faced with a profusion of actual landscape forms."[36] To reconcile the landscape with the land itself, these artists "sought a formula with which to balance the demands of place-specific landscapes with those of national meaning."[37]

Enter the train. The railroad in these paintings was the "identifiably New World image," that "unmistakably American" sign of progress imposed on the maelstrom of specific spaces that had to be evacuated in order for national meaning to emerge. Susan Danly argues that "images of the railroad in the western landscape can be seen as direct expressions of the ideology of Manifest Destiny. . . . In landscapes of the Hudson River School, the railroad makes a gradual and incidental incursion into a pastoral setting, but in images of the western landscape, the train dramatically divides the undeveloped wilderness from the civilized world."[38] As for the compositional problems caused by the continent's geography, "what could be a better compositional device than . . . a railroad running in a straight line toward infinity?"[39] This notion of the railroad as the "straight line" in the American landscape speaks not only to its ability to ground a painting from a compositional point of view but also to its ability to spatialize land that is otherwise unproductive and undeveloped. The railroad transforms a landscape that cannot be read via the usual signs (industry, construction, orderliness) into an "official landscape," which can be divided, marked, and surveyed for official use. It transforms the anti-functional into the functional, and it destroys a land that was seen as worthless, devoid of features, and resistant to extraction in order to bring forth a landscape that could be "productive."

The technology of train travel in the nineteenth century heightened the aesthetic work that the railroad was supporting. The aestheticization of land via landscape painting—the imposition of a singular national meaning upon terrestrial formations that were diverse and not necessarily awe inspiring—was emphasized by the increasing physical smoothness of railroad travel. David Schley points out that "whereas overland travel had formerly required sojourners to negotiate rocky passageways or confront muddy roadbeds, movement by rail was smoothed and standardized, guided by straight, flat iron rails."[40] Travel no longer required the passenger to bounce over rocky roads, to be at the mercy of the elements, or even to exert any physical effort into locomotion; rather than casting one's eyes downward or to the horizon in an attempt to keep oneself safe while on the road, the train passenger could simply look out his window and appreciate the terrain without actually having to experience it physically. Steam engines provided consistent and fluid locomotory power without requiring the traveler to do much of anything. The relative smoothness of railroad transport was part of how the train forever altered people's experience of the land, for as Schivelbusch writes, the railroad seemed to be "independent of outward nature and capable of prevailing against it."[41]

The presence of Native Americans in images that are meant to proclaim the Manifest Destiny of the nation exemplifies what Manu Karuka calls the "counter-sovereignty" of US politics, that a "recognition on the part of the United States" of prior and ongoing Indigenous collective life provides a substructure to stabilize U.S property claims."[42] Karuka argues that this "constrained" acknowledgment of Native American presence is "logically necessary for the functioning of US rule of law. As counter-sovereignty, US sovereignty is in perpetual reaction to the prior and primary claims of Native peoples on the territories that the United States claims as its own. Seen in this light, US sovereignty will always be an unfinished project in perpetual crisis of unraveling."[43] The railroad in paintings of Manifest Destiny elucidate how settler claims to land are always already conceived in relation to the prior presence of Indigenous peoples: the manifestation of US counter-sovereignty depends on the existence the Native American figure. While the trope of the "dead Indian" or "noble savage" is a familiar one to anyone who has read American literature of the nineteenth century, what I am discussing here is slightly different: the notion that the Native American must be present as a part of the landscape for the meaning of the railroad to take hold. The presence of the Native American makes legible the modernity and exceptionalism of the railroad. Much as the railroad gives shape to the relative unproductivity of the continent's interior, so too does the figure of the "Indian" make clear to the nation its technological and imperial progress. The inclusion of Native American figures in some of the most famous images of the American West points to how the railroad is never truly free of its racialized underpinnings, tied as it is to notions of progress, democracy, and liberty, especially in the nineteenth century.

If the train organized a space that was otherwise flat geographically, the "Indian" brought temporality and depth to the same scene. By his or her existence, the Native American enabled the railroad to become Progress, with the figure of the Indian becoming the ground (literally and figuratively) on which the railroad could be built to accrue meaning.

John Gast's lithograph *American Progress* (originally published in 1872) is perhaps the most famous painting of Manifest Destiny; it also represents many of the issues that I have been discussing to this point. The painting bears the alternative titles of *Westward Ho* and *Manifest Destiny*, and the reasons why are abundantly clear when one looks at the image. In the center, gliding purposefully over the landscape of the West, looms the allegorical female figure Liberty. Her larger-than-life body is draped in diaphanous white cloth; clutched in her hand is a telegraph wire, which she is unspooling as she moves west. Beating a retreat before her figure (on the left side of the painting, heading west) are wild animals (bear, buffalo) and Native Americans. Trailing behind Liberty (on the right side of the painting) are white settlers, farmers, covered wagons, stagecoaches, and, of course, two trains running on separate, parallel tracks. Aikin describes how "everyone [in the painting] hurries westward from right to left with patriotic abandon, [with] the people and machines . . . virtually the only features in the otherwise empty and directionless landscape."[44] Aikin's description of an empty landscape is not entirely accurate, however. The landscape to the right of Liberty— which represents the civilization and settlement of the east—is bathed in warm light. Rolling green hills slope gently down toward a body of water filled with boats. The rising sun can be seen peeking out over this bucolic and domesticated landscape. The landscape to the left of Liberty is markedly different. This side is darker (presumably not yet the recipient of dawn's early light), and there are ominous clouds roiling to the left. The gentle hills on the right side of the painting become snow-capped jagged peaks on the left side. The right side is ordered, light, and full of commerce, while the left side is chaotic, jagged, and dark, a miasma of running bodies and animals.

The presence of Native Americans, fleeing in advance of Liberty and the railroad, enables us to see how the train imposes order on a space that is depicted as disorganized. The railroad occupies a prominent place in the painting, with both lines running directly behind the

Figure 1.1. *American Progress*. Oil on canvas. By John Gast, 1872.

transformative figure of Liberty. The tracks of both trains also represent the only straight lines in the painting's otherwise undulating composition. And here we have the first example of what I alluded to earlier in my citation of Hobart's theory of deanimation: the Native figures are not absent but *in the process* of being absented. The viewer is witnessing their spectacular erasure. The painting's stark division does not signal the binary between civilization and absence; it depicts the process by which land becomes incorporable. While Liberty, the railroad, and the settlers glide serenely and sedately toward the nation's destiny, the Indians in the painting have a frantic energy, evidenced by the strong lean of their bodies toward the left. All the Indian figures are also looking over their shoulder as they run from the advancing vanguard of "civilization." The central figure in the group of Indians occupying the left foreground raises his arm with a weapon in anger and defiance. The figure on horseback is hunched over, while the Indian figure in the rear of the group looks up in terror. Two Indian figures are carried out on a travois, faces obscured to the viewer, heads bent in what seems to be illness or defeat. Farther in the background, just visible adjacent to the cable wires that Liberty carries in her right arm, a group of faint figures stand in a group, directly in the path of the train that occupies the background of the painting. They are no more detailed than stick figures, their racial identity only identifiable by the teepees that stand next to them. Gast's decision to have the Indians look back at the approach of the railroad is evocative of Benjamin's Angel of History; as they move inexorably into the future, they are witnesses to the onslaught of history that will eliminate their presence.

The train's status as the maker of space in time in Gast's painting can be seen again in one of the most famous prints in the Currier and Ives's catalogue, *Across the Continent: Westward the Course of Empire Takes Its Way*.[45] *Across the Continent* is the work of Frances Flora Bond Palmer, the artist responsible for many of the Currier and Ives's prints depicting the railroad, steamboat, and wagon trains. As John Gladstone notes, it is Palmer's ability to "evoke nostalgia in contemporary scenes" as well as her "perennial optimism" that made her the most important and popular artist for the Currier and Ives workshop.[46] Like *American Progress*, *Across the Continent* is a panoramic scene. The print depicts a small town sitting on the edge of the frontier in the American West. The town is crammed into the lower left of the image, filled with log cabins and industrious settlers. Mountains and a vast plain fill in the upper portion of the lithograph. David Nye describes the wilderness in the lithograph as "vague and unformed, in contrast to the foreground where a new town has sprung into existence, impelled into life by the railroad."[47] By the time the lithograph was sold to the American public in 1868, the Transcontinental Railroad was nearing completion, meaning that this image was "both a vision of the recent past and a prediction of the future. It uses space to represent time: the new community in the foreground is the present, the empty land ahead of the train is the future."[48]

It is this merging of space and time that is particularly of interest in terms of the railroad and the representation of Native American figures in the nineteenth century. Bisecting the lithograph, from lower right to upper left, is a line of railroad tracks with a locomotive billowing gray smoke pulling out of the station of the frontier town. On the lower right, facing the wall of black-gray smoke that is about to completely obscure them, two Native American men on horseback look in the direction of

Figure 1.2. *Across the Continent: Westward the Course of Empire Makes Its Way.*
Hand-colored lithograph. By Frances Flora Bond Palmer, from the workshop of
Nathaniel Currier and James Merritt Ives, 1868.

the departing train. The railroad track marks a line of separation between the Native American riders and the "wilderness" on the right and
the white settlers and "civilization" on the lower left; both are dwarfed
in terms of space, however, by the frontier that lies in front of them.
The railroad in *Across the Continent* is not just opening the frontier for
settlement and civilization; it is creating the space of the nation itself,
bringing order and a sense of time's passage. Nye's characterization of
the wilderness depicted in the image as "vague and unformed" only
tells part of the story; the lithograph also portrays the wilderness is untapped, full of potential for industry and commerce. This is not merely
an image of Native Americans being kicked off land that was theirs but
rather a representation of how peoples and land that are considered "un-
geographic" are conceived by the visual conventions of Western imperialism, in which space and time exist only once they have been used to
emplot Western civilization. The train is the sign of that emplotment,
the signal of the formation of space and time. The train in *Across the*

Continent does not traverse the landscape and horizon—it creates both. Space does not exist until the railroad arrives, meaning that Indigenous populations were never truly spatially a part of the land in the first place.

It is important to note that these are images that are not necessarily viewed as outdated culturally, even though they were in vogue over a century ago. The Currier and Ives print, in particular, continues to circulate and accrue cultural capital (a print of the lithograph sold at auction for a record $62,500 in 2019). To see how railroad creationism still permeates imaginings of the American West, one need only look at the production logo for Jerry Bruckheimer Films (JBF), the namesake company of Hollywood producer Jerry Bruckheimer, who has been responsible for a string of blockbuster films dating back three decades: *Top Gun*, the *Beverly Hills Cop* franchise, the *Bad Boys* franchise, *Armageddon*, *Pearl Harbor*, *Black Hawk Down*, the *Pirates of the Caribbean* franchise, and the *National Treasure* franchise. A production logo (also sometimes called a vanity logo) is the short piece of film that is usually seen at the beginning of films or at the end of television shows (think of Leo the Lion roaring at the start of MGM films). JBF has several iterations of its production reel, but the one that is of particular interest in this case is the version that was released in tandem with Bruckheimer's 2013 film *The Lone Ranger*, directed by Gore Verbinski and starring Johnny Depp and Armie Hammer.

Bruckheimer's production logo is the latest in a long line of visual works that use the railroad as a way of representing the putative desolation of lands that were already occupied. *The Lone Ranger* was produced in partnership with Walt Disney Studios, so the film opens with perhaps the most recognizable production and company logo in Western cinema: Sleeping Beauty's castle surrounded by an arc of fairy dust with the stylized signature of Walt Disney emblazoned across the bottom of the screen. As the camera zooms in, Sleeping Beauty's castle seamlessly transforms into Tsé Bit' a'í, known in English as Shiprock, the famous rock formation that is part of the Navajo Nation in New Mexico. (It should be noted that the First Transcontinental Railroad, which plays a crucial role in the film's plot, does not traverse New Mexico.) The film creates an equivalence between Sleeping Beauty's castle—an ersatz version of the castle at Neuschwanstein, which is in turn a late nineteenth-century copy of medieval Gothic architecture—and Shiprock, the most

Figure 1.3. Jerry Bruckheimer Films production logo, 2013.

sacred site for the Navajo nation. This seamless movement between two sites suggests how easily and extensively Navajo (and by extension, Native American spaces) are despatialized in the service of global and imperial economies. The camera speeds up as it approaches Shiprock and suddenly enters a tunnel bored directly into the rock. After a few seconds of darkness, the viewer finds herself in the tunnel at eye level with railroad tracks, the light of an oncoming train racing toward the camera/viewer and the sound of the locomotive growing louder. The train barrels over the camera, and the viewer catches a glimpse of its wheels rolling at high speed over the tracks. The perspective then changes, and the camera is now at the front of the train, presumably on the cowcatcher given its low perspective. As the train races out of the tunnel, it emerges onto a darkened plain that is starkly at odds with the mesa country of its entrance. Lightning strikes dot the horizon until a dead tree comes into view and is struck by lightning, transforming it into a living, green thing, at which point the image is framed and "Jerry Bruckheimer Films" appears.

The lightning strike as the concluding image of the logo not so subtly points to Jerry Bruckheimer Films (and Jerry Bruckheimer) as the source of a transformative creative power, one that can literally bring life to lifeless things. The railroad tracks and the logo's use of the phantom ride, one of the oldest film techniques and genres, position JBF at the end of a literal and metaphorical railroad line. With its invocation of the phantom ride, which I discussed in the introduction, JBF also aligns itself with the earliest days of filmmaking, suggesting that Bruckheimer is a modern-day heir to the visionaries who founded the industry. The railroad links Bruckheimer to that history. JBF's production logo shows us the pervasiveness of the narrative of US railroad creationism. The logo reel depicts the railroad as roaring through Tsé Bit' a'í, a sacred space for the Navajo people. This is not historically accurate as Shiprock most definitely does not have a train tunnel running through it; however, the fact that it features so prominently in a production logo trumpeting the creative powers of Hollywood is instructive. My point is that our imaginative lives are saturated with this concept that the train created the nation. What is noteworthy is how ordinary this association has become, so much so that the image of a train barreling through the religious grounds of a nation becomes an example of American exceptionalism. The production reel makes clear that where once there was nothing, the railroad brought forth life.[49]

Snowpiercer

Beyond the inclusion of the railroad and the Native American figures, however, both *Across the Continent* and *American Progress* share an unusual compositional characteristic. As I noted earlier, Aikin makes the claim that "almost all pictures of the great migration employ leftward movement" in the composition of the image.[50] This preference is not characteristic of European landscape paintings, and there is no tendency in American landscape painting more broadly to favor a leftward composition. Aikin persuasively argues that Americans may be more "compass oriented" than others, not because Americans are more geographically literate, but because Manifest Destiny relies on compass-oriented metaphors to persuade. The importance of the compass in defining American spaces is evident in the importance and prestige of the post of surveyor in the early days of the republic (George Washington and Abraham Lincoln both started their professional careers as surveyors). Because of the "unknown" nature of the continent's interior, Congress set up the Public Land Survey and sent surveyors out to "impose a rectilinear grid of true compass directions on the natural features of the landscape."[51] This mania for orientation along the cardinal directions explains the placement of state borders in the western half of the United States, often in defiance of geographical features. Settlers used the compass points to orient their streets, towns, and homesteads (which explains the proliferation of numbered street names). So strong is this compass orientation that incredibly, the western United States is the "only part of the world that looks like a grid from the air."[52] It is easy to see how the train fits into this obsession with orienting the land to match the story of Manifest Destiny: it is the straight line that will lead the nation to its political and geographic destiny. Our conception of the nation's history is inextricable from its spatialization; space dictates the story we tell and the story we tell about ourselves is a highly spatial one.

Bong Joon-ho is not American but an awareness of directional orientation is strikingly apparent in his film *Snowpiercer*. Whereas the leftward movement of railroad creationism is meant to impose a gridded order on land that seems disorienting, the rightward drive of *Snowpiercer* has another goal: to overturn the engine that orders the lives of everyone on the train. Set in 2031, Snowpiercer is a train with an "eternal engine" that circumnavigates the globe annually on a precise schedule. Onboard are the last survivors of a manmade disaster. Seventeen years prior to the movie's start, the world's governments released a chemical into the planet's atmosphere that was meant to counteract the effects of global warming. Rather than moderating temperatures as anticipated, the chemical caused a chain reaction that instead plunged the entire planet into a deep freeze that has made it uninhabitable.[53] The few remaining human survivors board Snowpiercer, which was built, engineered, and is run by the mysterious magnate Wilford (Ed Harris), who exercises total control over the lives of everyone on the train. Although Snowpiercer can be seen as a modern-day ark, the train is anything but safe. Those who paid for their spots on the train live a life of unbelievable luxury in the cars near the engine. The vast majority of Snowpiercer's passengers, however, have not paid and live in squalid conditions in the tail section. Guards from the train's elite section brutally maintain order and periodically appear in full riot gear to murder, maim, and kidnap those in the tail section. Realizing that the police are armed but no longer have bullets, Curtis (Chris Evans) takes the lead in a tail-section rebellion after two children, Timmy and Andy, are brutally taken away from their respective parents. Advised by the kindly Gilliam (John Hurt), Curtis believes that previous insurrections (including one called the Revolt of the Seven) have failed because the rebels failed to take the engine. Curtis enlists the help of Namgoong Minsoo (Song Kang-ho), who helped design the train's doors and who insists on bringing along his daughter, Yona (Ko Asung), a so-called train baby who exhibits clairvoyant qualities. As the group of rebels fight their way through increasingly luxurious and decadent train cars, their numbers are decimated by Wilford's henchmen. Only Curtis, Namgoong, and Yona make it alive to the engine. Wilford welcomes Curtis into the engine room and reveals that he and Gilliam have been working together since the train first launched to ensure its ability to sustain life. Tail section rebellions (like the Revolt of the Seven) were allowed to proceed in order to control the population of the train. Wilford offers Curtis the chance to take over Snowpiercer. Stunned to realize the extent to which his life has been controlled by Wilford and Gilliam, Curtis seems on the brink of accepting the offer until Yona breaks in and reveals the truth behind the engine's walls and floors: the "eternal engine" is disintegrating, and Wilford has been ordering the kidnapping of children like Timmy and Andy from the tail section to replace parts that have become obsolete. Realizing the futility of creating a more just social order on a train that literally runs on the bodies of children, Curtis sacrifices his arm to extract Timmy from the engine. Curtis and Namgoong then detonate an explosive, using their bodies to shield Timmy and Yona. The blast derails the train, causes a massive avalanche, and presumably kills everyone except Timmy and Yona, who emerge from the wreckage and catch a glimpse of a polar bear, a sign that life has returned to the planet.

Although most articles about the film have concentrated on its critique of the relationship between capitalism and climate catastrophe, my argument will focus on the how the film uses the train to launch an incomplete critique of settler colonialism embodied by the character of Yona, who is half Korean and half Inuit. Wilford and his cronies intensify the railroad creationism that is implied in the paintings of Manifest Destiny. In a speech to the tail section, Minister Mason (Tilda Swinton) articulates a view of life on the train that prizes order above all else: "We must all of us in this train of life remain in our allotted station. We must each of us occupy our preordained particular position." This order is not arbitrary but is "prescribed by the sacred engine. All things flow from the sacred engine. All things in their place. All passengers in their sections. All water flowing, all heat rising pays homage to the Sacred Engine." This is railroad creationism taken to its logical extreme. The train transforms life so that order is possible. It transforms an inhospitable and completely hostile landscape into something approaching regulation and order. The promise in the paintings of Manifest Destiny is that the train brings with it modernity, exceptionalism, and civilization; in *Snowpiercer*, the onset of climate catastrophe means that the state no longer has to maintain that pretense of benevolence and progress to pacify its inhabitants.

Mason's railroad creationism insists that the train creates a new kind of order, one that still relies on "natural" laws such as the law of thermodynamics ("all water flowing, all heat rising") to naturalize the social hierarchies imposed by the engine. While that order is disciplined and brutal, it can be seen from certain perspectives as aesthetically pleasing and can even offer a measure of tranquility.[54] That is why the train's inclusion in landscape paintings is so crucial: it imparts order and beauty to a scene that might otherwise seem blank. Bong makes this point in the film with his depiction of Wolford's engine room, which is encased in a lattice of polished steel and furnished sparely if richly. The pleasure of silence and simplicity that the engine room offers is, of course, also a façade, as Yona reminds Curtis when she pulls away the panels to reveal children in the works.

The film's critique of railroad creationism, then, is a critique of the belief that technology, whether in the form of a chemical released into the upper atmosphere or in the form of an "eternal" train, can transform or save our planet and our lives. Bong renders this critique in filmic terms with his decision to spatialize the insurrection of the tailsectioners. In an interview with *Vice* magazine, Bong explains the decision-making process behind filming the rebellion:

Within the frame, me and the DP [director of photography] shot the film so that left would be the tail section of the train in the back, and right would be the engine at the front of the train. So you always get the feeling of going from left to right. Whenever you see Curtis moving to the front of the train, you're almost always seeing that principle in effect."[55]

Figure 1.4. Still from *Snowpiercer*. Directed by Bong Joon-ho, 2013.

Like the paintings of Manifest Destiny, the film is strongly aware of directional orientation. Unlike those paintings, however, that direction is rightward/eastward. The camera often tracks down the length of the car with the lens at a 90-degree angle to the train's central long axis so characters appear in profile as they move right. Given the space constraints of the train, Bong also makes use of diagonal or recessional composition to emphasize the left-to-right movement. The scene in which the revolutionaries enter the school train is emblematic of the way that film represents settler spatialization. Curtis and his crew, with Minister Mason in tow as a hostage, enter a schoolroom on their way through the train cars. The children are cherubic and immaculately dressed, and their school environment is like that of an elite private school. The blond schoolteacher, who looks like she stepped straight out of a frontier fantasy in a long floral print dress, lacy collar, and sensible shoes, is heavily pregnant and maniacally cheerful, about to teach a lesson on Wilford's life and the history of the train. As the tailsectioners move slowly through the school car, the school children and teacher remain curiously indifferent to their presence. The tailsectioners are the dynamic figures in the scene and are shot from a variety of angles as they inch slowly forward but in positions that always maintain a rightward movement. The children in contrast remain seated at their desks, and their teacher's movement also seems slow and unsteady (at least until she pulls out a machine gun and starts shooting the tailsectioners). If American notions of its national space are defined by the fact that our "physical, historical, and psychological conquest of the continent proceeded inexorably westward"—a certainty that was taught to us in pedagogical settings like the one depicted at this moment in the film—then *Snowpiercer* can be read as an attempt to counter that relentless westward drive, which has defined American settler colonialism since the founding of the republic.[56]

The figure that the film invests with this critique is Yona, Namgoong's daughter. As the tailsectioners walk slowly rightward, the schoolteacher tells the children the history of the Revolt of the Seven, whose frozen bodies come into view as the camera slowly pans right. As she shares her lesson (which is couched in the good-bad binaries of so many grade-school history lessons), Namgoong quietly tells another version to Yona. He identifies the figure at the head of the seven as an Inuit woman who worked as a maid in the front section and tells his daughter that this woman knew everything about snow and ice. Believing that life off the train could be sustained, she and six compatriots escaped the train only to freeze to death before they crested the first hill. Her body and those of her comrades—frozen in mid-stride—stand as a monument to tailsectioners' irresponsibility and stupidity (from the perspective of the teacher and the elite whom she represents) and a reminder of the human cost to revolution (from the perspective of Namgoong and his daughter). Namgoong and his daughter's recessional orientation rightward offers a physical counterpoint to the story of triumph, progress, and individual greatness offered by the schoolteacher.

Although we know that the leader of the Revolt of the Seven was an Inuit woman, the film never reveals that this woman was Yona's mother.[57] When Namgoong looks out the window and sees the bodies of the seven, the audience is unaware that he is looking at the remains of his partner and his daughter's mother, and there is nothing in the film that hints at the possibility that Yona's mother was Indigenous. The absence of Indigenous representation in a film that makes a settler colonial critique is clearly troubling on a number of levels, including but not limited to the fact that the leader of the Revolt of the Seven is never named, Yona is never identified as half Inuit, and the actress who was cast in the part of Yona is not of Indigenous descent. Centralizing the train highlights the film's unpacking of settler ideologies of space, but it still renders the experience of the Indigenous characters invisible and disconnected from the critique it is exploring. Even in the new "new world" in which Yona and Timmy find themselves, the Indigenous woman, who first theorized that life off the train was possible and sacrificed to test the possibilities of life off the train, remains erased both on the level of plot and body. It is clear that Yona's own Inuit heritage is unknown to her, meaning that even though Indigenous knowledge has saved mankind, Indigenous people remain erased from any "new" history that is about to be written.

Repurposing the Railroad

If *Snowpiercer* represents a rebuttal to the visual economies of Manifest Destiny and railroad creationism, then we can see a similar critique in the art of Jaque Fragua. Fragua's installation pieces *Stop Coal, Untitled 2012,* and *Untitled 2015* reverse a narrative that essentially insists that the "Indian" is a figure upon which the railroad is built. His work "repurpos[es] his culture's iconography" to "conceptually subvert our overconsumption of misappropriated Native American design and identity."[58] One of the ways that Fragua subverts this "overconsumption" and "misappropriation" is by inverting the relationship between land, railroad, and Native American. Rather than being the surface upon which the train inscribes civilization (productivity and consumption), the Native American becomes the agent of inscription. Fragua's acts of graffiti on freight trains that are in situ transform the train as the expression of Manifest Destiny and settler colonialism into the surface upon which Fragua writes Native American continuing presence.

Fragua's reversal of who inscribes and onto what surface plays on early twentieth century popular images of the railroad and the Native American. The visual rhetoric is particularly visible in railroad advertising of the early twentieth century. With the threat of Indian aggression described by Palmer in the 1860s a relic of the past, the relationship between Native and railroad changed at the turn of the century. Whereas the paintings of railroad creationism represent the Native American as

peripheral to the march of progress, precisely because the figure represents such a threat to the nation, early twentieth-century advertisements
for leisure travel positioned the Native American front and center in
their campaigns, part of a broader marketing strategy to increase leisure
ridership of railroads in the face of falling profits. The commodification
of the Indian had everything to do with increasing passenger train ridership, which had dropped after the economic downturn of the 1890s.
The boom in railroad construction in the 1880s meant that companies
were competing against each other for passengers. And as railroad travel
became an increasingly commonplace aspect of American life, no longer
could the promise of novelty, comfort, and convenience woo complacent
riders onboard. Given this, railroad companies like the ATSF and other
western lines increasingly turned to tourism to make up numbers.

These economic pressures are reflected in the way that railroads advertised their services for passengers. In the early days of train travel,
railroad ads tended to consist of maps that emphasized the distance that
the train would travel on a line. The late nineteenth and early twentieth centuries marked a transition into advertisements that trumpeted
"appeal[s] of place," in which consumers were sold on the unique characteristics of the cities or resorts that served as the stops for railroad networks.[59] Railroad companies whose territories covered the western half
of the country began a concerted effort to sell to consumers the romance
of the "Old New World."[60] In partnership with the advertising and hos-
pitality industries, railroad companies were instrumental in bringing
to the public's attention the "western wonderlands" of California and
the Pacific Northwest.[61] "The railroad's objective [during what has been
called advertising's 'golden age' from c. 1900–1950] was . . . to persuade
tourists, potential settlers, sportsmen, and health-seekers to book passage on company trains and coastal steamships."[62] To lure curious passengers eager to see last of the frontier, railroads actively commissioned,
sponsored, and bought artworks for use in their advertisements, bro-
chures, and merchandise to proclaim the wonders of landmarks and
cities that were on their routes. No other railroad was as active in the
production and commercialization of western-themed art as the ATSF.
The ATSF not only bought such art, it also commissioned artists to create the canvases, often providing transportation, food, and lodging to
the artists in exchange for the paintings themselves.

ATSF art featured the landscape and the Native peoples of the American West, and their advertising emphasized the fact that both were
on the verge of passing into history. Artists hired by the railroad were
charged with capturing the grandeur of the landscape "before it disap-
peared" as well as the "dying race" of Native Americans who lived on
those lands.[63] In naming its flagship passenger train the Chief in 1926,
the railroad was doubling down on its strategy to lure tourists by linking landscape to Native American bodies and cultures. The Chief was
famous for being the first all-Pullman passenger train from Chicago to
Los Angeles. In dozens of advertisements from this period, the stylized
face of an Indian chief—sometimes young, sometimes old, always in
full headdress—gazes out at potential passengers. Most of the advertisements are based on the paintings of Hernando Gonzallo Villa (1881–
1952), a commercial artist who was one of the few artists of Mexican
descent active in the Southern California arts scene of the early twentieth century.[64] The ATSF's use of the Chief to describe its train service
is suggestive of how the Indian body is subsumed in this era into the
service of the train. The famous tagline "The Chief . . . is still chief"
represents a curious mélange of binaries. The text of the advertisement
equates the sign "the Chief" with the train, while the image makes the
association between the sign and the human figure depicted. The move
between text and image—or to put it more precisely, the desire for that
move to be seamless and frictionless—depends on the Native American
no longer being present. The mutability of the Chief's face, sometimes
painted realistically and sometimes presented in a more stylized fashion, also plays into the merging of text and body that I am referencing.
The text, the train, and the body of the Indian, in other words, are all
collapsed together in these ads. As the Indian becomes "the face" of the
train, the railroad company can write on this evacuated body whatever
messaging it wants.

During the early twentieth century, the Native American came not
only to symbolize the "appeal of place[s]" like California or the Southwest; his body became the place itself.[65] In a 1900 advertisement for the
Northern Pacific Railroad, the railroad line is mapped perfectly onto
the body of a Native American figure, who is lying face down on the
ground, his face and neck projecting over a rocky edge. The railroad
line forms the outline of the Indian's back, from his toe (represented by

Figure 1.5. *The Story of a Railroad Wonderland.* Northern Pacific Railroad, 1900.

St. Paul, Minnesota) to his forehead (representing Portland, Oregon) and down one of his long braids (representing San Francisco, the line's terminus). The Winnipeg branch forms the outline of the Indian's right leg, which is bent at an accommodating 90-degree angle to maintain the map's spatial and geographical accuracy. Unsurprisingly, given what the advertisement is about, the Yellowstone Park branch line is positioned at the center of the image, above the Northern Pacific's large logo, right at the center of the Indian's waist. Other important stations—Spokane, Seattle, Vancouver, Lewiston—are located on other parts of the Indian's body (the top of his shoulder, the top of his head, the tip of his feather headdress, and his shoulder blade, respectively). Many of the cities on this route—Winnipeg (Cree and Ojibwe), Spokane (Spokane), Seattle (Duwamish), Tacoma (Puyallup), Missoula (Salish)—name the tribes that inhabited these lands. The image is striking for both its highly de-tailed draftsmanship (from the fringes on the figure's buckskin suit to the wrinkles around his eyes, nose, and mouth) and its perfect confla-tion of the Indian with the train and the landscape. Whereas once the Native American was depicted attempting to blow up train tracks (see for example, Theodore Kauffman's oil on canvas *Westward the Star of Empire*, ca. 1880), by 1900, he has literally become the ground on which the train runs. The Indian body provides the ground for settler practices only when settlement has already occurred.

Fragua's works strongly refute the collapsing link between Native American and land that the ATSF and other railroads promulgated. His installations do not depict Native American figures; rather, they reenvision iconic Native American images to reveal the presence of Native Americans on lands that are often imagined as having no past beyond the nation. Although he works in a wide range of media, my focus here will be on Fragua's work as a graffiti artist. Graffiti is usually thought to be situated in urban streetscapes and its practitioners in such cases are often young, male, and disenfranchised. While it is often understood to be illegal, graffiti depends on being displayed in public but inaccessible spaces (such as on the concrete barriers of a highly traveled freeway). Urban geographers like Toni Moreau and Derek Alderman have argued that graffiti "serve[s] as a tactic for challenging and offering alternative meanings for public space and for who belongs or whose ideas count within these spaces."[66] The ordered and productive spaces that Palmer imagines the railroad creating out of the chaos of the Native American lands is a perfect manifestation of what Moreau and Alderman call an "exclusionary geograph[y]." Graffiti is meant to disrupt that exclusion. In the popular imaginary, graffiti and tagging are construed as territorial markers for gangs with vaguely "harmful effects" on the communities in which they appear. But urban geographers tend to point to graffiti as "indicators of social tension," "acts of dissonance," and "registers of social trauma, cultural meaning, and political expression."[67]

Graffiti is most often associated with the city, and indeed, Fragua is perhaps most famous for a piece of street art titled *Untitled (One-liner)*, *2014*. Using bright red paint, Fragua painted "THIS IS INDIAN LAND" in eight-foot letters on a temporary construction wall in downtown Los Angeles on the corner of South Eighth Street and Main. Someone reported the graffiti to the LAPD as a "hate crime"; posting the image on his personal Instagram was enough to get him kicked off the social media platform for violating its terms of service.[68] Fragua's "Graffiti on a Train" series is not set in urban environments, however. The locations are clearly rural, devoid of people and buildings. For example, Fragua's *Stop Coal* depicts an abandoned freight car on which Fragua has painted the phrase "Stop Coal" in a distinctive style of lettering that is meant to invoke Native American design. The darkened freight car sits in the shadow, between expanses of dirt and weeds in the foreground and a clear blue sky in the background. Visible in the distance is a green interstate sign, which indicates that the freight car is situated next to a well-traveled road (Fragua also paints his graffiti on abandoned billboards along highways). Fragua has explicitly noted that the political message behind *Stop Coal* was meant to draw attention to the toxic impact of coal mines on the bodies and environments of the Hopi and Navajo peoples in northern Arizona.[69] Fragua explains that he feels "like the landscape talks to me and then I translate what the landscape is saying onto the actual environment," a statement that elides the fact that Fragua's graffiti work is almost never done on the land itself.[70] Rather, Fragua situates his critique on the surfaces that call attention to the nation's history of exploitation: abandoned billboards, which he identifies with the commodification of Indian culture and images, and the train, which was fueled by coal in the nineteenth century and enabled the settlers to intensify their profit-seeking extraction of natural resources.

Fragua's environmental message is part of a long history of Native resistance to resource extraction in the name of "productivity" (to borrow Palmer's term from the start of the chapter), a history that was on full display during the #NoDAPL movement. The Native nations that camped out in and around Standing Rock, North Dakota, in solidarity with the Oceti Sakowin to protest the construction of the Dakota Access Pipeline constitute an "Indian Problem" for the state. According to Nick Estes, "Controlling the 'Indian Problem' has always meant maintaining unrestricted access to Native lands and resources and keeping Indians silent, out of view, and factionalized."[71] The policing of Indians' bodies described by Estes is fully backed by the images of Indians that appear in the paintings of railroad creationism and in the advertising images of the ATSF. Estes's rich historicization of the protests at Standing Rock reveal the long history of environmental catastrophe that settlers have wrought on the lands they occupy; as all the texts that I have cited in this chapter indicate, the train was an integral part of that eradication process. Fragua's exhortation to "Stop Coal," inscribed on the wreckage of the very machine that has historically enabled the exploitation of Native lands, inverts the usual process of settlement. Rather than being a tool of the colonizer to make the land legible and to disembody the Native subject into some kind of romantic figuration of landscape, Fragua transforms the train into the very ground that the Native figure has traditionally occupied in settler discourse. To put it another way, Fragua's graffiti art "revitalize[s] [a] politics of place" that the train has historically tried to despatialize.[72]

This reversal of the role that the train has played in Native American history can also be seen in Fragua's other works. The freight cars in *Untitled 2012* and *Untitled 2015* are sprayed in the same rhythmic pattern that evokes Native American design. While *Untitled 2012* and *Untitled 2015* do not contain any overtly political message, Fragua's choice of design on the freight cars asks us to take seriously the surface on which his text is inscribed. In a highly instructive article on the complexities of graffiti, Ella Chmielewska argues that inscription is a more accurate concept for describing graffiti's relationship to text and materiality rather than the more commonly theorized concept of icon, which is understood to appeal directly to the viewer without language.[73] The "Graffiti on a Train" series offers an avenue for Fragua to challenge the narrative propagated by the railroad advertisements that the train is the domesticator of Native lands and peoples and that it made it possible for settlers, tourists, and passengers to safely visit the spaces that were once considered uninhabitable and in danger of being "lost." Whereas in the paintings of Manifest Destiny and in the railroad advertisements of the early twentieth century the Indian is seen as being in the process of being expelled from the land or as a part of its romanticized past, Fragua's inscription on the train car inverts the entire narrative, inscribing that which has been used to inscribe. This notion of inscription is particularly visible in a technique Fragua calls "one-liner," in which he wraps "whole buildings, billboards, [and] train cars" with "a single continuous line," the shape of which is inspired by Native American design.[74] Fragua claims to enjoy the one-liner technique because it is "therapeutic; there [is] a frequency, pattern, rhythm, and syncopation happening while I was painting."[75]

The one-liner is present in both of Fragua's *Untitled* graffiti works. The shape that he creates invokes the landforms of northwestern New Mexico, which is filled with deep canyons, valleys, cliffs, and mesas. Fragua's design on the freight cars echoes the geography that surrounds the Jemez Pueblo, another inversion of the putative relationship between rail and land. Fragua's use of a "single, continuous line" evokes the image of the train in nineteenth century visual culture: the single straight line that would lead the nation to the Pacific and civilize the land and peoples within. Only rather than the train marking the land to make it legible to settler economies and governance, in Fragua's work, the land marks the train to make visible histories of Native extermination.

Despite its public and highly visual nature, graffiti is ephemeral. Fragua notes that his works are usually painted over within a week; this was the case with *Untitled (One-liner), 2014.* He attributes this erasure to a "visceral" fear that his text elicits. He also accepts and celebrates the fact that street art is not meant to be preserved: "When you paint something, eventually the environment gets to it, and it starts to wear down. The sun bakes [the work] and things start to fade. The paint starts to come through and I love all of that stuff."[76] In contrast to paint, inscription cannot be easily erased even if the text itself is painted over. Just as railroad tracks crisscrossed this nation in an attempt to bring to heel the land underneath it and to eradicate the Indigenous population, Fragua's inscription on the train cars will remain, a palimpsest that reemerges from time to time before being hastily blotted out. Such blotting, Fragua suggests, is also not permanent. The belief that the train can stamp out the Native and bring forth the nation is itself the very material that Fragua uses to resist that narrative. The train has become the surface for Native American resistance.

2

The Chinaman's Crime

The railroad with which the Chinese are most associated in the United States is the First Transcontinental Railroad. That is because the Chinese were instrumental in that railroad's completion, laying track in the Sierra Nevada Mountains and finding ways to blast through the rock that made this portion of the track the most difficult terrain any railroad company had ever attempted to build upon. Chinese work on the railroad and its afterlives in Chinese American history, memory, and culture are the focus of my next two chapters, but in this chapter, I want to consider how a nation that was uneasy about the presence of the Chinese used the railroad to emphasize their racial difference. I turn to Willa Cather's short fiction about the Chinese not only because she is the American author most associated with the American frontier but also because her stories capture how anxieties about the Chinese are always entangled with questions about the nation's modernity and exceptionalism—all of which are embodied by the train.

Cather's "The Affair at Grover Station" (1900) is narrated by an un-named traveler, who meets an old acquaintance, "Terrapin" Rodgers, while riding on a train in the West. Rodgers proceeds to tell the narrator the story of the murder of Lawrence O'Toole, a popular agent at Grover Station, Wyoming. The villain of the story is Freymark, a mysterious railroad agent and professional gambler who has a personal and profes-sional antipathy toward the upright O'Toole. When Rodgers discovers that Freymark is not the "Alsatian Jew" he has advertised himself to be but really of Chinese descent, he declares that this fact "explain[s] every-thing."[1] It explains why Freymark, a man of about thirty, has the "yel-low, wrinkled hands" of a "centenarian," although he takes "the greatest care" of them.[2] It explains his "unusual, stealthy grace," his "sallow [and] unwholesome looking" face, the "impudent red lips," and the sense that there is something "in his present, or in his past, or in his destiny which isolate[s] him from other men."[3] Most important of all, the story implies that it is Freymark's Chinese blood that leads him to murder O'Toole in cold blood at Grover Station before hiding the body on an eastbound freight car and returning to Cheyenne to dance at the governor's inaugural ball with O'Toole's sweetheart, Helen Masterson. After dancing with the love of his murder victim, Freymark steps on a train and vanishes, never to be tried or punished for the crime he committed.

In many ways, "The Affair at Grover Station" presents a familiar, early twentieth-century justification for Chinese exclusion. It warns that the Chinese have no place in America, and if they are allowed to sneak in, as Freymark has, the consequences for the hard-working men who represent the best of the US frontier and the virtuous women who love them will be dire if not disastrous. In this regard, Freymark seems to fit in with the cast of Chinese villains who populate the cultural landscape of the late nineteenth and early twentieth centuries. From Frank Norris's depictions in "The Third Circle" (1909) of the Chinese as kidnapping, drugging, and then enslaving white women, to Jack London's fantasy of a race war between China and the United States in "The Unparalleled Invasion" (1910), to the evil, world-conquering machinations of Sax Rohmer's Dr. Fu Manchu (first introduced in 1913 with *The Insidious Dr. Fu Manchu*), Chinese fictional characters such as Freymark reflected and reinforced the widespread early twentieth-century belief that the Chinese presented a real and imminent threat to the nation, a belief that reached its hysterical heights with the passage of the first Chinese Exclusion Act in 1882 but that resonated for much of the twentieth century. Jacob Riis, who deplored the miserable conditions under which many immigrants lived in the New York City slums in *How the Other Half Lives* (1890), nevertheless wrote in the same volume that the Chinese "are in no sense a desirable element of the population . . . [and] serve no useful purpose here"; in fact, "they are [such] a constant and terrible menace to society" that the "severest official scrutiny, [and] the harshest repressive measures are justifiable in Chinatown."[4]

Despite the seeming unanimity of anti-Chinese sentiment throughout this period, the manner in which the Chinese were depicted in popular fiction was anything but monolithic. Each Chinese figure, Freymark included, offers a slightly different version of a complicated historical story, one that has little to do with the experiences or histories of the Chinese in America and instead has everything to do with US anxieties regarding the limits of its national identity and emerging global power. In attempting to account for the depth of anti-Chinese sentiment and the diversity of its literary manifestations, a productive but relatively unheralded conversation has emerged among literary scholars regarding the archaeology of Asian racial formation in the early twentieth century.

These viewpoints are by no means mutually exclusive; in fact, they overlap and build on each other in important ways, but each focuses on a slightly different trope within anti-Chinese discourse to explain the power and persistence of Asian racialization. For Colleen Lye, Asian racialization in the early twentieth century was built around economic tropes, and she argues that the association between Asians and economic modernity characterizes much of that discourse—both in its "negative" manifestations (yellow peril) and in its "positive" ones (model minority).[5] David Palumbo-Liu argues that Asian racialization had everything to do with the nation's attempts to "manage" the modern, which was particularly linked to conquering the Pacific Rim.[6] Robert G. Lee presents extensive historical evidence that the Chinese were imagined to be contaminants, infecting and weakening every aspect of US life they touched, from labor to urban spaces, from gender relations to domestic arrangements.[7] For these critics, the key to understanding the racialization of the Chinese in the early twentieth century is to analyze what Lye calls "modernity's dehumanizing effects."[8]

I want to build on the conversation that I have summarized above to argue that "The Affair at Grover Station" offers a particular and peculiar twist on the usual anti-Chinese rhetoric, one that I will attempt in this essay to parse and make meaning of. The wellspring of Chinese amorality and the justification for their exclusion is not rooted merely in an inherently violent or uncivilized nature; rather, the story argues that Freymark and his ilk should be excluded from the nation because they are *old*, and not just old, but *too* old. In other words, what is most noteworthy about Rodger's Sinophobia is its emphasis on the ancientness of the Chinese as a race. "The Affair at Grover Station" goes to great lengths to assert the fact that Freymark commits this premeditated murder because he belongs to "a race that was already old when Jacob tended the flocks of Laban upon the hills of Padan-Aram, a race," Rodgers goes on to note, "that was in its mort clｏ h before Europe's swaddling clothes were made."[9] Rodgers staunchly beｌ ｸves that Freymark murders

O'Toole because of the "sluggish amphibious blood" that flows through his veins.[10] The antiquity of Chinese civilization has rendered its citizens walking anachronisms—forever foreign both in terms of space *and* time—and therefore unfit for inclusion into the United States.

The problem with this verdict is that Freymark does not seem to be aware of the fact that he and his race have been relegated to the dustbin of history. This, I would argue, is the central conundrum that troubles "The Affair at Grover Station": the Chinese never seem to recognize their irrelevance and so fail to fade away accordingly. On the contrary, the Chinese do not merely cling to the modernity that America exemplifies, they thrive in it. Rodgers grudgingly but repeatedly showcases Freymark's genius for maneuvering himself through the US landscape. Rodgers describes Freymark as a shrewd if dishonest businessman with an "insatiable passion for gambling."[11] Freymark's murder of O'Toole is a technical feat as well as a diabolical one; he takes a train down to Grover Station from Cheyenne, murders O'Toole, disposes of the body, performs the dead man's work in order to allay any suspicions, and then catches another train back to Cheyenne in time for the ball—all in the absence of any eyewitnesses who can definitively place him at the scene of the crime.[12] Thus, the story's insistence on Chinese exclusion based on their atemporality as citizen-subjects masks a much deeper anxiety: that the Chinese are actually incredibly adept at maneuvering themselves through modernity, rendering the United States a belated newcomer to the modernity that it had believed itself to epitomize.

The story's anxiety that the Chinese actually embody—rather than threaten—US modernity is exemplified and complicated by two interconnected tropes that are central to the story. The first is the railroad and Freymark's relationship to it. As I discussed in the introduction, for much of the nineteenth century, the railroad was a potent symbol of US Manifest Destiny, the very thing that justified and exemplified US exceptionalism. Yet in "The Affair at Grover Station," it is Freymark who is most closely linked with the railroad. He was the station agent at Grover Station before being caught in financial shenanigans by the scrupulously honest O'Toole; after his dismissal, Rodgers explains that Freymark "went into cattle" and often "sent cattle shipments our way."[13] His success in murdering O'Toole depends on his ability to navigate train schedules as a passenger and his knowledge of the railway business as a freight agent; because he is a prized customer, Freymark can request that the train make unscheduled stops at his ranch outside of Cheyenne. Freymark is last seen riding on the Union Pacific railroad, free presumably to create another identity and insinuate himself into the life of another town in the West. Freymark's association with the railroad—and the fact that he uses it to commit and then flee from his crime—is perhaps the most convincing indicator that the story's attempt to relegate the Chinese to the ancient past cannot succeed. If the train is the stage for national identity in the turn-of-the century United States, then somewhere riding the rails, the Chinese linger, hidden, fungible, and able, surprisingly, to blend in.

The second trope that informs the story's anxieties regarding the Chinese is one that will be familiar to Cather readers: that of memory. As much as any work of fiction within Cather's canon, "The Affair at Grover Station" is an anxious meditation on the nature of memory-making itself—*how* memories are formed and recalled—and the narratives that are conjured by certain memories. It is a story about mnemonics, or the signs that we must interpret to make certain memories available. Freymark, as we shall see, transforms himself into a mnemonic device, essentially asserting that any act of memory on the part of the characters will have to take him into account. In inserting himself into the memory-making process, he also implicates the railroad; indeed, it is while riding a train, "sitting on the rear platform of an accommodation freight that [is] crawl[ing] along through the brown sun-dried wilderness between Grover Station and Cheyenne," that Terrapin Rodgers decides to tell his tale to the story's frame narrator.[14] Freymark's co-optation of memory and his association with the railroad emblematizes the story's concern that the Chinese can shape national narratives, even when their presence is demeaned and minimized. The story emphasizes the antiquity of China in an attempt to control the kind of memories they provoke—things easily relegated to the past, irrelevant to the workings of an US present—but it simultaneously presents a lingering anxiety that the Chinese can not only control that modernity (as Freymark controls the railroad) but also the meaning-making processes that bind the nation together. Freymark's ability to ride the rails undetected marks the train system as possibly contaminated by the invisible presence of the Chinese. It is precisely because the Chinese are perceived as being anachronistic—that is, out of their time—that their presence disrupts the nationalist narratives that are central to the nation's imagined community.

The Chinese and Temporality

The relationship between temporality and racial difference is vital to understanding the threat that Freymark poses in "The Affair at Grover Station." As I stated earlier, the Chinese cannot be assimilated, but not merely because they are heathens, contaminated, and less than human. Instead, these qualities are the results of their own racial, cultural, and political obsolescence. What distinguishes the Chinese from other racialized groups (and makes them fascinating to Americans from the nineteenth century to the present) is the perception that although China was once a highly civilized and cultured nation, it now lingers stubbornly in a world that has moved beyond it. Theirs is a race that is characterized not by belatedness in relation to the white man, which is the relationship that Homi Bhabha argues exists between the colonizer and the colonized, but by metachronism, the erroneous placement of a person or event after its actual date.[15] Their continued existence and interaction with Americans therefore represents a disruption of a narrative regarding progress, race, and nation.

A preoccupation with temporality and metachronism pervades much anti-Chinese rhetoric. Stuart Creighton Miller maintains that "China was viewed as singularly impervious to nineteenth-century ideals of progress, liberty, and civilization to which an emergent modern America was committed."[16] The Chinese were often associated with death simply because they themselves were seen as part of a culture and civilization near death. Senator James Blaine, a vociferous champion of Chinese exclusion, argued that Americans had "the right to exclude that immigration which reeks with impurity and which cannot come to us without plenteously sowing the seeds of moral and physical disease, destitution, and death."[17] A cartoon published in the September 25, 1869, issue of *Harper's Weekly* starkly captures the notion of the Chinese as living anachronisms in relation to the United States.[18] The cartoon, titled "The Last Addition to the Family," shows a woman, embodying the United States, holding in her arms what initially appears to be an infant.

Closer inspection reveals the baby to be an ancient Chinaman, with a long queue of black hair, a deeply wrinkled face, and a sinister expression about his eyes. The woman's pose in the cartoon suggests maternal solicitude, and her face is set with what seems to be parental resolve as she gazes upon the infant in her arms. The image is fascinating because it emphasizes the idea that the relationship between the United States and China is generational and thus defined by each nation's place on a timeline. The grotesque image of the Chinaman suggests the ambivalent registers of the nation's construction of Chinese difference. On the one hand, the helplessness and weakness that characterize the Chinese is imagined as a form of infanthood and thus evokes a sense of moral and familial responsibility that fits in with imperialist fantasies. With noble mien, the United States resolves to cherish and care for a nation that clearly violates all principles of domesticity and personhood because it has a duty to civilize. On the other hand, however, the image also evokes a sense of disgust as well as pity. China as a nation is forcibly represented as having entered its "second childishness" but without any sense that "mere oblivion" is about to follow, as Shakespeare tells us. This bizarre image of the Chinese man as at once infantile and ancient powerfully suggests how metachronistic and out of synch the Chinese and Chinese culture are with the modernity that the United States represents. But this combination also makes clear that the Chinaman still has a long life, as it were, ahead of himself, one that the United States will have to take into account in its role as exemplar of the modern world.[19]

Part of what makes Freymark fascinating to Rodgers and other characters is the sense that he is a man out of his time, that there is something "in his present, or in his past, or in his destiny which isolate[s] him from other men."[20] Prior to the revelation of Freymark's racial identity, Rodgers thinks of him as "a blackguard," "queer," and "uncanny."[21] Early in the story, the secret of Freymark's Chinese ancestry is revealed by a cousin of O'Toole's who worked as a journalist in London. Freymark is indeed from Paris, but he is not a Jew, as he initially purports to be; rather, his ancestry "date[s] from farther back than Israel."[22] Rodgers and O'Toole also learn from this source that Freymark is exceedingly sensitive about his Chinese lineage and eager to enter society as a white man; his adoption of a "Jewish patronymic" is an attempt to "account for his oriental complexion and traits of feature." Despite Freymark's attempts to mingle in respectable society, Rodgers and O'Toole learn that while in London, Freymark engaged in "exceedingly questionable traffic"; later, Rodgers again asserts mysteriously that Freymark was involved in "peculiarly un-savory traffic" and that his activities, not to mention his race, would have "disbarred [him from] almost any region outside of Whitechapel."[23] The invocation of Whitechapel, an area associated in the Victorian world with prostitution and, most infamously, Jack the Ripper, gives the reader a sense of the nature of Freymark's underworld ties and the threat he po-tentially poses to the beautiful Miss Masterson particularly and to white womanhood more generally.[24] Rodgers's construction of Freymark's isolation along a timeline rather than through other exclusionary rheto-rics (such as biology, religion, or politics) reflects the particular strain of anti-Chinese discourse in the twentieth century that I discuss above.

The temporal displacement that the narrative continually touches on is also reflected in its structure. Rodgers's narration of O'Toole's murder is surrounded by a framing story that is narrated in the first person by an unnamed college friend of Rodgers. This frame narrator is out West on a geological expedition and recounts meeting Rodgers by chance in Gro-ver Station. While the two men are riding a train car back to Cheyenne, the frame narrator asks to hear the story of O'Toole's murder. Cather often used this framing technique in her stories, most famously in her novel *My Ántonia* (1918), to explore what Lisa Marie Lucenti calls "the architecture of . . . remembrance."[25] In the case of "The Affair at Grover Station," the frame does not merely highlight the narrator's intensive in-terest in making meaning of the past. The framing story acts as another form of temporal displacement, further separating the Chinese from the "here and now" of Rodgers and his college friend in an attempt to locate them more firmly in the "there and then" of the story's own past. Placing Freymark in the past, even if it is the immediate past of the story, con-tains his presence and controls what he is capable of doing in the pres-ent. In addition to the story's temporal containment, Rodgers is warned by his superiors not to repeat the story, an admonishment that is obvi-ously meant to control Freymark's presence, or at least, to control knowl-edge about his presence. Rodgers ignores the warning of his employers and recounts the story to the unnamed framing narrator, partly because he is deeply troubled by what has transpired and partly with the idea of shaping the listeners' understanding of events and O'Toole's blamelessness in them. By the story's end, neither strategy—containment nor repetition—has worked in limiting the impact that Freymark has had on the other characters.

The story's insistence that Freymark's presence can be displaced both temporally and geographically speaks to its anxiety that the Chinese are not as irrelevant as the US wants to believe. The story's description of Freymark falls in line with Colleen Lye's proposition that the United States has historically constructed Asian exceptionalism as an "unusual capacity for economic modernity [that] extends to moments when the effect of racial discourse has been hostile ('yellow peril') as well as admiring ('model minority')."[26] The story's anxiety regarding the Chinese propensity for economic modernity can be seen in Freymark's name itself. In German, *frei* means "free," and *mark* was the currency of Germany in the late nineteenth century. We can thus interpret his name as meaning "free money" or "liberated money." That the struggle between Freymark and the various characters in the story is inextricable from economic issues can also be seen in the description of O'Toole, who is described as having a "face that served him as a sight draft, good in all banks."[27] It seems counter to the story's logic that O'Toole's open face and honest demeanor should bring to mind systems of borrowing and institutions of lending (drafts, banks), while Freymark's sinister mien and crafty manner are associated, linguistically speaking at least, with currency as gifts. However, Lye's theory of US constructions of Asia reveals this seeming contradiction to be two sides of the same coin. In this case, Freymark's name along with his widely recognized skill in gambling and his ability to master the technology of the railroad to commit his nefarious deeds all seem to suggest that despite the corrupting effects of China's great age, it produces men who excel at accumulating capital and manipulating technology. As Lye suggests, the Chinese have historically been perceived as a threat to the US precisely because of their ability to embody both the "yellow peril" and "the model minority," stereotypes that she argues are really different facets of the same racialized discourse. Cather's portrayal of Freymark makes temporality a vital and constitutive component of the Chinese exceptionalism that Lye describes rather than an irreconcilable element outside of it. The agedness of Freymark's Chinese blood does not make him any less adaptable to the modern United States; in fact, it makes him all the more skillful in furthering his economic interests, in moving noiselessly from place to place undetected by anyone, and ultimately in committing a crime for which he will not be punished.

These two strands of thought regarding the Chinese—that they are culturally metachronistic and simultaneously hyper-competent nego- tiators of modernity—necessarily had a profound impact on how the US viewed itself as a nation. The presence of the Chinese in the United States highlights the difference between the two countries in terms of their histories; if China is imagined as a country with too much past, then America becomes the nation with too little. The ease with which Freymark navigates modern life—trains, schedules, firearms, capital— raises the possibility that it is not the Chinese who have outlived their own time but the United States that has arrived belatedly into its own; the angst that Rodgers feels over O'Toole's seeming lateness to the ball, especially after Freymark makes his appearance, echoes a cultural appre- hension that US exceptionalism is merely another way of talking about its laggardly relationship to the temporality that defines modernity. To borrow a formulation of Aamir Mufti's regarding the Jews and Europe, being Chinese in America "puts into question any settled identification of *this* place with *this* people and *this* language."[28]

"Dead Things That Move": Cather's Chinese Fiction

Cather's representation of the Chinese as the living dead is not unique to Freymark and "The Affair at Grover Station." Unlike "The Affair," "A Son of the Celestial" (published in the *journal Hesperian* in 1893) and "The Conversion of Sum Loo" (published in the *Library* in 1900) are set in Chinatown and are character sketches rather than full-fledged narratives. While "The Affair"—with its prairie setting, idealization of frontier life, evocative prose, and a framing narrative device—is more readily identifiable as a Cather work, all three stories make the meta- chronistic nature of the Chinese their focus. Although the Chinese figures in "A Son of the Celestial" and "The Conversion of Sum Loo" are not nearly as villainous as Freymark, they inspire in the other characters a similar level of fear, resentment, and, most interestingly, exaspera- tion. These three stories—all published in the first decade of Cather's professional writing career and which I am dubbing Cather's Chinese fiction—provide a new perspective on Cather's attitudes toward racial difference. While several critics have written about Cather's representation of Jewish and African American characters, none have considered how the Chinese figure into Cather's fiction. Read together, the three stories make clear that Cather's work contains an untapped archive of materials regarding the Chinese in the United States—an archive that does not necessarily contain any accurate information on the lives of the Chinese who worked and lived here but rather that indicates how anti-Chinese discourses were constructed, utilized, and adapted.

Published in the same year as "The Affair at Grover Station," "The Conversion of Sum Loo" is the most sentimental and arguably most sympathetic of the three stories in terms of its treatment of the Chinese. It recounts the attempts of several missionaries with the Heavenly Rest Mission Home to convert Sum Chin, a successful San Francisco merchant, to the Christian faith. Sister Hannah of the mission convinces Sum Chin and his young wife, Sum Loo, to baptize their only son, Sum Wing. Hannah's triumph in bringing the couple to Christ is marred by the intense discomfort she feels when she is in Sum Chin's presence, a discomfort that stems from his demeanor, which is characterized by a "passive, resigned agnosticism, a doubt older than the very beginnings of [her own] faith. . . . It is such an ancient doubt, that of China, and it has gradually stolen the odor from the roses and the tenderness from the breasts of women."[29] Like "The Affair," "The Conversion of Sum Loo" constructs Chinese-American relations in temporal terms, emphasizing the deadening quality of Chinese culture, especially when placed in proximity to US ideals. Unlike Freymark, Sun Chin is a family man who has consciously chosen to assimilate into the US through gender, domestic, and religious conventions. Despite these attempts, Sister Hannah perceives Sum Chin as a threat, not because he represents an immediate physical danger but because of his ability to suck the life out of the innocent things around him. The descriptions of roses that have no scent and breasts that are no longer tender suggests a slower, more seductive form of corruption, one that fascinates as much as it terrorizes. The unexpected death of the baby leads Sum Chin to accuse the "Jesus people" of murdering his son; Sister Hannah then witnesses a terrifying ritual in which Sum Loo, to regain her husband's favor and bear another son, burns the New Testament, one page at a time, as a sacrifice to a fertility god.[30] Horrified by what she has seen, Sister Hannah withdraws from the Chinese mission trip she had agreed to undertake, not because, the story suggests, she lacks religious zeal but because she realizes the ultimate futility of Christianizing Chinese people at all. The nation's duty to Christianize and civilize its Chinese inferiors cannot override the revulsion that China inspires in America's dutiful and modern subjects.

The theme of Chinese antiquity can also be seen in "A Son of the Celestial: A Character Sketch," which describes the life of Yung Le Ho, a San Francisco artist who crafts "painted silken birds, and beautiful lacquered boxes," "bronze vases," "ivory gods," and "carved sandalwood" with such skill that he is compared to Michelangelo.[31] The narrative explicitly mentions the Chinese Exclusion Act and states "that it was not because of the cheapness of Chinese labor that the bill was enacted" but rather the fear of China's "terrible antiquity" that "weighed upon us like a dead hand upon a living heart."[32] Both church and state fear a people "who had printed centuries before Gutenberg was born, who had used anesthetics before chloroform was ever dreamed of. Who, in the new west, settled down and ate and drank and dressed as men had done in the days of the flood."[33] This description of Chinese difference is notable in that it contains a tension. On the one hand, the story portrays the Chinese as nearly sui generis, predating technology, modernity, and even the Flood. And yet this description of the Chinese also betrays a lingering respect for the achievements of their civilization. It is this tension within US orientalism that distinguishes this particular racist discourse from others and that Cather's Chinese stories seize on so consistently and forcefully.

Yung is an opium addict and forms an unlikely friendship with a painter and another addict named Ponter. Ponter professes to like Yung, but in the middle of the brief narrative, he delivers a screed against the Chinese that ends with his berating Yung. Here, any trace of grudging admiration is gone, and Ponter expresses fear of and, surprisingly, frustration with the Chinese:

> Your devilish gods have cursed you with immortality and you have outlived your souls. You are so old that you are born yellow and wrinkled and blind. You ought to have been buried centuries before Europe was

civilized. You ought to have been wrapped in your mort cloth ages before our swaddling clothes were made. You are dead things that move![34]

Ponter's attack expresses impatience that Chinese individuals have refused to die when it is so clear that their civilization has already passed on. But Ponter's frustration might also stem from the fact that although both are artists, only Yung is successful. Yung is able to capitalize on the craze for Oriental objects, even as he smokes up most of the proceeds from his sales. Like Freymark, Yung might be a "dead thing that move[s]," but he is still better than Ponter at understanding US consumer preferences, creating products that will appeal to American orientalist tastes, and selling his work to the public. Ponter's anger stems not just from Yung's decrepitude but also from the success that Yung has as an artist, a success that far outstrips Ponter's.

Strikingly, the language that Cather uses here to describe the Chinese ("You ought to have been wrapped in your mort cloth ages before our swaddling clothes were made") is recycled in "The Affair at Grover Station." The repetition of this language in two different stories indicates an uncharacteristic carelessness on the part of Cather, who was well known for the meticulous care with which she wrote, revised, and shaped her prose.[35] This act of self-plagiarism suggests that words have essentially failed Cather in describing the Chinese and the horror that they inspire in Americans, whether they be drug addicts like Ponter or hard-working frontiersman like Rodgers. The absence of an adequate vocabulary for expressing one's horror at the Chinese seems directly tied to the way in which they undermine the temporality of the nation. In her essay on fiction "The Novel Démeublé," Cather talks about narrative's transformative power to transform "tiresome old patterns" and the "meaningless reiterations" into the "stage of a Greek theatre" or into a "house into which the glory of the Pentecost [has] descended."[36] The Chinese, however, seem impervious to that kind of transformative, almost religious, power—they are tied to the "meaningless" and to the "tiresome" even in the language used to describe them.

Yung's death in "A Son of the Celestial" is particularly useful in helping the reader understand the finale of "The Affair at Grover Station." At the end of "A Son of the Celestial," Yung asks Ponter to have his body sent back to China after he dies. Ponter comes across Yung's corpse one morning after a long opium bender. Standing over the body, Ponter exclaims, "Your heart has been dead these last six thousand years, and it was better for your carcass to follow suit" (528). "The Son of the Celestial" reduces the Chinese body to a "carcass" before dematerializing and then banishing that body with burial back in China. In stark contrast, in "The Affair at Grover Station," it is the body of the murdered O'Toole that reappears in graphic form at the story's terrifying climax. The morning after the ball, Rodgers, still none the wiser about what has happened to his friend, goes down to Grover Station to investigate O'Toole's disappearance. During the course of his search, he finds a large pool of drying blood on O'Toole's pillow. Filled with dread, Rodgers goes to sleep in O'Toole's room only to be confronted that night by the dead man. Rodgers instantly recognizes O'Toole with his "broad, high shoulders," wearing his dress clothes and moving "silently as a shadow in his black stocking feet," "as though his limbs had been frozen."[37] Rodgers goes on to note that his "face was chalky white, his hair seemed damp and was plastered down . . . his eyes were colorless jellies, dull as lead" and most horribly of all, O'Toole's "lower jaw had fallen and was set rigidly upon his collar, the mouth was wide open and was *stuffed full of white cotton!*" (original italics).[38] Unable to speak, O'Toole takes up a piece of blue chalk and writes down a series of letters and numbers, which Rodgers realizes refers to a train car. Using this information, Rodgers is able to locate O'Toole's body, which has been stashed on a train car bearing the serial number that O'Toole had provided. When Rodgers goes to identify the body and retrieve O'Toole's personal belongings, he reveals that the fingers of O'Toole's corpse were "covered with blue chalk."[39]

Rodgers's description of the violent wounds and the blue chalk on O'Toole's body implies, of course, that it was not a ghost that visited him that night (as we might expect) but rather the actual body of O'Toole himself, reanimated and transported across hundreds of miles of track to make certain that his absence (and therefore his presence) could be accounted for. This also explains why the only piece of information O'Toole's reanimated body imparts to Rodgers is its location, as opposed to the killer's identity. The story's emphasis on the physicality of O'Toole's body suggests that its hard turn into the realm of the supernatural is not about solving a crime or exacting frontier justice; rather, it expresses fears about the nature of the potential relationship between

Chinese and American bodies in the United States. According to Sarah Juliet Lauro and Karen Embry, zombies terrify us because they represent the loss of control, agency, and consciousness; they manifest the enslavement of ourselves to our bodies.[40] As Mark McGurl contends, of the monsters that populate our world, "only zombies make this fundamentally social and self-accusatory charge: we the people are the problem we cannot solve. We outnumber ourselves."[41] This notion of bodies over which we have no control is particularly pertinent to the story's representation of the Chinese. Freymark does not need to become a zombie, because, according to the narrative, he already is one.

O'Toole's transformation into a zombie by Freymark's hand simultaneously insists on the presence of the white male body while also expressing a deep fear that the white man will become Chinese. In other words, although O'Toole and Yung are both "dead things that move," the two stories draw an important distinction between them; even in death, the text insists on the presence of O'Toole's body and a form of consciousness, whereas it is only in death that Yung's body and soul are perfectly in accord and at peace. Managing Chinese bodies, whether in "A Son of the Celestial" or in "The Affair at Grover Station," means banishing Chinese bodies from the US landscape as soon as possible and emphasizing the physical presence of white male bodies, even when—or especially when—those white male bodies are corpses. The story mitigates the threat that Freymark poses by claiming that the white male body can still assert itself and cannot be erased from the country. Ironically, in insisting on the inviolable connection between the nation and whiteness, "The Affair at Grover Station" transforms O'Toole, its symbol of white masculine superiority, into a dead thing that moves, that is to say, a Chinese. The intertextual connection between the corpse of O'Toole and the immediate banishment of Yung's carcass is linked to a fear that the memory of the Chinese man will linger even after the bodies of white men have passed away.

Remember Me

As I noted above, Rodgers attributes Freymark's brutality to the f ct that the Chinese are an anachronism, the antithesis of US openne s, individuality, and modernity, qualities that are exemplified by O'To(le.

Because of their metachronistic status, their presence makes certain kinds of memory impossible and others impossible to ignore. Freymark himself makes this point before the discovery of O'Toole's body, during an enigmatic conversation with Miss Masterson at the inaugural ball. He wonders to Miss Masterson, as he "thrust[s] out [his] impudent red lips," "'If I can teach you to forgive, I wonder whether I could not also teach you to forget? I almost think I could. At any rate I shall make you remember this night. *Rappelles-toi lorsque les destinées / M'auront de toi pour jamais séparé* [Remember, when the fates / have parted me from you forever].'"[42]

At first glance, Freymark's use of this line of poetry seems to be an acknowledgment that the two are about to be separated because of the crime he has committed. But Freymark's injunction to remember carries with it another, much more sinister meaning. Although Rodgers knows about Freymark's racial identity at this point in the story, Helen still does not. Thus, she is not aware, as the reader is, of the sexual threat that lurks behind Freymark's comments: the imperative to "remember" accompanied by the "thrust" of those "impudent red lips." The story implies that Freymark's desire to sexually dominate is not limited to Helen; later, we learn that Freymark murders O'Toole by shooting him in the mouth and then inserting white cotton to prevent the blood from flowing out. The intimacy that both the murder and the handling of the corpse must have required, bringing Freymark into close contact with O'Toole's sleeping and then lifeless body, is clearly meant to cause a shudder in the reader. But there is something excessively emasculating about Freymark's act of violence, an excess that hints at the sexual threat that the Chinese were constantly accused of posing. It is not enough that he shoots O'Toole; he must point the gun in his mouth in a symbolic rape and then complete the emasculation of O'Toole by stuffing his mouth with cotton. Indeed, if we read the insertion of the cotton into O'Toole's mouth as another act of violation, then Freymark essentially rapes him twice, the second time while the man is dead. Freymark's necrophilic treatment of O'Toole is not just a sign of his race's moral corruption; it also is a statement about the state of the Chinese civilization and its life force. Like Yung in "A Son of the Celestial," who should be dead before he was even born, Freymark is so ancient that the only "natural" sex partner the story can imagine for him is a corpse.

The ominous manner in which Freymark essentially commands Miss Masterson to remember this night foreshadows what we learn at the story's end: that her true love is dead, and she will, naturally, be unlikely to forget that he never made it to Cheyenne to escort her to the ball. However, it is within the context of the story's discourse surrounding memory that we begin to understand the true threat behind Freymark's citation of this line. The short verse that Freymark quotes is from a poem titled "Rappelle-toi" by Louis Charles Alfred de Musset. In the poem, the narrator exhorts his beloved to remember him, though they are about to be separated. Since the poem forms a crucial part of my reading, I shall quote the English translation of the stanza (lines 20–28) in full:

> Remember, when the fates
> Have parted me from you forever,
> When grief, exile and the years
> Have withered this despairing heart;
> Think of my sorrowful love, think of the supreme farewell!
> Absence and time are nothing when we love.
> For as long as my heart shall beat,
> It will always say to you:
> Remember.[43]

Freymark's invocation of a poem that is obsessed with the act of memory has nothing to do with romantic sorrow, even though the circumstances seem to call for that kind of rhetoric. The rest of the poem asserts that even death will not be able to stop the poet's heart from commanding his lover to remember him: "For as long as my heart shall beat, / it will always say to you: / Remember." The act of remembering depicted here is not shared between two equals; rather, it is a command from one to another. Its status as a command is emphasized by the fact that the stanza begins and ends with that single word.[44] The sandwiching of the poem between the commands to remember suggests a loop in which the narrator is ordering the listener to remember to remember. Freymark takes advantage of his metachronistic status and inserts himself into the act of memory by becoming a mnemonic device. By making the beating of his heart an admonishment to Helen to remember, Freymark transforms his own body into an instrument of memory. So if we consider what it is exactly that Freymark is asking Helen to remember, it turns out he is not asking her to remember his love or devotion, as we might expect from a suitor; instead, he is ordering her to remember the fact that he will always be ordering her to remember, no matter where he is, and even after his death. By ordering her to remember him, he is, in other words, inserting himself into the act of memory itself.

How does Cather's representation of Freymark—as one who belongs to a culture that should be a memory but instead controls the process of memory-making—work with or against the historical erasure of the Chinese within the United States? The recursivity of Freymark's command to Helen to remember memory speaks to a pervasive apprehension within the story that the narrative's attempts to contain the Chinese by categorizing them temporally as premodern have already failed and will continue to fail in the future. As Lisa Lowe argues in *Immigrant Acts* (1996), assimilation into the US nation-state has always meant "adopting the national historical narrative that disavows the existence of an American imperial power."[45] Lowe argues that "narratives of immigrant inclusion" are "driven by the repetition and return of episodes in which the Asian American, even as a citizen, continues to be located outside the cultural and racial boundaries of the nation."[46] Cather's determination to represent Freymark and the Chinese as a memory strikes me as an attempt to control or contain Chinese racial difference by insisting on a certain place for them within the national narrative; if the Chinese are a memory, then they cannot be relevant to the present. The problem with this strategy, as the story makes clear, is the gnawing worry over what Chinese past-ness means about American present-ness. Despite the attempts to immobilize and eliminate the literal and figurative presence of the Chinese, the story professes profound anxiety that they will always be remembered, against the collective will of Americans such as Rodgers or Miss Masterson, and that their experiences will not and cannot be forgotten or eradicated as intended.

Figuring the Chinese

Cather's consistent linkage of the Chinese with mnemonics, as exemplified in this story, seems to contradict a history that has striven to erase the experiences of the Chinese, particularly in relation to labor. While there is no evidence to suggest that Cather herself was aware of the role of Chinese labor in the completion of the railroad (none of her Chinese characters are railroad workers), her story—and its linkage of the Chinese and the railroad with themes of memory—nevertheless opens up the question of what it means to forget the Chinese. In closing this chapter, it seems important to try and wrestle with the question of how a story like this interacts with the nation's amnesia around the railroad, the Chinese, and their labor.

Freymark's association with the railroad inevitably recalls to the modern reader's mind the history of Chinese workers in the United States, specifically, the extensive use of Chinese workers by the Central Pacific Railroad to complete the Transcontinental Railroad in 1869. (Ironically, the story notes that Freymark uses the Union Pacific Railroad to escape the authorities.) Although the story calls to mind an erased history of Chinese labor, I am not suggesting that we should read "The Affair at Grover Station" because it offers us clues about the actual lived experiences of those Chinese workers who worked on the railroad. Rather, I want to suggest that the railroad offers itself as a potential way to think of the relationship between the material history of Chinese labor and exclusion (a history that has been nearly erased) with a discursive history of Chinese representation that is well documented in a variety of sources. In this vein, I think of my reading of "The Affair at Grover Station" as part of an excavation, not to recover the lives of the "real" Chinese who populated the West and the frontier but to get a better sense of the mechanisms by which they were excluded as a group and then imagined as individuals. It is important for that reason to note that "The Affair at Grover Station" begins with our unnamed narrator on a geological expedition "digging for fossils."[47] Digging through the nation's geological past is an apt metaphor for thinking about how "The Affair" wants to forget and then imagine the Chinese; uncovering the nation's bones means uncovering the representational mechanisms that first contained Chinese bodies and produced Chinese figures like Freymark. Thus, the search through the nation's buried past also necessitates bringing to light the means by which laboring, racially othered bodies were transformed into figures of anxiety and fear. In its representation of Freymark, "The Affair at Grover Station" does not so much echo the erasure of Chinese labor from the annals of US history as reveal the logic behind that erasure and the nationalist anxieties that pervaded it. In its attempt to contain the memory of the Chinese, the story unveils the discursive formations that governed the construction of the Chinese. These rules can never be acknowledged, but they nevertheless define the racialized system under which the Chinese lived. Works such as Cather's "The Affair at Grover Station" should be reexamined because these texts enable us to trace the conditions under which Chinese American identities came to be constituted. For better or worse, they offer a genealogy for the formation of Asian America.

3

Telling Stories

The Transcontinental Railroad as Chinese American Narrative

He had maps, with sections of the railroad numbered. He
pointed out the gravesites, haphazardly described at the end
of each section. He'd been told that there would be markers,
or cairns, or something.
—Sky Lee, *Disappearing Moon Café*

"They told me—the other Chinamen on the gang. We've
been telling stories ever since the strike began."
—David Henry Hwang, *The Dance and the Railroad*

The Transcontinental Railroad looms large in Chinese American culture. The writers Maxine Hong Kingston, Brian Leung, Peter Ho Davies,
Sky Lee, Frank Chin, and Lisa See and the playwright David Henry
Hwang have all made the railroad an important part of their fictional
and dramatic imaginings. Artists Mian Situ and Zhi Lin have painted
and photographed it. Chinese American activists have reenacted significant moments of its construction. Its popularity is no doubt attributable
to the central and complicated place that the railroad—particularly the
Transcontinental Railroad—occupies in the Asian American imaginary,
central because Chinese laborers played such an indispensable role in
its construction and complicated because these contributions have been
erased and generally ignored by the nation. Historians Sucheng Chan,
Gordon Chang, Iris Chang, Gary Okihiro, and Ronald Takaki have done
much to fill in the gaps regarding the Chinese and the railroad, but it
would seem that literary Asian America's preoccupation with the railroad is fueled in part by this seemingly intractable contradiction: that
it's a highly visible signifier of Chinese lives, communities, and experiences that have otherwise been made invisible.[1] All at once, the railroad

stands as a monument to the labor and ingenuity of thousands of Chinese workers, as a manifestation of the economic exploitation that they endured, and as the quotation above from Sky Lee's novel *Disappearing Moon Café* suggests, as an unmarked grave for an untold number of men who died in its shadow. It is the cause and sign of Chinese American erasure.

It is the interplay between visibility and invisibility, presence and absence, that particularly drives the representation of the railroad in the Chinese American works that serve as the focus of this chapter and chapter 4. Both of these chapters explore the railroad's place in contemporary Chinese American culture but from different perspectives. The focus here is on how Chinese American authors David Henry Hwang, Frank Chin, and Maxine Hong Kingston relate the problem of the railroad to the problem of textuality. Hwang's *The Dance and the Railroad* (produced in 1981), Chin's "Riding the Rails with Chickencoop Slim" (published in 1977), and Kingston's "The Grandfather of the Sierra Nevada Mountains" (hereafter shortened to "The Grandfather"), a chapter from *China Men* (published in 1980), represent the train as a sign of both the presence of the Chinese in the United States (since the railroad would never have been built without their labor) and their absence (since little is known about the lives of individual Chinese railroad workers and their contributions to building the railroad was never acknowledged). These works thus offer the railroad not only as a key for understanding Chinese American subject formation but also as a strategy for narrating Chinese American experiences in the face of marginalization and expunction from the nation's history.[2] Like the relationship between signifier and signified, the train functions as a vehicle for figuring Chinese workers and conceptualizing an absent Chinese American past.

This chapter begins by examining why the railroad is such a compelling device in contemporary Asian American critical discourse, suggesting that its attraction stems from the fact that it serves both as a powerful justification for Chinese inclusion into the United States and as an effective rebuttal to popular stereotypes about Asian American masculinity. The railroad, however, plays a more complicated role in Chinese American literary works than as a symbol of Chinese resistance to racist discourses. The rest of this chapter examines how *The Dance and the Railroad*, "Riding the Rails with Chickencoop Slim," and "The Grandfather" figure the railroad as text, which is another way of saying that in these works, the railroad does several things: it "exists in the absence of the thing to which it refers" (i.e., the Chinese laborers who built it), it must be interpreted by its readers (in this case, the authors themselves), and it generates ever more text and stories.[3] I argue that by making the railroad a kind of text in their respective works, these authors are able to explore the absences, traces, and contradictions that constitute their experiences.

The Dance and the Railroad resignifies the train, transforming it from a symbol of Chinese American exploitation to a generator of stories, art, and movement. The train itself or work on the railroad is never shown on stage in the play; rather, all of the action takes place in a clearing in the Sierras above the Chinese workers' campsite. However, the train does not need to be present for it to do its work; it becomes homologous for creation, imagination, and formation. It is this link between cultural practice and labor practice that the play (even down to its title) explores. Similarly, for Chin, the railroad acts as an engine for the production of multiple kinds of stories. The railroad in "Riding the Rails" not only inspires stories, it also generates narratives that are foundational to Chin's sense of himself as a Chinese American man. The generative nature of the train enables Chin to construct a version of himself that is temporarily outside of the racism that he and other Chinese men have confronted.[4] However, these stories and the art of storytelling in general are highly gendered in Chin's imaginings. Chin looks to the railroad to connect himself to his grandfather and other forefathers, but the fact that these stories must be mediated by the presence of female figures (like his mother) represents an irreparable loss. In "Riding the Rails," the stories that Chin tells about the men who work on the train can exist outside of the influence of mothers and daughters; it is an idealized space for the telling of stories because it is a homosocial space that rigorously excludes women. The train can generate stories because it is an exclusively masculine space; women are portrayed in Chin's railroad works as the end of the story and storytelling.

Kingston's approach to the railroad takes a few different forms. Rather than portraying the railroad as *producing* a gendered form of narrative, as Chin does, Kingston represents the railroad *as* narrative, one that must be read and interpreted for clues about her grandfather's life. This concept of the railroad as text does not preclude Kingston from figuring the train as a descendant to her grandfather and an ancestor to her. By transforming the railroad into a system of signifiers that promises but can never fully capture the lives of the Chinese railroad workers, Kingston calls attention to the contradictions that are constitutive of Chinese American history and experience and how the figure of her unknown and unknowable grandfather nevertheless informs her sense of self and community. It is important—and no coincidence—that two of the authors (Chin and Kingston) negotiate with memoir in narrating the relationship between the railroad and Chinese American self through history. In the final section of this essay, I consider how all three authors use the figure of the train to negotiate the conventions of ethnic memoir and life writing. The railroad disrupts the assumption that memoir is manifest, progressive, simply a matter of telling the author's version of "truth," or reflects one individual's lifelong process of identity formation.[5] It instead reveals how Asian American writers' lives are subject to the peculiar workings and history of Asian exclusion, in which visibility and invisibility are in constant tension with each other.

Missed Connections

As I have noted throughout this book, part of the reason why the railroad has such a hold on writers like Hwang Chin and Kingston is that the railroad has such a hold on the nation.[6] The Transcontinental Railroad was one of the most visible, ambitious, and prestigious engineering projects in American history, widely hailed as a technological marvel and a key symbol of American exceptionalist rhetoric. Like no other accomplishment of the nineteenth century, it gripped the nation's imagination. As I noted earlier, Trachtenberg calls the railroad "the most conspicuous machine of the age," a "symbol of mechanization and of economic and political change."[7] It made visible the exercise of corporate power, even as it introduced modern technological advances into the everyday lives of Americans.[8] Richard White makes a similar claim that the railroad was perceived in the nineteenth century as "the epitome of modernity. [Americans] were in love with railroads because railroads defined the age. The claims made for railroads by men who wrote about them were always extravagant."[9] The notion of the railroad as a prerequisite for and symbol of American modernity combined with the grandiose discourse it inspired calls to mind Sau-ling Wong's use of "necessity" and "extravagance" as "contrasting modes of existence and operation" through which Asian American literary history could be conceptualized.[10] The railroad captures both of these concepts for the nation and for the men who built it: a "contained" and "survival driven" enterprise and at the same time one defined by a rhetorical and expressive excess.

This hyperbolic approach to the railroad within US culture informs Asian America's interest in the subject but not for similar celebratory reasons. Rather, Asian American historians and writers focus on the railroad because that nationalist hyperbole masks the extent to which the entire enterprise relied on Chinese labor. The Central Pacific Railroad and the Union Pacific Railroad companies began laying down track for what would become the Transcontinental Railroad in 1863. The Union Pacific built westward, and the Central Pacific built eastward, with the idea being that the two tracks would meet and be joined together at Promontory Summit.[11] The Central Pacific, however, faced a far more formidable challenge than the Union Pacific in laying down track, having to traverse more mountainous terrain (including the Sierra Nevadas) under more difficult weather conditions. In 1865, after hiring an initial crew of fifty Chinese workers in response to a threatened labor strike, Charles Crocker, the Central Pacific's chief contractor, made the decision to add three thousand Chinese laborers to the Central Pacific payroll.[12] By the time the railroad was completed in 1869 over 12,000 of the Central Pacific's 13,500 workers were Chinese, and over 80 percent of all the grading done between Sacramento, California, and Ogden, Utah—through the treacherous Sierras—had been completed by the Chinese.[13]

Despite strong initial reservations about their ability to handle the backbreaking work necessary to lay the rail, the Chinese wound up being a boon for the chronically delayed and short-on-cash Central Pacific. As Alexander Saxton notes, the Central Pacific saved tremendous amounts of money by taking on the Chinese as laborers. Saxton writes that in aggregate, the railroad paid the Chinese about two-thirds of what their white colleagues made. This estimate is based on wages paid to "unskilled" labor. However, as Saxton points out, many of the Chinese workers engaged in labor that normally would have been categorized as "skilled" (e.g., laying track and handling explosives); they therefore should have been paid at an even higher rate. Saxton estimates that the Chinese were probably being paid less than a third of what a comparable white worker might make doing the same work.[14] Working conditions were difficult and extremely dangerous, and as a result, the mortality rate was high; according to Iris Chang's estimates, three laborers died for every two miles of track laid.[15] Men were buried in avalanches, frozen in snowstorms, or blown apart by the explosions that were required to blast through the solid rock. Once the line was finished, none of the Chinese were retained by the railroad as brakemen or engineers, although a few were kept on in remote outposts for track maintenance. Most of the Chinese workers were fired immediately upon the railroad's completion; they even had to pay their own return passage on the trains they had helped build. Public acknowledgment of the Chinese contribution to the completion of the Transcontinental Railroad was virtually nonexistent. No Chinese workers were included in the celebratory photographs marking the occasion, and no Chinese were invited to participate in the various municipal celebrations that occurred along the line. With the exception of a few Central Pacific Railroad executives, no public figure commended the Chinese for their accomplishments.[16]

As this brief history makes clear, Chinese laborers were twice victimized, their labor exploited by railroad companies and then their accomplishments and sacrifices expunged from the nation's memory and history. Asian American historians have done much to fill in the gaps in this historical record, uncovering the extent of Chinese contributions and the economic and physical costs that these men incurred. But when the railroad is discussed in Asian American historiography, it is usually analyzed in one of two ways. First, the railroad is often positioned as a justification for Chinese—and therefore Asian American—inclusion into the nation. Emphasizing the crucial role the Chinese played in one of the most important and public nation-building endeavors ever undertaken within the United States understandably validates Chinese claims to citizenship. It also highlights the hypocrisy and injustice of US attitudes toward the Chinese and immigration. The problem with this kind of discourse is that it suggests that migrants and laborers coming into the United States must somehow "prove" their right to belong through their contributions to nation- and/or empire-building projects;

it turns immigration and immigrant labor into a version of model-minority politics.

The second use of the railroad in Asian American histories tends to focus on how Chinese laborers on the railroad counter the most entrenched racist and sexist narratives about Chinese American masculinity. Gary Okihiro writes that the Chinese transcontinental workers were "exemplars of true masculinity and manly virtue."[17] Despite their relatively small stature compared to their white compatriots (Iris Chang notes that the average Chinese man stood at four feet ten inches and weighed about 120 pounds), they "hauled heavy tracks and ties, bored tunnels through granite mountains, and bound the nation with bands of steel."[18] To Asian American male writers like Frank Chin, these railroad men epitomize Asian American manhood: "No wimps they, who sweated and cursed, struck for higher wages, and clambered over rock faces and defied death in baskets suspended over ledges."[19] In a history that is all about the feminization and marginalization of Chinese men, the railroad is a moment that rings differently. The notion of Chinese men engaging in this kind of physical labor clearly counters prevailing racist views of Asian men as effeminate and asexual. The problem, however, is that insisting on the manliness of Chinese men working on the railroad only reaffirms a highly sexist and patriarchal conception of masculinity and posits some kinds of labor as being more valuable or more heroic than others. The laundryman and the waiter—two other archetypal figures for Chinese masculinity in the nineteenth century and beyond—also engage in work that is physically taxing; and yet because these occupations are associated with the feminine and the domestic (cleaning, washing, and food preparation), the men who engage in them are viewed as being absent of manly virtue. It is this feminized figure that writers such as Frank Chin often rail against, the figure that inspires the "racist love" of white America.[20]

While these two paradigms for understanding the railroad in Asian American historiography and criticism have been vital to the field as a whole and are clearly in play in the texts under consideration here, I want to suggest that other literary and critical forces are also at work. An approach to these texts that focuses solely on the train as a vehicle for reclaiming a "virtuous masculinity" or justifying Chinese inclusion tells only a part of the story. This chapter moves beyond the notion that the railroad is a metaphor for Chinese experiences in the United States and considers instead how the railroad itself functions as text that Hwang, Chin, and Kingston set out to interpret. David Eng and Iyko Day are two scholars whose work seeks to rethink the railroad in an Asian North American context. Both present readings of the railroad and Asian American labor that highlights what Day calls the "visual interplay" between race and capital (in the case of her readings) or between race and visibility (in the case of Eng's).[21] In *Racial Castration: Managing Masculinity in Asian America* (2001), Eng provides an analysis of Chin's and Kingston's narrative treatments of the famous champagne photograph, which captures the ceremonial joining together of the Union Pacific and Central Pacific Railroads at Promontory Summit, Utah, on May 10, 1869, but which does not depict any Chinese laborers. Eng proposes that *China Men* and *Donald Duk* "rework dominant history through an emphatic shifting of the visual image."[22] For Eng, the recreation of the champagne photograph, important as it is, reinforces the notion that the camera conveys truth and historical authenticity.[23] Eng suggests that the absence of the Chinese in this photograph spurs the authors to come up with "new methods of looking," specifically by challenging the supposed transparency and veracity of photography itself. In Eng's estimation, Kingston and Chin "work against [the] notions of mimetic realism" that underpin much of our understanding of photography and instead challenge the reader or viewer to "look awry at what the visible image would have us most readily apprehend."[24]

Eng argues that Chin and Kingston focus on the visual as a means of querying the historical invisibility of the Chinese.[25] Day also opens her analysis of the railroad and Asian labor by examining an absent image: the sketch of a Chinese laborer's face made by William Van Horne on the back of the telegram sent in 1885 to Canadian prime minister John A. Macdonald announcing the completion of the Canadian Pacific Railway. Day notes that she cannot include a reproduction of this image in her book because of a refusal on the part of the Canadian Pacific Railroad, "a multi-billion dollar corporation," to allow it. The CPR's refusal to allow for the inclusion of the image in an academic book constitutes yet another attempt to repress the role of Chinese labor in North America precisely because it suggests the constitutive role of said labor in the consolidation of white settler nationhood for the US and Canada.[26] Van

Horne's sketch of a Chinese laborer's face is surrounded by doodles and jottings of numbers, "calculations that seem indicative of Van Horne's financial worries during the railroad's construction."[27] Day's reading of the railroad relies on the "peculiar fungibility of the Asian alien" that Van Horne's sketch evokes; the railroad prompts a "reconsideration of the relation between . . . the concrete specificity of racialized labor and the abstract, universal equivalence of money."[28] Day argues that Chinese North American authors "queer the disembodying effects of an accelerating temporal logic of equivalence that constitutes abstract labor. What unites their distinct texts is a recurring theme of substitutions . . . which function collectively to expose how racial, sexual, and gender difference operates as a degraded substitute within the capitalist logics of white settler colonialism."[29]

Both Eng's and Day's readings of the railroad rely on the notion that the railroad represents a kind of substitution; for Eng, that the photograph becomes a stand-in for "a transparent historical record and 'truth,'" while for Day, the Chinese laborer becomes a stand-in for abstract labor, which within the ideology of romantic anticapitalism, is equated with a "quasi-mechanized labor temporality" that is "excluded from normative social relations and domestic temporalities."[30] What links these readings with my own is their emphasis on the absence of Chinese bodies and labor in the signification of the railroad. While Eng theorizes that absence via psychoanalysis and Day does so via Marxist critique, I am interested in teasing out the relationship between Chinese labor and the railroad from a semiotic/textual perspective. The enforced erasure of the Chinese and their labor from the nation's history prompts the authors to focus on the railroad as a means of reconsidering not only how texts are constructed and who gets left out of them but also how to read a text when one knows it contains elisions and exclusions. Interpreting the railroad—trying to understand what it can and cannot convey—illustrates the difficulties of grasping and narrating the Chinese American experience. The railroad is a subject that Chinese American authors have invested with a good deal of significance in their works, as a historical object, a link to a familial past, a technological apparatus requiring mastery, and a part of the physical environment. It is this intimate, tangible, and material knowledge of the railroad combined with all the absences that the railroad evokes—absence of knowledge on the part of most Americans about the Chinese role in the railroad, absence of recognition as to Chinese contributions, the enforced absence of Chinese laborers to speak about their experiences on the railroad— that makes the railroad such a useful cognate for text and textuality, especially as they relate to racial identity. In making railroad text, the authors offer a strategy for dealing with Chinese American erasure that goes beyond the project of insisting on the presence of the Chinese in the United States. Hwang, Chin, and Kingston suggest that the Chinese American experience is defined by the interplay between presence and absence, and these texts represent attempts to reconciling these two seemingly incompatible conditions.

David Henry Hwang: Performing the Railroad

The Dance and the Railroad emerged out of Hwang's desire to dramatize an "actual historical incident." [31] Hwang spoke of "reclaiming our American past," explaining the importance of representing the 1867 Chinese railroad workers' strike because it and other incidents "remind us that in historical fact these were assertive men who stood up for their rights in the face of great adversity."[32] Esther Kim Lee periodizes Asian American drama into several waves and considers *The Dance and the Railroad* as part of a second wave that was still very much attentive to the Asian American politics of the first wave (which in Lee's reckoning includes Wakako Yamauchi and Frank Chin). Despite this emphasis on the historicity of the events depicted in the play, Hwang cultivates what Lee calls a "California cool" style in his writing, with characters speaking dialogue that "sounds . . . Southern Californian."[33] According to Lee, the anachronistic nature of the dialogue is an attempt on Hwang's part to counter the orientalism that is often embedded in "Chinese" English: stilted, heavily accented, and overly formal.

The Dance and the Railroad debuted in 1981 at the Joseph Papp Public Theater and starred well-known Chinese Americans actors Tzi Ma and John Lone, with Lone also undertaking directorial duties. The play was revived in 2013 in an Off-Broadway production at the Signature Theatre.[34] The action centers around two Chinese railroad workers, Lone and Ma, during the course of a strike by Chinese railroad workers against the Central Pacific. Lone, the embittered older man who has been in

Gold Mountain for several years, trained in the Cantonese opera as a youth and practices his steps on a mountaintop away from the camp.[35] Ma, who has been in America for about four weeks and still seems to believe the other Chinese workers' stories about how the snow in Gold Mountain is "warm," is interested in learning the discipline and pesters Lone to teach him. He is particularly interested in playing the part of Gwan Gung, a heroic general of Chinese myth who was deified after his death. When Lone excitedly tells Ma that the strike is over after nine days, Ma insists that they perform an opera about his own life because he has "just won a great victory" and therefore has earned the right to "immortalize my story."[36] At the opera's conclusion, Ma discovers that the Chinese railroad workers had to compromise in terms of hours and wages, a fact that enrages him. He bitterly tells Lone that he now agrees with Lone's earlier assessment of the railroad workers as "dead men" who have accomplished nothing in America.[37] The final scene is of Ma returning to work, vowing to "toughen up" and declining to continue with his opera training because he hasn't "got time to be the Second Clown."[38] Lone asks Ma to take the opera props down the mountain and resumes his dance practice as the sun rises.

Perhaps surprisingly in a play that focuses on Chinese railroad workers, *The Dance and the Railroad* does not depict Lone and Ma working on the railroad. In fact, the railroad does not appear at any point in the play. However, the physically taxing nature of the work that the men are required to do is a recurring theme throughout the play, with Lone complaining that the "mountain turn[s] muscles to ice" and with Ma admitting near the play's end that the "rock doesn't give in." The absence of the railroad on the stage and the emphasis on Lone's and Ma's bodies as sources for the production and transmission of Chinese cultural practices inverts the historical record on the Chinese railroad workers, which usually emphasizes the intense physicality of the labor they undertook. Instead of standing as the sign of Chinese American exploitation, the play resignifies the train as a generator of stories, art, and movement. The train's absence on stage even as Lone and Ma begin the formation of a small artistic community on the mountaintop highlights the link between labor and art. The two men cannot stop talking about how the two types of movemen —one association with work, the other with imagination— become a fcnt for a reimagining of both.

This notion of the creativity that springs from the railroad camp is articulated most frequently by Ma, who possesses a more fluid notion of the relationship between railroad labor and performance practice. Ma associates the railroad with acts of "play[ing] soldiers, sing[ing] songs, [and] tell[ing] stories."[39] When Ma regales Lone with tales of what he plans to buy with his anticipated Gold Mountain wealth—rides in a "gold sedan chair with twenty wives fanning me," a "stable of small birds to give to any woman who pleases me"—Lone asks him what stories he will tell about his time on the railroad. Ma responds, "I'll say, 'We laid tracks like soldiers. Mountains? We hung from cliffs in baskets and the wind blew us like birds. Snow? We lived underground like moles for days at a time.'"[40] When Lone asks Ma incredulously where he has heard all these stories from, Ma replies, "They told me—the other Chinamen on the gang. We've been telling stories ever since the strike began."[41] The storytelling possibilities of the railroad work extends to the environment in which the men work. Ma and Lone's opera of Ma's life anthropomorphizes the Mountain into a worthy opponent for heroic protagonists, who speaks in verse as Ma does "battle" with it: "Hit your hardest / Pound out your tears / The more you try / The more you'll cry / At how little I've moved / And how large I loom." When Ma tells Lone that he is going to make himself the hero of his own opera ("You said I was like Gwan Gung. . . . well, look at the operas he's got. I ain't even got one"), he is making the case that the life of an ordinary Chinese railroad worker contains enough heroism and valor to be the source material for the highest forms of art.[42] It is this link between cultural practice and labor practice that the play explores.

As the creative practitioner of the play, Lone initially misunderstands the relationship between his life on the railroad and his life in art, understandably viewing the two as rigidly separate. At one point during Ma's opera training, Lone questions Ma's ability to dedicate his life to the art. Ma's problem, in Lone's eyes, is that he "think[s] [opera practice] is the same as working on the railroad"[43] (74). Lone insists that the labor entailed in performance is diametrically opposed to the labor of railroad building; if Ma is going to learn the art of opera from him, Ma will have to echo Lone's belief that railroading transforms the Chinese workers into the dead. By the play's end, Lone realizes his mistake in bifurcating the railroad from art. Unfortunately, the same experience that led him to reconsider that divide has triggered in Ma the opposite response. Ma now hurries to work because he has no time for opera. Ma does not consider the Chinese concessions to end the strike a sign of Chinese survival but a harbinger of Chinese death. Lone's recommitment to his practice and Ma's abandonment of it after the strike suggest how the relationship between railroad and artistic production can be obscured by not totally severed.

Frank Chin: Universal Brakeman

The railroad's significance in Frank Chin's works cannot be overestimated. Eve Oishi states that the nineteenth-century Chinese railroader is "the original heroic Asian American figure," the figure with which he most identifies.[44] John Goshert argues that "the railroad operates as the master referent" in Chin's work for US racism against Asians.[45] According to Viet Nguyen, the masculinization process that Chin's protagonists undergo to enter US society involves negotiating spaces of "violent character formation," which in the case of his novel *Donald Duk* involves visiting "the heroic past of the Chinese railroad worker."[46] As many have noted, Chin's antiracism is deeply invested in recuperating Asian American masculinity from the clutches of a white society intent on portraying it as compliant, foreign, and silent.[47] It is this collective emasculation of Asian men into Uncle Toms that Chin finds particularly galling as it robs Asian men of all kinds of patriarchal privilege to which their gender might otherwise allow them access. One of the more critical ways in which Chin attempts to counter these discourses is to emphasize the linguistic agility of Chinese American men. Chin's exuberant use of language resists racism's silencing (and therefore emasculating) power. At the center of Chin's narratives are protagonists who exhibit what Daniel Kim has described as a kind of vernacular masculinity: the ability to use language to "repeat parodically and subversively the languages that constitute the center."[48] Chin's protagonists and narrators work furiously to fill by whatever means necessary the silence that white racism has placed at the heart of Asian American manhood.

It is this project of reclaiming a vernacular masculinity that has been lost to history that makes the railroad so important to Chin. But the thread that connects Chin to this Chinese American masculine vernacular is always under threat, and in some cases, the threat comes from the female members of his own family. The short work "Railroad Standard Time" (1988) narrates Chin's attempts to get to San Francisco in time for his mother's funeral. The opening of the story focuses on the familiar issue of legacy: What does a legacy mean when the history behind it cannot be recalled or articulated? The story opens with Chin's memory of receiving his long-dead grandfather's railroad watch from his mother soon after his grandmother passes away. The watch itself is impressive: an Elgin with "[n]ineteen-jewel movement. American made. Lever set. Stem wound. Glass facecover. Railroad standard all the way."[49] The economical use of language in this description, with its staccato pacing, is highly uncharacteristic of Chin's usual writing style, and yet this tension between the terseness of this passage with Chin's more recognizable stream-of-consciousness type narration is highly telling. Despite the fact that the story revolves around his grandfather's railroad watch, Chin notes that he never knew him. But at the moment that the watch becomes his, in his mother's kitchen, he understands that the watch carries with it his mother's hope that it will somehow connect him more tightly to his Chinese heritage. His mother passes on the watch, believing that somehow "Chinese would be easier for [Chin] to understand. As if my mother would say all the important things of the soul and blood to her son, me, only in Chinese from now on."[50] The railroad watch becomes a stand-in, in much the same that the railroad is in Asian American literature: a conflicted symbol of all the words and histories that have been forgotten because they were never deemed worthy of remembrance in the first place. Chin imagines that the watch is invested with the immigrant hope that somehow the symbol/the object can bear the weight of all that has been forgotten.

What should be an important moment of (unspoken) communication between a mother and her son quickly transforms into misogynistic invective as Chin blames his mother for not being able to answer basic questions about his grandfather. He describes her voice as "woozy," "her throat and nostrils full of bubbly sniffles."[51] His mother's inability to connect the son to his grandfather means that "the solemnity of the moment [is] gone, the watch in my hand turned to cheap with the mumbling of a few awful English words."[52] Later, on hearing of his mother's death, Chin bypasses his mother in his family tree by directly addressing his unknown grandfather, calling on him to "ride with me . . . your grandson, the ragmouth, called Tampax."[53] The stories that Chinese men tell are strangled by the women who stand between them. The narrative of Chinese American masculinity is fragile, a chain that can be broken by the inarticulate mumbling of an intervening maternal figure. Nowhere in the text does Chin consider the story behind his mother's supposed inarticulateness; her linguistic difficulties are not contextualized within a history of anti-Asian exclusion or violence. Indeed, Chin deposits all the blame for his family's lack of knowledge about its own history squarely on his mother's shoulders. Chin clings to the notion that the railroad watch represents that connection when he says, "I like to think my grandfather was a good man. Even the kiss-ass steward service, I like to think he was tough, had a few laughs and ran off with his pockets full of engraved watches."[54] But because Chin never knew his grandfather's "name nor anything about him" and because the stories of him are filtered through his "mother's face," he realizes he won't pass along the watch as an heirloom to his own son, even though he has told countless people that he would do exactly that. Chin's mother (and by extension, all women) represent the end of the line.

Where mothers fail, the railroad steps in. While the watch fails to forge connections between generations (partly, the story suggests, because it has been handled by a woman), Chin imagines the railroad fulfilling that role, enabling an unbroken chain of connection between men. In "Railroad Standard Time," the presence of a woman chokes up the narrator's storytelling rather than opening it up. In "Riding the Rails with Chickencoop Slim," Chin's mother plays a more marginal role in the narrative. Without her fumbling English, Chin can transform the railroad into a producer of narratives and stories, even as he recognizes it as a historical cause of Chinese American erasure. Because Chin associates the train with narrative, it inspires the creation of more narrative and through that, a sense of himself as a Chinese man who might be connected to other Chinese men and laborers. The railroad's generative quality enables Chin to imagine himself as a different kind of subject, one who is not defined by his skin color, physical appearance, his name, or his relationships to women It enables the joyfulness that infuses Chin's account of himself when he's working on the railroad. But the railroad also reminds Chin of how masculinity is defined by racial difference. The expansive self that Chin creates for himself cannot be sustained because this history of anti-Chinese racism can never be left behind for long.

This intertwining of railroad and narrative is evident from the start of "Riding the Rails with Chickencoop Slim," which recounts Chin's memories of driving trains as the first Chinese brakeman on the Southern Pacific Railroad. Chin begins the narrative by explaining what he calls "the Universal Brakeman story"; that is, "every man on every railroad who's ever turned a wheel or pulled a pin has his own version of the story of the brakeman or switchman who gets 'coupled up.'"[55] In keeping with Chin's fantasy that the train is a masculine and highly homosocial space, the phrase "coupling up" is not meant to conjure up images of romantic partners in the first throes of love, but rather to something much more ominous: a person who is pinned between the coupling devices of two trains as they are joined together. What unites all railroad men, according to Chin, is the desire to tell stories about the unbreakable union between man and train. With the Universal Brakeman story, we are introduced to the notion that the railroad is a generative if risky space for storytelling and the making of self. The version of the Universal Brakeman story that Chin prefers involves a man who is pinned between two cars but somehow remains conscious and lucid. While his coworkers try to figure out how to uncouple the cars without killing him, the victim proceeds to eat a sandwich, cuss at his colleagues and rescuers, and harangue the unfaithful wife who hurries to the tracks when she hears about the accident. Only when the cars are finally decoupled does the man "die sudden. Like a damn breaking. Blood!"[56]

That this version of the Universal Brakeman story is Chin's favorite may not be surprising to readers. The brakeman in Chin's iteration of the story unleashes angry diatribes against his coworkers for their incompetence and his wife for her unfaithfulness. With rhetoric that will seem familiar, the brakeman rails against the woman who has betrayed him and the brotherhood of workers to which he should belong. However, Chin's take on the Universal Brakeman also precisely encapsulates the fertile relationship between railroad and narrative. The image of a man coupled to the train, who can only live and speak while he is literally bound to the track, sets the stage for Chin's own conflicted relationship to the railroad: on the one hand, the cause of Chinese suffering and on the other, a source for its anguished articulation.

If working on the railroad presents Chin with the opportunity be the "straight-talking, straight-shooting" masculine subject that he valorizes, it does so by allowing him to gain power over words themselves. Controlling the engine is a way to control the discursive power of language.

> As I walked out onto the tracks, I would alert myself for the sight of the engine. And I'd say, "Hey, look at me! I'm going to get in that thing and make it do what I want. I'm going to make that thing go!" That was a fact. I carried the orders to make it go. And that made me more than just a hundred and thirty pound Chinese boy claiming the rails laid by his ancestors. I was above history. I was too big for the name of a little man, Frank Chin. No, sir. I was a thing: brakeman! That's the person I remember being, the one I enjoy remembering on the railroad, the image I love.[57]

The importance of this brakeman identity does not stem from the fact that it instills a sense of belonging to the nation; this is not a moment about claiming America or validating Chinese inclusion into the nation. Instead, by marking the shift from "Frank Chin" to "brakeman," Chin evokes the Universal Brakeman, transforming himself into the protagonist of a narrative that is foundational to the train, the hero of every story that the workers tell, not just his own. This identity is not caught up in a web of racializing or racist discourse but in Chin's eyes is simply the person who can "make that thing go!" The social categories that we associate with racial difference—names, physical characteristics—are shed; even the line between object and subject is blurred as Chin describes himself as both "a thing" and a "person": brakeman. It is not that Chin becomes white when he is working on the train; it is that the train makes it possible for him to—temporarily—transcend whiteness. The railroad creates this fiction of a self that is beyond names and beyond history. Chin equates the ability to control the train with linguistic mastery; both the train and language enable his self-transformation. By "making the train go," Chin essentially gains control of language that is so often used to categorize and marginalize him and others like him.

Chin's representation of the train transports him outside of the confines of a racialized history and space and fills him with a sense of pleasure in his own "little" body. He has the right to name himself what he wishes (he is brakeman rather than China man), and he speaks of this moment with "enjoyment" and even "love." However, Chin cannot remain brakeman forever. His access to this identity outside of racializing discourse is provisional and brief. While working as a brakeman on the train offers Chin the opportunity to create and imagine a universal self, its effects are not permanent. As Chin notes, the freedom the train offers is deceptive because "in the vastness of speed, you become roomy enough to accept the knowledge that the railroader you believed in, the steel and iron version of John Wayne, Gary Cooper, Westerner you were and still are is no good." Serving as brakeman on the train inflates Chin's sense of himself to such an extent that he can acknowledge and even endure the idea that the railroaders he idolizes and for whom he should feel an affinity, are based on racist histories that posit white masculinity as the unattainable ideal. Chin's emphasis on how the railroad makes space for bodies like his own is ultimately "no good." One can see the inability of Chin to carve out a permanent space on the railroad for his self-authorization at the end of the passage where he describes himself as brakeman: "That's the person I remember being, the one I enjoy remembering on the railroad, the image I love."[58] In this sentence, Chin is not describing a single self but rather three different selves: "the person I remember," "the [person] I enjoy remembering," and "the image I love." As Chin moves through each position in sequence, the self he was on the railroad becomes increasingly distanced from him, going from "the person I remember" to "the image I love." As the train moves along on an ever-retreating horizon, so too does this idealized self that Chin briefly inhabited.

Again, it is important to note that Chin is not trying to recoup the train as a nationalist space for his own inclusion but rather reflecting on the multiple and complex narratives that it produces. Chin goes on in the passage to note:

The independent, self-reliant, walk-tall, common sense, personal-experience-favoring good man doing what a man has to do who built the railroad and made it work a hundred years ago, who led civilization and learned only from his mistakes and shot straight and dealt square, the iron rider, Marlboro man in this part of the Twentieth Century as a real man is racist, bigoted, politically and socially prejudiced against all reform and book learning and finds it difficult to acknowledge the existence of a world beyond the railroad and his home.[59]

The ideals that the nation associates with the train—of John Wayne and Gary Cooper, of men doing the "right" thing and being square dealers and straight shooters—are limited by the social pressures and histories with which all men, whatever body they occupy, must grapple. For these men, it is easy to forget that there is a "world beyond the railroad," one that is filled with injustice, racism, and intolerance. But for Chin and Chinese men like him, their ability to disconnect from those realities can last only so long and go so far. Chin's assumption of a more lyrical voice and a stream-of-consciousness style in this passage (which characterizes much of his work but is notably absent throughout most of "Riding the Rails") converges with his realization that the power the railroad confers is not sustainable; at the moment that he is reminded that he fills the role of "John Wayne, Gary Cooper, Westerner" incompletely, he reverts to an undisciplined vernacular that reasserts his power through his ability to manipulate language. While the railroad provides a space for Chin to imagine his own subjectivity as universal, that moment is limited by the history of the West and the railroad itself.

The Binding and Building Ancestors of Maxine Hong Kingston

Unlike "Riding the Rails," *China Men* is an extended attempt to reconstruct the experiences of one Chinese worker on the Transcontinental Railroad: Kingston's paternal grandfather, Ah Goong. Going to America is something of a tradition for the men of Kingston's family. *China Men* as a whole chronicles the experiences of her great-grandfather, grandfather, and father on "Gold Mountain"; the final chapter recounts her brother's experiences fighting in Vietnam during the war and then returning home to California.[60] Given the fact that Kingston is often positioned as the poststructural feminist in contrast to Chin's essentialist cultural nationalist, it is perhaps surprising that *China Men*, much more so than "Riding the Rails," initially seems so invested in the canonical narrative of "claiming America" for the Chinese via the railroad. Kingston insists that the Chinese

> built railroads in every part of the country—the Alabama and Chatta-
> nooga Railroad, the Houston and Texas Railroad, the Southern Pacific,
> the railroads in Louisiana and Boston, the Pacific Northwest, and Alaska.
> After the Civil War, China Men banded the nation North and South, East
> and West, with crisscrossing steel. They were the binding and building
> ancestors of this place.[61]

Kingston's list of railroads emphasizes that the Chinese lived throughout the United States, not just the West or California. But in this passage—especially in the last sentence—she raises issues outside of inclusivity and exclusion, hinting that the Chinese and the train are interconnected with her ambiguous use of the pronoun *they*. The Chinese men who worked on the railroad are clearly meant to be considered the "binding and building ancestors," but the trains themselves also bound the nation together. My point here is that even in a passage that is all about using the train to legitimate Chinese inclusion into the nation, there is an implicit conflation of railroad and Chinese. To borrow Kingston's own language, railroad and Chinese laborer are bound together and built upon each other.

Like Chin, Kingston emphasizes the generative work of the railroad, how it structures her family histories as well as producing tales. The railroad and the China Men who built the train in the nineteenth century are inextricably woven into the spaces of Kingston's twentieth-century childhood and family. "The Grandfather" opens with her description of how the "train used to cross the sky. [Our] house jumped and dust shook down from the attic."[62] Having been told that her grandfather built the Transcontinental Railroad, Kingston and her siblings mistakenly believe that he built the railroad tracks that run over their home, that he "had set those very logs into the ground, poured the iron for those very spikes . . . built the railroad so that trains would thunder over us."[63] Not only does the train affect Kingston's physical environment, but its detritus has infiltrated the house itself. Kingston writes that her family retrieves items from the railroad tracks and brings them home; they use the square logs "for benches, edged the yard with them, made bases for fences, embedded them in the ground for walkways" while the spikes make useful "paperweights, levers, wedges, and chisels."[64] The interpenetration of railroad and domestic space suggests how inextricable the railroad is in the constitution of this Chinese American family. With the railroad structuring her sense of space and time, Kingston can query the distinctions between national, racial, and personal histories. At the start of her chapter on Ah Goong, Kingston notes, "Once in a while an adult said, 'Your grandfather built the railroad' (Or 'Your grandfathers built the railroad.' Plural and singular are by context)."[65] The *s* that differentiates *grandfather* from *grandfathers*, that differentiates a personal relationship from an abstracted one, is crucial to understanding Kingston's multifaceted relationship to the railroad. Depending on how one frames identity, the railroad is something at once personal and public, a part of the stories about an individual family as well as a part of the histories of all Chinese living in North America.

This suggestion that *Chinese* and *railroad* can stand in for each other—or that the one can speak for the other—pervades the entire chapter. While it is indisputable that *China Men* works to carve out a place for the Chinese in American history, Kingston's insistence on Chinese presence is rendered in more complicated terms by her treatment of the railroad. While she has no written documents detailing the life of her grandfather in the United States, she does have a text. She writes, "Grandfather left a railroad for his message: We had to go somewhere difficult. Ride a train. Go somewhere important. In case of danger, the train was to be ready for us."[66] In a sense, the rest of the chapter—indeed, the rest of the book—is an attempt to decipher what the messages left by the past might mean. Kingston presents a series of possible interpretations of the message punctuated by belief that the train will take her where she needs to go as well as away from danger.

The problem, of course, is that the message is irrecoverable and that no amount of interpreting on Kingston's part will ever make her grandfather's life (or the lives of his fellow workers) totally available. Although Kingston can never arrive at the message that her grandfather left, her attempt nevertheless allows her to forge a Chinese American identity that is constituted horizontally across space and vertically across time. The train affords her the opportunity to connect herself to a community of unknown and unknowable ancestors. The connection is achieved by grafting the train into her own family genealogy. Ah Goong's work on the railroad increases his potency, only in the latter's case, that potency is sexual. Whenever he is lowered in a basket down a sheer cliff to plant dynamite in the rock, Kingston writes that Ah Goong stands up tall and ejaculates out into space, declaring as he does so, "I am fucking the world!"[67] "The world's vagina was big, big as the sky, big as the valley. He grew a habit: whenever he was lowered in the basket, his blood rushed to his penis, and he fucked the world."[68] Ah Goong's sexual arousal is the direct result of the beauty of his surroundings and the fear he lives with daily; it also speaks obliquely to the impact that strict anti-miscegenation laws and anti-immigration laws prohibiting the legal entry of Chinese women had on Chinese men in the United States. But Kingston none-theless represents this moment as an act of joyful independence, one that is outside of the strictures of patriarchal heterosexuality.[69]

While this sexual act resists the normativization of white heterosex-uality and the historical desexualization of Chinese men, it would be incorrect to call this moment nonreproductive. Ah Goong's terraphilia produces offspring, according to Kingston, and that is the railroad it-self. Again, Kingston imagines the relationship between Chinese and the railroad in conflicted terms, at once the destroyer of life because of neglect and greed (she has several scenes in which she describes Chinese workers being blown up by dynamite or nitroglycerin or getting caught in landslides and avalanches) but also the fruit of Chinese labor—in Ah Goong's case, literally. The final image of the chapter is a family myth that Ah Goong emerged from the fires of the San Francisco earthquake with a child of his own: "He had built the railroad out of sweat, why not have an American child out of longing?"[70] For Kingston, the railroad is that American child, and the genealogy of her family is intertwined with it.

Memoir and the Railroad

Thinking about Hwang's, Chin's, and Kingston's use of the railroad as a kind of art or text leads me to a question regarding both works: What role does the railroad play in the narration of the Chinese American experience? This question is particularly important given the fact that two of the three works discussed in this chapter explicitly take the form of memoir to explore the relationship between Chinese American identity and the past; it also serves as a bridge into chapter 4, which focuses on how Chinese American artists reenact key moments in the construction of the Transcontinental Railroad as a way of exploring the gaps between identity and history. How does the link between railroad and text inform our understanding of memoir as the vehicle through which subjects can constitute identity?

Hwang's, Chin's, and Kingston's concern with text and its ability to bear witness to the past explains why all three authors are invested in thinking of the railroad as a form of memoir. While no one who is familiar with Kingston would argue with my claim that she actively embraces (even as she also reimagines) memoir and life writing, my proposition that Hwang and Chin are exploring the notion of life writing might initially seem dubious. By putting *The Dance and the Railroad* into conversation with memoir, I am not suggesting that there are autobiographical elements in the play. Rather, I would argue that the play's intervention into the "master narrative of history" destabilizes the terms through which categories like fiction or memoir are constituted.[71] If we apply Colleen Lye's useful formulation that memoir and fiction are not oppositional but are rather "alternative narrative strategies [for] representing Asian American character," then it becomes possible to read *The Dance and the Railroad* through the lens of memoir rather than as an example of memoir.[72] My claim about the relationship between these authors and memoir might seem even stranger in the case of Chin given his vociferous diatribes against this specific category of writing in multiple essays. He has called autobiography and autobiographical fiction a "traditional tool of Christian conversion," one that is inextricably linked to its confessional past and that "advance[es] the stereotype of Chinese culture [as] so foul, so cruel to women, [and] so perverse" that they seem to endorse the notion that Chinese history and people must be destroyed.[73] Autobiographies fulfill white fantasies regarding Chinese backwardness and misogyny, and they "promise and demand Asian racial extinction."[74]

Chin's suspicion of autobiography is not without merit, especially given its traditional role in American letters as the genre that readers expect ethnic authors to wield to prove their assimilation and trumpet American exceptionalism. Autobiography has been the privileged site for immigrant and ethnic self-expression since the late nineteenth century, a genre that has historically supported the notion, as expressed by Louis Adamic, that "immigrants were Americans before they landed [in the United States]."[75] On the subject of Asian American memoir in particular, Colleen Lye has noted how the genre "traces the conversion of the model minority into the Asian American," while Lisa Lowe has written of the "intense social value accorded to the autobiographical genre."[76]

Despite these strong objections, I would suggest that all three authors are engaging with the notion of memoir in productive and complex ways. While the conventional view of the autobiography conceives of it as a "means to impose order on . . . experience[s] that [are] both disruptive and confusing," Hwang, Chin, and Kingston deploy the railroad to highlight precisely how disruptive and confusing the experiences of ethnic subjects can be especially in relation to a historical past that is present or visible (as the railroad is) and simultaneously inaccessible.[77] The railroad gives these writers not one story but rather multiple stories; it does not impose order but rather is a sign of the disorder that often shapes the lives and experiences of subjects of color. I would go further and suggest that Hwang, Chin, and Kingston transform the railroad into a kind of memoir, an imperfect record of lives that were never deemed worth remembering or memorializing in the first place. Reading *The Dance and the Railroad* through memoir means we can trace the arc of Long's realization that the distinction he makes between the art of opera and the labor of railroad work is not as hard and fast as he once thought. The play makes the case that the artistry that he has spent a lifetime mastering has a parallel in the labor of the Chinese railroad workers; one is not possible with the other. The historical imaginings of Asian America are not possible without its labor, both historical and current. For Kingston, "the smell of [the] burned flesh" of Chinese laborers remains seared into the physical landscape itself. She notes that the workers who died while building the Transcontinental Railroad were "buried or cairned next to the last section of track they had worked on" (138). Her representation of the train as a form of inscription makes visible the bodies and experiences of the Chinese laborers who lived and died in order to finish the Transcontinental Railroad. The railroad is a memoir for those workers but one that is characterized by a succession of "voiceless tropes" that cannot represent the subject it purports to speak for.[78]

The train instead reminds us of the silence that surrounds the lives of Chinese American laborers, one that renders them visible but nevertheless "deprived of voice and condemned to muteness."[79]

While Kingston imagines the railroad as the partially legible and highly material remnant of Chinese railroaders' attempts to make an impact on the US landscape, Chin takes a different approach. The railroad's ability to proliferate narrative and constitute subjects connects Chin to his fellow railroad workers, regardless of race. But it also finally enables him to connect with the unnamed and forgotten Chinese laborers of the First Transcontinental and other railroads. If the train acts as a memoir in his text, it is one that memorializes forgetting rather than remembering. Ruminating on his unheralded railroading experiences, Chin recalls that his mother found his career on the Southern Pacific to be "very satisfying . . . because she sees my extraordinarily unsung railroad career as being somehow very Chinese" (85). Later, Chin himself espouses the link between Chinese identity and loss when he writes that there is something "very Chinese" about being forgotten. As the first Chinese brakeman on the Southern Pacific, Chin's accomplishment is as little known or heralded as the work of the Chinese who worked on the Transcontinental Railroad. But what binds Chin to these men is not the fact that they helped build the nation or accomplished feats that were thought to be dangerous and impossible. Rather, what connects them and makes them "very Chinese" are the railroad and anonymity. Chin emphasizes that point when he goes on to note, "Like the Chinese who chipped roadbeds out of solid granite at the rate of six inches a day, I achieved anonymity" (85). His point is not to attempt to single out his achievements or the achievements of his Chinese predecessors but rather to reveal how complicit narrative structures such as memoir or history are in the erasure of marginalized subjects. Anonymity can be achieved only by those whose accomplishments are not worth recognition in the first place. *The Dance and the Railroad*, "Riding the Rails," and "The Grandfather" make clear that spaces like the railroad can never completely speak for the dead. It is an imperfect repository for the lives and experiences of Chinese laborers.

Hwang, Chin, and Kingston portray the railroad as the enabling factor in their own emergence as Chinese American subjects. At one point in her narrative of Ah Goong's life, Kingston bluntly declares, "No

China Men, no railroad," rightly suggesting that the Chinese were indispensable to the building of the Transcontinental Railroad, and that
it would never have been built if not for the labor of China Men.[80] But
The Dance and the Railroad, "Riding the Rails," and "The Grandfather"
suggest that the inverse of that statement is equally true: "No railroad,
no China Men." Just as the Transcontinental Railroad would have never
existed without the Chinese men who built it, Chinese Americans could
never have emerged as they did if it had not been for the railroad. The
positioning of the railroad as memoir thus questions the assumption un-
derpinning autobiography and memoir that "life produces autobiography as an act produces its consequences."[81] *The Dance and the Railroad*,
"Riding the Rails," and "The Grandfather" reveal how the railroad—with
its violent erasure of Chinese labor and its hypervisible place within the
nation—produced the conditions of possibility for the formation of Chinese America. Just as in the case of the train, stories that these authors
tell "disfigure to the precise extent that they restore" the experiences of
Chinese Americans.[82] Figuring the railroad as memoir highlights not
the triumphant recovery of Chinese laborers and Chinese Americans
but the particular problematics of narrating the Chinese American
experience.

4

Remembrance and Reenactment at Promontory Summit

> She looks for a promised chapter but finds in those pages
> only a few lines, herself reduced to something crude and
> unrecognizable.
> —C. Pam Zhang, *How Much of These Hills Is Gold*

In chapter 3, I argued that Chinese American writers used the Transcontinental Railroad as a way of thinking about the relationship between narration and Chinese American identity. In this chapter, I want to revisit the issue of Chinese America and the Transcontinental Railroad from a different perspective, namely the significance of Chinese American reenactments—in person, in texts, and art—of key historical events in the construction of the railroad. This chapter will focus on Chinese American reenactments of what are popularly known as the champagne photo and the golden spike ceremony, both of which occurred at Promontory Summit, Utah, and marked the official completion of the Transcontinental on May 10, 1869. It is important to note that these are not the only reenacted moments in the history of the Chinese and the Transcontinental Railroad; just to name one other example, Chinese Americans often hike the ten miles of track that a "small army of Chinese coolies" laid in twelve hours on April 27, 1869, just outside of Promontory Summit.[1] My purpose in considering Chinese American reenactments of these key events in nineteenth-century American history is to consider what it means to reenact events or moments in time that were never fully or properly enacted in the first place. Chinese American reenactments denaturalize the binary between enactment and reenactment, suggesting that all reenactments are unfaithful and that all originals are performative. For example, while the historical record tends to present the champagne photo and the golden spike as two distinct moments of celebrations that represent an originary moment in American history, Chinese American reenactments make clear how

Figure 4.1. Promontory Summit, Utah, May 10, 2014. Photograph by Corky Lee.

these momentous occasions of national formation are dynamic, inter-sectional, and even chaotic. Reenactment in this case is not to correct the historical record or to argue for a more inclusive perspective of an event (although these things may wind up happening). Instead, Chinese American reenactments undo narratives of mastery and discourses of wonder that such moments are meant to invoke. They call into question the authority of the moment that they seem to memorialize.

To drive home this point, let us begin this chapter with a reenact-ment. On May 10, 2014, a group of 200 individuals, consisting of Chi-nese Americans, Asian Americans, and Chinese nationals, gathered at Promontory Summit, Utah, to pose for a photograph. The occasion was the 145th anniversary of the completion of the Transcontinental Railroad, but this was not an ordinary celebration. In what was touted as a "pho-tographic act of justice" by photojournalist Corky Lee, who took the picture, the assembled group deliberately reenacted the famous cham-pagne photo—the moment that the Central Pacific and Union Pacific railroad lines were joined to form the Transcontinental Railroad on May 10, 1869.[2] The 1869 champagne photo—taken by Andrew J. Russell and officially titled "East and West Shaking Hands at Laying of Last Rail"—depicts railroad executives, local officials, and laborers—all white and all men—crowding around the Union Pacific No. 119 and the Central Pacific Jupiter as they face each other on the track. As the most famous photograph associated with the railroad (and arguably one of the most famous photographs in nineteenth-century America), the 1869 image notoriously does not include any of the approximately twelve thousand Chinese men who were employed in building the railroad. And although this absence is now widely acknowledged, it still lingers in official ways. For example, the National Park Service website, which contains a legend that names every man in the 1869 champagne photograph (even those men whose faces are partially obscured or hidden), does not mention the absence of the Chinese at all, only noting at the bottom of its web-page that "a Chinese contingent from the Central Pacific" was present at the Promontory Summit celebrations. Present, but not photographed.

It is this erasure that the 2014 Chinese American-led group clearly wishes to both note and reverse.[3] The 2014 reenactment received positive coverage from local newspapers like the *Salt Lake Tribune* as well as national news sources, such as NPR. A sense that justice has been delayed but ultimately served pervades these news stories. They implicitly impose a progressive narrative on American race relations, suggesting that the nation's problems can be ameliorated simply by the passage of time. Racial injustice is presented as the regrettable ignorance of a previous era and not the result of structural inequalities; the 2014 reenactment appeals to the nation precisely because it fits into an easy narrative of "righting an old wrong." As Vanessa Agnew argues, this constitutes one of the fundamental appeals of historical reenactments generally. Not only can such reenactments reflect an interest in a "colorful, familiar history," they also serve a political purpose. As a form of "history from below," reenactment "provides an important public service and gives voice to hitherto marginalized positions."[4] In the popular imagination, reenactment promises to "honor the sacrifices and accomplishments" of the ordinary individuals who participated in the signal events in a nation's history; it offers the possibility that those "from below" can provide a course correction to history, decades or even centuries after the event it is meant to reenact.

Under this popular framework of reenactment, the 2014 photograph might be seen as a final and, to some, satisfying response to this particular phase of Chinese American history. This chapter, however, views reenactment as the beginning of the story rather than its conclusion. For one thing, the 2014 photograph is not a perfect reproduction of the 1869

Figure 4.2. "East and West Shaking Hands at the Laying of the Last Rail" (the champagne photo). Promontory Summit, Utah, May 19, 1869. Photograph by Andrew J. Russell.

photograph; it clearly intends to evoke the earlier image without copying it. If historical accuracy is not the goal (and in the genre of historical reenactment, it often is), then what purpose does this and other Chinese American reenactments have? To borrow Agnew's language, what "service" do these Chinese American reenactments provide, either to the Chinese American or the wider national community?

In the remaining pages, I examine how Chinese American reenactment offers a genealogy of the railroad and the nation that is contrapuntal to official histories that trumpet destiny, progress, achievement, and modernity. Inspired by the 2014 photograph and the questions it raises regarding reenactment as a form of political and cultural work, this chapter examines how the reenactment of historical events connected to the Transcontinental Railroad —particularly depictions of the golden spike ceremony and the champagne photo—disrupt nationalist narratives of origins and exceptionalism. The reenactment does more than question nationalist narratives; it also undoes the temporalities embedded in those narratives that silently confer authority onto these moments, transforming a performance into an "original." Underlying this chapter—perhaps underlying any critical consideration of the Chinese in nineteenth-century America—is an uneasiness about what reenactment can mean or not mean when historical information detailing the lives and experiences of excluded groups like the Chinese in the United States is so scant as to be nonexistent. I hope that this concern is evident to the reader throughout the chapter, but I address the issue specifically at the chapter's beginning, attempting to articulate the historical and temporal problems that arise when we talk about Asian American reenactment. I then move on to the examples of reenactment that will serve as the case studies, starting with the 2014 photographic reenactment before moving on to examine literary reenactments of the golden spike and the champagne photo in Peter Ho Davies's novel *The Fortunes* (2017) and C. Pam Zhang's novel *How Much of These Hills Is Gold* (2020). These literary works queer their reenactments by disrupting the supposedly natural chronology between origin and reenactment. I mentioned Kingston's grandfather's terraphilia in the previous chapter (as he masturbates, he thinks of himself as fucking the earth) as queering the policing and disciplining of Chinese railroad workers. I would like to extend that argument in this chapter and argue that *The Fortunes* and *How Much of These Hills Is Gold* suggest that reenactments queer the authority of history by performatively enacting failure. Their approaches, which reflect on some of the most objectified and invisible figures in Asian American history—the Chinese miner or railroad worker or prostitute—disrupt historical narratives that emphasize accuracy of representation for those that are imperfect or askew. Zhi Lin's multimedia installation *Chinaman's Chance on Promontory Summit: Golden Spike Celebration, 12:30pm, 10th May 1869* (hereafter shortened to *Chinaman's Chance*) also obscures the supposedly clear lens of history, in this case, by looking at events literally from behind. I conclude this chapter with a brief rumination on what it means to research or teach about the nineteenth-century Asian American experience with twentieth or twenty-first century materials. While I do not find these types of temporal leaps to be at all problematic—I would not be writing this book if I did—I nevertheless think there must be a theoretical or conceptual reckoning of sorts within Asian America literary studies regarding long nineteenth-century Asian American cultural production. If anything, early Asian American cultural production makes clear the contradictions—perhaps tenable, perhaps not—within Asian American studies as a field.

When the Past Remains So

As I have made clear, I am not interested in acts of reenactment that are meant as moments of recovery. Rather than thinking of reenactment as a way of bringing "back to life" the events and individuals of the past, I am interested in Chinese American reenactment as a form of queer relationality that highlights rather than obscures the ways in which the Chinese American present can never recover the past, especially when that past is, to borrow Saidiya Hartman's brilliant formulation, "a death sentence, a tomb, a display of the violated body, an inventory property, a medical treatise on gonorrhea, a few lines about a whore's life, an asterisk in the grand narrative of history."[5] How is it possible to understand the experience of those in the past whose lives have been erased from the historical record?[6] How can one reenact the experiences of an individual or a group when there is no archive to record even the most basic pieces of information about their experiences?

In his study *None Like Us: Blackness, Belonging, Aesthetic Life* (2018), Stephen Best asks for a reconsideration within African American studies of the relationship between the past and the present, and particularly the central role that the slave plays in structuring that relationship. Best questions the "primacy" that the slave "has come to assume . . . in black critical thought," uncomfortable with the assumption that the supposed "continuity between the slave past and our present provides a framework for conceptions of black collectivity and community across time."[7] Best's questioning of the role of the slave in accounts of African American politics resists a scholarly ethos that tends toward "recovery" and/or "melancholy" in its expression. Rather than a politics premised on "racial belonging rooted in the historical dispossession of slavery," which he finds limiting and problematic, Best instead advocates for a queer "non-relationality between the past and the present," one that focuses on "forms of unbelonging, negative sociality, abandonment, and other disruptions that thwart historical recovery."[8] Reading the relationship between past and present as a queer non-relationality means scholars might be required to "resist the impulse to redeem the past and instead rest content with the fact that our orientation toward it remains forever perverse, queer, askew."[9] *None Like Us* describes a historical figure and an intellectual history that is specific to the African American experience, but the questions that Best poses about the nature of the relationship between a traumatic communal past and the radical politics of the present can be transported across disciplinary and community lines. Best's formulations on the relationship between the lost or erased past and the scholarly apparatus of our present is productive in thinking about the historical absence of those Asian American or Asian diasporic figures—like the Chinese railroad worker—whose words and experiences are inaccessible to us in the present but who are nevertheless conceived of as vital to the practice of our contemporary identities and politics.

Best's move to queer the relationship between the past and the present is particularly useful in thinking about reenactment. I argue that Chinese American reenactments of the completion of the Transcontinental Railroad derive their meanings not only from their invocation of historical events but also from their own deliberately imperfect replication of these events. The purpose of Chinese reenactment is not to repeat an originary enactment; rather, the *re* in *reenactment* is meant to interrogate the very assumptions that lead to the original's gaining that status in the first place. This method is in sympathy with strategies such as Hartman's practice of critical fabulation or Joseph Roach's theory of surrogation. Like Hartman, I consider how Chinese American artists rearrange story elements in the interest of "jeopardiz[ing] the status of the [original] event, to displace the received or authorized account, and to imagine what might have happened or might have been said or might have been done."[10] The 2014 champagne photo makes clear that its 1869 counterpart is, to borrow a phrase from Roach, "an elusive entity," one which is reinvented every time a reenactment takes place.[11] In other words, the process of reenactment can never succeed in its goal of replacement/replication—and is certainly not meant to here—precisely because the original event itself is always already a fiction, misremembered, "selectively, imaginatively, and . . . perversely" in the words of Roach, or queerly in the words of Best.[12]

2014

The 2014 reenactment at Promontory Summit breaks many of the unofficial rules of historical reenactment. The participants are dressed in modern clothes and holding signs. As I noted earlier, the group consists of men, women, and children; no attempt is made to replicate the positioning of the men in the 1869 photograph. Furthermore, the 1869 photograph prominently features two men shaking hands in the center of the picture. The 2014 photograph, on the other hand, is staged quite differently. This one has the participants all grouped together directly facing the camera. There is no central pair exchanging handshakes. The Chinese are smiling broadly; the 1869 participants are not. For all these reasons, the 2014 reenactment would never be labeled "hardcore" or "superhardcore," according to the categories that informally circulate among US Civil War reenactors, who are generally the most numerous and best organized of historical reenactors.[13] The cheerful indifference evinced by the 2014 participants to duplicating the 1869 photograph emphasizes the most spectacular failure of all: the failure of whiteness. In refusing (whether consciously or not) to align their bodies and faces with the poses of the 1869 photograph, these Chinese American reenactors are signaling that whiteness may not be the originary moment worth replicating after all. Reenactment ostensibly offers a way to "fill in the blank spaces of the historical record and to represent the lives of those deemed unworthy of remembering," but only if the reenactment is a failure.[14]

The highly visible nature of this failure reminds us that questions of Chinese American reenactment must take into account frameworks that examine Asian American embodiment. There is a rich vein of scholarship that explores these relationships. In performing and revising the past, Asian Americans are drawing upon a particular dynamic, what Karen Shimakawa has called "national abjection," a position that requires a constant oscillation "between visibility and invisibility, foreignness and domestication/assimilation."[15] According to Shimakawa, it is the oscillation between these dyads, performed by and on Asian American bodies, "that mark the boundaries of Asian American cultural (and sometimes legal) citizenship." Abjection is the "psychic, symbolic, legal, and aesthetic dimensions of national identity as they are performed by Asian Americans."[16] Shimakawa offers a way of constructing Asian American identity as related to and a product of the nation—or "occupying the seemingly contradictory, yet functionally essential, position of constituent element *and* radical other."[17] Whereas Shimakawa draws primarily on a mixture of psychoanalysis and affect studies to define the stakes of Asian American performance, Joshua Chambers-Letson turns to the intersection between performance and law. Performance as an embodied act can be used by the state as a means of controlling and disciplining individuals, but it can also be deployed by marginalized subjects to disrupt "the containment of the theatrical frame secured and held by the government."[18] Building off of Shimakawa's work, JuYon Kim has argued that Asian American racialization is marked by a similar central tension: the spectacularity of the racially marked Asian American body performing the mundane, the quotidian, or the routine. Kim defines the "mundane" capaciously, inclusive of acts such as "inflections of speech, gesture, daily routines" that exist at the "limits of conscious action."[19] It is the mundane that marks "where racial divides [can] be crossed—or not."[20] Kim argues that it is these "everyday enactments" that are the ground upon which Asian American racial difference has been both externally imposed and internally constituted. It is also in the performance of the everyday that Asian American subjects can "manag[e] racial and national identifications" by "including ritual, mime, cross-racial role-playing, and caricature, with ethnographic and documentary elements."[21]

All these scholars offer a way of thinking about Chinese American reenactment of the completion of the Transcontinental Railroad as an unraveling of American erasure *and* an intensification of its stakes. The purpose behind these reenactments is not to show the Chinese as deserving of inclusion into the United States or to champion Chinese involvement in US history but rather to critique the more complex role that Shimakawa alludes to: that of the Chinese as functionally essential *and* radically other. Those complementary roles are reflected in the 1869 photograph in which the product of Chinese labor is hypervisible and celebrated even as Chinese bodies are banished from the memorialization. The 2014 reenactment transforms that historical moment—imbu d with its own grandeur and conspicuously silent on the erasure it h is perpetrated—into a moment of the racial mundane, a transformati n that ironically highlights what Kim calls the "body's ambiguous relationship to the behaviors that it enacts."[22] It is this ambiguous relationship between racial body and behavior that occupies the heart of the 2014 reenactment of the champagne photo. The performance of these reenactments reflects on the unsettling dynamic between erasure and hypervisibility. In invoking the 1869 photograph, the Chinese/American reenactors call attention to themselves twice over: by occupying the same ground; and by assembling together and as racialized subjects in a purposeful way in a large group to have their photograph taken. With the 2014 reenactment, the spectacle entails the performance of both the mundane and the historical on the part of Asian American subjects.

The 2014 photograph and other Chinese American cultural and literary reenactments of this moment reveal that these seeming moments of authentic origin—whether they involve the putative completion of the Transcontinental Railroad or the founding of the nation—are always fictions, reiterations, and performances repackaged as legitimate and legitimating. By examining some of the visual works that purport to capture the original moment of completion, we can see how narratives of authenticity accrue over time. Just prior to the taking of the 1869 champagne photograph, Central Pacific president and governor of the state of California Leland Stanford "drove in" the ceremonial last spike to signal the end of construction. This moment—or more precisely, its aftermath—is captured in Alfred Hart's stereograph titled "The Last Rail Is Laid—Scene at Promontory Point, May 10, 1869."[23] Unlike the champagne photograph, in which the two engines are photographed facing each other, in "The Last Rail Is Laid," the camera is pointing down the tracks, to the east. Leland Stanford stands in the center of the photo holding up above his head the long handle of the hammer he just used. Directly to his right stands a woman (perhaps his wife), and in front of him is a small child. Workmen and other officials surround Stanford and crowd the railroad, a sea of dark clothes punctuated briefly by ghostly white faces. In the background, crowded with people, sits the Union Pacific engine 119. Note the difference between this photographic image and the romanticized depiction of the moment in Thomas Hill's 1881 painting *The Last Spike*.[24] In Hill's painting, Stanford is a dominant figure in the center of the frame. Even though he is surrounded by a crowd of workmen gazing adoringly at him (two of them are on their

Figure 4.3. "The Last Spike Is Laid." Promontory Summit, Utah, May 14, 1869.
Photograph by Alfred A. Hart.

knees at his feet, looking up into his face), Stanford stands apart from
the others. Rather than awkwardly holding up the hammer (as he does
in Hart's stereograph), Stanford leans casually and easily on it. In both
images, the engines themselves are secondary to Stanford. Hill's vision
clearly dovetailed with official narratives of the railroad as this painting
for many years graced the California state capitol in Sacramento.

These two moments celebrating the nation contain several elisions
and illusions. The "last" spike that Stanford drove into the rail was made
of pure gold, which means that it was not functional. Pure gold is very
soft; given its malleability, there was no way that it could be driven into
a regular iron-tie rail. So railroad executives commissioned a special rail
of soft laurel wood, pre-drilled with several holes and manufactured by
a company in San Francisco that specialized in billiard cues. Stanford
tap-tapped the golden spike into his ceremonial laurel wood tie (by one
account, he missed the spike on his first swing), before stepping aside
to let two Chinese railroad workers drive the final last spike into the tie.
While there is no photograph of Stanford's strike (perhaps because he
missed), Andrew Russell did take a shot of the Chinese workers working
on the last spike. And while the chronologically earlier event is usually

considered the originary one, from which all subsequent reenactments arise, in this case, the presence of the Chinese laborers and their labor upset that timeline that posits the West as the modern and the East as the atemporal. Stanford may have driven his "last spike" first, but in the end, he was only mimicking the movements of the Chinese workers who followed him.

Let me be clear. I do not raise these issues to argue that the Chinese "got there first." My purpose is not to correct the historical record or chronology of events with the idea of proving Chinese primacy in narratives of the Transcontinental. Rather, it is to point out that even on that day, multiple versions of the golden spike moment were circulating. One would become enshrined in the narrative of the nation, and the others would fall to the side. However, traces of those other versions remain. But this is exactly what that 2014 photograph launches: an investigation into the nature of origins and authenticity and the historical record. A genealogy of Chinese American reenactment of this particular moment in the nation's history exemplifies how the performance of Chinese American identity constitutes an "intricate unraveling of the putative seamlessness of origins," the seeming justice (read, whiteness) of American technology and progress.[25] The ceremonial moment that the Chinese American reenactment invokes is itself a performance, not of modernity, mastery, or Manifest Destiny but of anxious racialized,

Figure 4.4. "Chinese at Laying Last Rail UPRR" [*sic*]. Promontory Summit, Utah, May 14, 1869. Photograph by Andrew J. Russell.

gendered, and imperial nationhood. The Chinese American reenactment is not a "relentless search for the purity of origins." It is not meant to lionize or authorize the "authenticity" of the 1869 champagne photo but to highlight the fictiveness of that photo, which was never the only story of the origins of the railroad.

The Golden Spike, Spiked

The 2014 reenactment at Promontory Summit is an embodied act, one that defiantly reminds the viewer not of presence but of absence—namely, the absence of Chinese Americans in pages and archives of US history. Embodiment does not fill in the absence left by US racism but rather highlights that absence, making jagged its smoothed-down edges. Textual reenactments of historical events are, of course, vastly different from embodied or visual ones, but they engage in a similar process that questions origins and reframes the fundamental components of history. The Chinese American authors who write of the Transcontinental Railroad employ what Saidiya Hartman calls "critical fabulation." Critical fabulation involves telling the impossible story—for example, the story of Black Venus—to amplify not the subject of the narrative but the conditions of impossibility that are intrinsic to the telling. In "Venus in Two Acts," Hartman writes that critical fabulation involves "playing with and rearranging the basic elements of the story," "re-presenting the sequence of events . . . from contested points of view," and "illuminat[ing] the contested character of history, narrative, event, and fact, to topple the hierarchy of discourse, and to engulf authorized speech in the clash of voices."[26] Critical fabulation works to "jeopardize the status of the event"; its method is confusion and its goal is disavowal.[27]

Reenactments of key moments in the construction of the Transcontinental Railroad play small but vital roles in Peter Ho Davies's *The Fortunes* and C. Pam Zhang's *How Much of These Hills Is Gold*, two contemporary Chinese American novels that have garnered a good deal of public attention and adulation in the past few years.[28] *The Fortunes* and *How Much of These Hills Is Gold* share not only a nineteenth-century setting but also an epic approach to Chinese American narrative that blends the historical with the fantastical. *The Fortunes* chronicles Chinese American history via the stories of four Chinese diasporic protago-

reenactment - past
constructing - future...

nists living in different eras: Ling, a Chinese worker in the pre-Exclusion era American West; Anna May Wong, the film star working in Hollywood in the 1930s; a young man who is friends with Vincent Chin and is with him the night he is murdered in 1982; and John, a professor traveling to China with his wife to adopt a child. For the purposes of this argument, I will be focusing on chapter 1, "Gold," which tells the story of Ling, a half Tanka-half European Chinese worker who migrates to San Francisco as a young man and winds up serving as a valet for Charles Crocker, one of the founders of the Central Pacific Railroad, before working on the Transcontinental Railroad himself as an explosives expert. Ling's proximity to Crocker and his work on the railroad means that he witnesses or participates in key historical events in the construction of the Transcontinental, including the construction at Cape Horn, the tracklaying bet of 1869 in which the Chinese laid down ten miles of track in one day, and the golden spike ceremony.

Ling is born in China to a Chinese woman who dies in childbirth and a European father who abandons him upon the mother's death. He is raised on a boat by Big Uncle and Aunty Bao, who ship him off to San Francisco when he is fourteen. Ling's desire to prove himself is driven by his triply marginalized status: he is orphaned, a Eurasian, and a member of the outcast Tanka ethnicity. Although he is Chinese, he does not feel that China is home. When Ling arrives in the US, he works as a washer and a delivery man for the gambler and laundryman Ng. Ling develops feelings for his employer's daughter Mei, who works as a prostitute in a lean-to adjacent to the laundry. By chance, Ling crosses paths with Crocker, who is in the early stages of constructing the railroad. Impressed by Ling's hustle and in need of a reliable supply of clean shirts, Crocker hires Ling as his personal valet. Ling works hard to please Crocker, anticipating his needs, listening to his stories, and deferring to his boss's opinion. Ling is desperate to "prove himself better than the ghosts' opinions . . . prove the Chinese better than they thought."[29] Crocker repays Ling's loyalty by purchasing a suit of clothes so that he can look like a "civilized fellow."[30] He takes Ling along when he visits a Chinese brothel and magnanimously offers to pay for Ling to have one hour with one of the prostitutes. He confides in Ling about his past business struggles and harangues him about his philosophy toward success. Crocker's mix of wealth, condescension, undisciplined physical appetites, and brutal business tactics inspire in Ling a desire to maintain Crocker's "trust in the Chinese."[31] It is because of Ling that Crocker takes a chance and hires Chinese railroad workers to replace striking Irish laborers. Ling is one of the first men to see the construction completed at Cape Horn, a rocky promontory located about fifty-seven miles east of Sacramento that marks the start of the Sierras and the first significant engineering challenge for the Central Pacific.[32] Finally realizing that Crocker is using him and that trying to prove the humanity of the Chinese to men who are determined to exploit them is a lost cause, Ling quits and takes a job on the railroad itself. Later, Ling is part of the Central Pacific work gang that lays ten miles of track in one day and is present at the driving of the golden spike at Promontory Summit. At the chapter's end, Ling, an old man, stares out across the San Francisco Bay, contemplating making a return trip back to China. American resentment against the Chinese is at an all-time high, competition for jobs is fierce, and the passage of the Chinese Exclusion Act means "no more Chinamen" and "no more women for those already there." Nevertheless, Ling "resist[s] being driven out," not because he hates China or because he loves the United States but more out of a sense of intransigence: "If what distinguished the Chinese from the rest was that they didn't mean to stay, well then, some of them *must* stay, and why shouldn't he be one? Him and the whores."[33] Ling identifies with prostitutes because like them he still bears the "stains" of shame, which in his case is being Eurasian and Tanka: "On Gold Mountain, at least, they were all simply Chinese."[34]

The novel's reenactment of Chinese American experiences on the Transcontinental Railroad works to question the very notion of authenticity and history. It does this in an unexpected manner; unlike many histories and narratives of the Transcontinental Railroad (see my discussion of Whitman's "Passage to India" in the introduction), "Gold" seems to *deflate* the accomplishments of the Chinese. In other words, rather than glorifying the accomplishments of the Chinese workers, "Gold" deliberately undermines many of the most cherished stories associated with Chinese resilience on the railroad. Perhaps one of the most enduring stories involves Chinese men being lowered in woven baskets (referred to as bosuns) from the cliffs of the Sierra Nevadas to chisel out railroad tunnels.[35] (This is a story that Kingston also cites in *China Men*.) When he first sees Cape Horn, Ling notes that

Chinese men had been "lowered in woven baskets to blast out this ledge, so the papers said, the wind spinning them like tops, then swatting them against the rockface."[36] Instead of feeling pride over this story, it fills his heart "with fear."[37] Later, listening to some of the railroad workers bitterly describe their work digging out of the rock, Ling asks them incredulously if they are not proud of their accomplishments, particularly being lowered in baskets to blast out the tunnel near Cape Horn. The men look at him in

> bemused impatience. Baskets? They didn't know anything of baskets. Men on ropes? Who would be so foolhardy as to dangle over a cliff? "They're not paying us enough for that!" Such modesty, Ling thought at first. He remonstrated with them. The feat was famous; they were celebrated for it as far afield as San Francisco! It had been in the newspapers!
>
> "Lies." The old man shrugged. "I was there. That's just a story made up by the bosses."[38]

Ling's boosterism for the "celebrated" feat of the Chinese is a façade; in posing his question, Ling is not necessarily looking for someone to share in his pride; rather, he is looking for someone to quell the misgivings he is beginning to feel about the Chinese role in building the railroad. The text recasts the historical events that it depicts as a series of elaborate lies told by executives like Crocker to extract the maximum amount of labor from the Chinese workers and to head off any objection to the replacement of Irish labor with Chinese. In revealing as false the stories about Chinese ingenuity and bravery—one of the few stories that portrayed the Chinese positively in the nineteenth century—and refusing a narrative of Chinese heroism, *The Fortunes* uses the Transcontinental to disrupt the imposition of model-minority representation into narratives of Chinese exclusion and exploitation. The takeaway from stories about the Chinese and the railroad should not be that the railroad proved Chinese worthiness for entry into the nation but rather that the railroad highlights how capital and the nation incorporate the spectacle of pliant racialized bodies to bolster their legitimacy and to mask profiteering. It is precisely this type of benevolent racialization that the 2014 photograph also rejects. These types of myths—as appealing as they may be to present-day readers—work in the service of power. They also prompt us to question the "straight" genealogy of event to representation. Ling goes out searching for a reenactment of the "famous" feat; what he gets instead is that stories of Chinese resilience ultimately only profit the "bosses." Ling's imaginative reenactment of the Chinese hanging in baskets near Cape Horn is simply a narrative of capitalist greed. Reenactment in the case of *The Fortunes* is not to justify Chinese American inclusion or prove Chinese excellence; it reveals the exploitation that is at the heart of all origin stories. Ling's desire to believe these stories—of the railroad as a sign of Chinese ingenuity or of Crocker's deeply buried decency and sense of fair play—is linked to his intense desire for a sense of belonging within a family and within a nation. The ultimate truthfulness of these histories would mean that Ling has finally found a home for himself in the United States, despite all the hardships he has endured.

Once he realizes the fraudulence of those moments, which have already been trumpeted to the nation, Ling cannot look at the railroad in the same way. Although he attends the golden spike ceremony as a worker, his perspective does not reflect a sense of accomplishment or triumph. Rather than the symbolism emphasized in the nation's history of the golden spike moment—the celebration, the technological exceptionalism, the moment when "DONE" is transmitted across the telegraph lines—Ling highlights those moments that reflect his experience of the nation. He sees the hypocrisy of the moment when Stanford "driv[es] a long fang of gold back into the earth" because he knows that it will "swiftly drawn out again and an iron spike inserted in its place."[39] He watches as Stanford, the former governor of California, offers a revised opinion of the Chinese as "quiet, peaceable, patient, industrious, and economical." He sees Stanford raise a hammer to drive home the last spike—and miss. His own participation in perhaps the most memorable feat in the history of the Transcontinental Railroad's construction—the laying of ten miles of track in one day—barely rates a mention in the narrative. Ling's story of the golden spike ceremony suggests that the supposedly original enactment of these moments were not worth witnessing, no matter what subsequent reenactments tell us.

Ling labels all these moments as examples of "seeing the elephant," which is how the Old Timers on Gold Mountain talked about having "seen it all." Ling realizes that all the supposed feats of the Chinese in building the railroad are examples of "seeing the elephant," only instead of filling him with pride, it heightens the alienation he feels about his life. Ling transforms the narrative of exceptional Chinese labor and the railroad into something ineffable and strange. It is not a narrative filled with pride over Chinese American accomplishments but a catalogue of all the ways that Chinese American bodies have been forced into acts of compliance that denied them their humanity and safety.

The Fortunes is able to reenact key moments in the construction of the Transcontinental Railroad because one of its central characters is a Chinese man. There is a correspondence between Chinese American narrative on the level of plot and character and the "real life events" that are being interrogated. That level of correspondence between narrative and history seems to be murkier in C. Pam Zhang's *How Much of These Hills Is Gold*. I will get the bad news out of the way first: the Transcontinental Railroad plays a very minor part in this narrative. The novel's account of its construction and completion takes up a few sentences. The protagonist of the novel, Lucy, is not even an eyewitness to this history; she can hear the cheers and the celebrations from the boardinghouse where she works as a prostitute, but she cannot see it for herself. Despite the seemingly small role that the railroad and its construction plays in the narrative, it is clear that the railroad has played an outsized part in Lucy's life, never more so than at the end, when her clientele consists almost entirely of the Chinese railroad workers.

Lucy has been peripheral to the story of the nation her entire life. Her abusive and alcoholic Ba is a gold prospector and a miner (not a railroad worker), her Ma is dead (so we think), and her younger sister, Sam, is a taciturn and impulsive presence with a strong internal code of right and wrong. Sam also prefers to wear men's clothes and keeps her hair shorn short; she usually keeps a rock or carrot in the crotch of her pants and as she grows up proves to be irresistible to the white women who want to sleep with her. The novel opens with the death of Ba and the two sisters roaming the brutal western landscape trying to scrape together two bits of silver with which to bury him; as they search, Ba's corpse, which is rolled in their mother's old trunk from China, putrefies and begins to fall apart. The sisters eventually separate as Lucy seeks domestic comfort and a sense of belonging while Sam prizes her freedom and working with her hands. After a lengthy flashback section, narrated by Ba in death, the sisters are reunited several years later and decide to make a fresh start in China, a trip that their mother always hoped to make. Before they can board the boat, gunmen catch up with Sam, who, it turns out, has stolen a motherlode of gold from a mining operation and dispersed it Robin Hood–style to the miners who had not been paid. To save Sam, Lucy agrees to give herself to the "gold man"; she does not tell Sam of her sacrifice and physically assaults her to force her onto the boat to China.

At the novel's conclusion, Lucy hears the celebrations of the Transcontinental Railroad's golden spike ceremony. As she thinks about the moment and ponders what her life has amounted to, she realizes that what she seeks is to be "claimed" by a land that forever unfurls in front of her, that land of her childhood. This is not the land of the "frontier" or of Manifest Destiny but something that has not been surveyed or parceled or exploited. The novel ends just before she opens her mouth to articulate that desire, and the reader is uncertain if she ever voices that wish aloud to anyone, a disavowal of closure and of inclusion.

My argument that Lucy's marginalized status actually makes her the ideal figure for Chinese American reenactment depends on Anne Cheng's theory of "the yellow woman," whose being has historically been defined by "ornamental forms and fungible surfaces" rather than "organic flesh."[40] In Cheng's account, the yellow woman is a racial formation that is permeated with loss; while that loss may not be recoverable, it can nevertheless be transformed into something productive.[41] To her own question of whether there is "room in the dehumanizing history of race to talk about a figure whose survival is secured through crushing objecthood," Cheng answers a qualified yes, as long as we who live in the present are "willing to confront the life of a subject who lives as an object."[42] Only then will we

> arrive not at an easy politics, but rather at an alternative track within the making of modern Western personhood, one that is not traceable to the idea of a biological, organized, and masculine body bequeathed from a long line of Enlightenment thinkers, but is instead peculiarly synthetic, aggregated, feminine, and non-European.[43]

This alternative genealogy of subjectivity—which emerges at the intersection between "thingliness" and "personness"—can "prov ke considerations of alternative modes of being and of action for subjects who have not been considered subjects, or subjects who have come to know themselves through objects."[44] Lucy's life as a decorative and highly prized object is one she takes up with precision and care. She observes her own thingification and studies it as assiduously as she once studied her schoolbooks. She morphs from a Chinese American woman with a family and a desire to belong into an object bought and paid for. Her transformation makes clear to her that she has always been an object—her life as a prostitute does not mark her entry into objecthood, only her awareness of it.

As the title indicates, gold is the central trope of the novel—the search for it and the safety that the family thinks it will provide them drive much of the plot and tragedy. Despite its relative absence in the text, the railroad exerts a pull on the narrative in less palpable but no less powerful ways. On the level of plot, it is the promise of railroad work that brings Lucy's Ma and 200 of her fellow villagers (called "the 200" by Ma) on a ship from China to the United States. Ba is one of the hired men charged with keeping an eye on the 200. The railroad does not materialize; according to the dates provides in the novel, Ma and the 200 arrive in the US in 1862, one year before the start of construction of the railroad and three years before the Central Pacific hired Chinese workers in large numbers. In waiting to be transported to the work site, one of the villagers is murdered by a white guard who was hired to watch over the workers. Ma and Ba hatch a plan for revenge that goes terribly wrong and ends with the 200—as well as the hired guards—being killed. Their lives after that moment are consumed with guilt over the deaths their actions caused.

From the start of this family's history, the novel associates the railroad with death and the destruction of the landscape. In *How Much of These Hills Is Gold*, the train represents not the opening of the frontier but rather the death of the land that is labeled "frontier." The massacre of Native American tribes has already soaked the land with blood, and the incessant horde of miners, prospectors, and railroaders "dig[ging] up streams and clog[ging] rivers" in their hunt for wealth have done the rest.[45] "Frontiersmen" have cut down trees to such an extent that the soil goes dry; they overfish, overhunt, and kill every green thing so that "when the dry season comes, a spark can set it all aflame."[46] The land has become so barren and choked with the death that corpses dangle from trees or lay unburied on the ground. On the day the railroad is completed, as Lucy lies in bed listening to the cheers and the speeches, she "tri[es] to summon up old images. Gold hills. Green grass. Buffalo. Tigers. Rivers. Trying to remember any story but the ones she spends her days selling. The images flicker like mirage, gone the moment she gets close. She stares as long as she is able, mourning what she can before it slips away. The trains have killed an age."[47]

This is the context in which the narrative "reenacts" the golden spike. From her room on May 14, 1869, Lucy "hears the cheer that goes through the city the day the last railroad tie is hammered. A golden spike holds track to earth. A picture is drawn for the history books, a picture that shows none of the people who look like her, who built it."[48] As a girl, Lucy was the pet of a local schoolteacher who claimed to be writing a book about the American West and wanted to observe Lucy and her mother closely as examples of their kind. She eventually finds the book that the schoolteacher wrote, "thick with dust, clumsily written."[49] The schoolteacher had promised Lucy that he would devote the book to an honest portrait of her people, to undo prejudices and hatred. Lucy finds that the promised chapter has become only a few lines, and her role has been "reduced to something crude and unrecognizable."[50] The juxtaposition of the schoolteacher's history textbook with the celebration of the golden spike emphasizes Lucy's awareness about her own irrelevance to the stories of the nation. As a Chinese woman living in the United States, Lucy understands that others "rewrite" her to "tell the story of Lucy's skin."[51] Anne Cheng writes of Lucy's fate in *Ornamentalism* when she discusses the fate of "the yellow woman," whose being has historically been defined by "ornamental forms and fungible surfaces" rather than "organic flesh."[52] The railroad and its memorialization are the culmination of the erasure of Lucy's identity and of "every Lucy that came before." The Transcontinental, then, not only signals the end of all that the West was and could have been, it also marks the death of Lucy's past and her future. All that is left is the shell.

History from the Other Side of the Tracks

How Much of These Hills Is Gold and *The Fortunes* portray history as it is lived by those who can never enact or reenact it. Zhi Lin's *Chinaman's Chance on Promontory Summit: Golden Spike Celebration, 12:30 pm, 10th May 1869* reflects on what those historical moments looked like for those who were present but not central—the Chinese railroad workers themselves. Lin creates an immersive experience of the champagne photo—in high definition with surround sound on a granite ballast. *Chinaman's Chance* does more than just give the viewer a sense of what it must have been like to be present at such a moment; Lin actually creates an experience in which the viewer is excluded from the champagne photo, just as the Chinese railroad workers were in 1869. The reenactment is not a reenactment of presence but a reenactment of absence.

The installation has two distinct elements to it. The first part is a short film that acts as an introduction to or contextualization of Chinese American work on the Transcontinental Railroad. The video provides a sketch of the history of the Central Pacific Railroad, the route of the Transcontinental, and the death rates for the Chinese laborers. Russell's champagne photograph is shown, accompanied by text that reads:

> Chinese workers, who had just finished laying the last rail, are absent from the famous photograph and most of the official records on the historical onsite celebrations. The reenactment of the historical meeting of the two locomotives and the champagne photograph takes place annually on the 10th of May at the Golden Spike National Historic Site in Promontory Summit, Utah.

The video next shows an image of an entry from the Central Pacific payroll and then a description of the film and how it was shot. Directly in front of the screen are track ballasts, upon which the video of the moving train cars seems to glide over. The use of material props in relation to the screen immerses the viewer in the scene. The stones that make up the ballast contain the names of 921 Chinese laborers written in red. These names were drawn "from existing Central Pacific Railroad payroll records" and according to the video "reveal the untold story behind the historical celebration and iconic image."

These introductory images assume a viewer with little knowledge about the Transcontinental Railroad and its construction (an altogether safe assumption to make) and are clearly meant to contextualize Lin's work. While I recognize that the historical contextualization is a nod to the reality that most Americans are unaware of the history of the Chinese in the US, the first part of the installation video also reflects an uneasy dynamic between the installation's seeming pedagogical goal (to educate viewers about the contributions of Chinese railroad workers) and its representation of the process by which national histories emerge. This first part of the video thus takes an additive approach to American history, while the second part of the video takes a deconstructive view. While these two goals do not have to be mutually antagonistic, *Chinaman's Chance* sets up a series of pressing issues about the nature of Chinese American experience in the nineteenth century, which can be boiled down to this: How can we interrogate reenactment when the viewer does not understand reenactment to be a critical act but rather sees it as an imitative act?

The second element of the installation is the reenactment of the champagne photo itself. Although the viewer may not realize it from the start, the installation positions the viewer as the Chinese railroad worker. As the video portion of the installation starts, we watch as a group of men in period dress (clearly railroad employees) aid in maneuvering two locomotive engines into position for what we recognize is going to be the champagne photo. As the two engines draw together, cowcatcher to cowcatcher, it becomes clear that the viewer is not with the other observers; instead, she is standing on the other side of the tracks, watching the action as it is happening, her presence obscured by the locomotives in front of her. This realization is driven home at the moment the photograph is taken. As the railroad employees get into position on the cowcatchers, bottles of champagne clutched in their hands, they turn their backs to the viewer. As the reenactment participants pose for the famous picture, the viewer senses the moment of photographic capture based on the stillness of the reenactors and the brief flare of reflected light from what is presumably a camera flash. On the soundtrack accompanying the video, we hear the echo of man calling out "D-O-N-E. Done," which was the text of the famous telegram that was sent to the rest of the country at the moment of the railroad's completion. Because of the viewer's position on

the other side of the tracks, away from the crowd, hidden by the two locomotives, we understand that her face will not be included in the frame,
despite the fact that she is present at the taking of the picture. Never has
the phrase "the wrong side of the tracks" been more accurate or relevant
than in this case. The viewer/Chinese railroad worker is watching her
erasure from history happening in real time.

This second element of *Chinaman's Chance* works very differently
from the first. It renders reenactment as a fraught practice, swathed in
multiple layers of mediation and a series of imperfect performances that
have no origin. The men in the video are reenacting a historical moment, mimicking the movement of the white railroad workers in the
champagne photograph as they get ready to pose for the camera. That
1869 version, however, was itself a performance, arranged for the benefit
of posterity and Andrew Russell's camera with enough forethought to
deliberately remove the Chinese workers from the frame. The viewer is
meant to embody—or reenact—the perspective of the Chinese railroad
worker. But again, that reenactment cannot be perfect, as the viewer is
surprised to find herself on the wrong side of the tracks and history, a
reaction that the Chinese workers would have surely not had the privilege of experiencing. This is reenactment as alienation rather than replication. And it highlights that the *re* in *reenactment* is always present in
enactment, whether or not those two letters precede the word. *Chinaman's Chance's* representation of the train captures the contradiction of
Chinese American experience, in which Chinese American presence is
obscured by the very thing it has helped to build.

Chinese American reenactment opens a door to thinking through a
vexing issue within Asian American studies that I have danced around
up to this point, namely, the challenges of considering the *long durée* of
Asian experience in this country given the relative paucity of what we
might call "primary" source materials that were authored or created by
Asian subjects living in the United States prior to the twentieth century.
Nowhere is this problem more acute than in the case of the Chinese railroad workers, who constituted almost 90 percent of the Central Pacific
Railroad's labor force and completed most of the work—grading, hauling,
blasting, and laying track—between Sacramento and Ogden, Utah, during the period of the Transcontinental Railroad's construction. Despite
the significance of these contributions, there are, to my knowledge, no

extant narratives written by these workers, in either Chinese or English. And while this fact may seem to indicate that Chinese railroad workers by and large did not write about their experiences building the Transcontinental, Asian American history tells us otherwise. The example of the Angel Island poems is instructive in this case. We know of the existence of these poems, which were carved with knives into the walls of the Angel Island Detention Center in San Francisco Bay by Chinese laborers, only because official attempts to destroy the poems (which were considered graffiti) by puttying over them had the assuredly unintentional effect of preserving them from decay; and because the etchings caught the eye of a curious state park ranger who was inspecting the ruins of the detention center prior to its scheduled destruction in 1970. If such a visible and seemingly durable example of Chinese American literary imaginings came within a hairsbreadth of being bulldozed out of existence without any of us being the wiser, it is not difficult to imagine the vulnerability of Chinese laborers' narratives, written on scraps of paper, or in journals and letters home that could be burned, mislaid, misdirected, or relegated to the trash. In *Ghosts of Gold Mountain: The Epic Story of the Chinese Who Built the Transcontinental Railroad* (2019), historian Gordon Chang argues that it is this absence of first-person documentation combined with mainstream unfamiliarity with Chinese life in America and a deprecation of the Chinese presence in the history of the country that has "rendered these workers all but invisible."[53] The historic and ongoing refusal on the part of the nation to acknowledge the extensive role that slaves, "coolies," and indentured laborers have played in its formation and rise to global power also goes a long way in explaining Chinese America's continued marginalization. Again, the nation would rather forget than reckon with its historic and ongoing reliance on exploited and dehumanized labor to smooth the gears of capital. As Chang notes, the "Chinese were not deemed sufficiently important or interesting to include in sweeping narratives about the rise of the nation."[54] Chang suggests that it is an absence of primary accounts that explains the nation's indifference to Chinese American history. I would argue, however, that the inverse is true, that the nation's indifference to Chinese American experience is the cause rather than the effect of these lost narratives.

In chapter 2, I noted that David Henry Hwang wrote *The Dance and the Railroad* because he wanted to produce a play that was based on an "actual historical incident" from Asian American history in which "assertive men . . . stood up for their rights in the face of great adversity."[55] Hwang's desire to ground his creative imaginings in a "historical incident" is not unusual within Asian American cultural productions, which are often driven by a desire to recover an "absence," or a "presence . . . [that is] all but invisible," within US history. In fact, much early Asian American theater was invested in dramatizing moments in Asian American history. Esther Kim Lee notes that Asian American drama of the first and second wave, which she dates to the 1970s and the birth of the Asian American movement, are committed to representing moments and events out of Asian American history "such as the internment of Japanese American during World War II and the creation of Chinatowns."[56] But Kim Lee's assertion about Asian American artists' investment in representing the past can be applied more broadly across representational genres. This desire to uncover or discover narratives about Asians in the US as a means of authenticating a contemporary Asian American presence does not just drive cultural representations, it also serves as one of the unspoken assumptions of the field of Asian American studies itself. The 2014 reenactment highlights the underlying problematic with this contemporary desire and perhaps within Asian American studies and history broadly, namely the tenuous relationship between the lives and experiences of those Asians who lived in the United States prior to or during the Exclusion era and the disciplines that we call "Asian American studies." The fundamental problem of Asian American studies is the fraught link between the sign and the signifier, a relationship that is based on a collective nudge and wink. The Chinese railroad worker is a figure around whom questions and assumptions about the field can coalesce. Reenactment makes clear what our investments should be, not in recovering this figure that was erased into oblivion but rather in determining how this figure can be a launching point for thinking through the epistemology of Asian American studies as a discipline. The figure of the Chinese railroad worker says more about how we understand Asian American identity then it does about the men who occupied that historical position. This is the useful impasse that the reenactments in *The Fortunes, How Much of These Hills Is Gold*, and *Chinaman's Chance* make visible.

5

The Jim Crow Train in African American Literature

On October 6, 2010, the *New York Times* published an op-ed by John Edgar Wideman titled "The Seat Not Taken." In it, Wideman confesses that for the past four years, he has been conducting what he calls a "casual sociological experiment" on the Amtrak train that carries him twice a week from New York City to his university teaching job in Providence, Rhode Island. Wideman writes that when he takes a vacant double seat at the start of the train's journey, the seat next to his almost always remains empty for the entire trip, even though the route is a popular and crowded one. After eliminating several possible reasons for this phenomenon (he does not have "excessive body odor or bad breath; a hateful, intimidating scowl; hip-hop clothing; or a hideous deformity"), Wideman concludes that his skin color must be the primary reason why his fellow train travelers choose not to sit next to him. Clearly, Wideman's logic relies on ableist and class-based assumptions, but it is hard to question the conclusion he reaches. Far from being angry about this fact, however, Wideman professes to enjoy the extra space and "the opportunity to spread out, savor the privacy and quiet and work or gaze at the scenic New England woods and coast." He goes so far as to confess that he looks forward to that moment when the train pulls out of Penn or Providence Station and all of the passengers, "including the ones who willfully blinded themselves to the open seat beside me," have settled into their spots, for it is then that he knows that the adjacent vacant seat is "free, free at last." Wideman's tongue-in-cheek enjoyment of this "privilege conferred [by] color" is tempered by the "disquieting" and "odd" fact that even in 2010, "with an African-descended, brown president in the White House and a nation confidently asserting its passage into a postracial era," the mostly white passengers who take this three-hour train ride do not wish to sit next to a Black man. For Wideman, riding the train becomes both a respite from the "congestion" of modern life and "something quite sad . . . [a]nd quite dangerous . . . if left unexamined. Posters in the train, the station, the subway warn: if you see something, say something."[1] Thus, during the course of Wideman's train ride up and down the northeast corridor, we move along a track that starts in our postracial present (in which a Black man can be a professor at Brown University or the president of the United States), runs through the broken dreams of the US's civil rights past, and ends in a Jim Crow America that is linked to our post-9/11 moment and the so-called war on terror. These temporal leaps, far from being abrupt or disordered, reflect a Black experience in which the "current moment, or 'now,' can certainly correlate with other moments but . . . that is [not] always the effect of a specific, previous moment."[2] Train travel makes clear the temporal disjunctures and spatial disciplines that African American subjects must confront on the train and beyond.

Wideman's piece is just one of the latest in a long line of African American literary works that have explored the vital role that the railroad has played in the formation and perception of racial identity and difference in African American culture in the past century. It is not exaggeration to state that the train is a central trope in the African American imagination, showing up in songs, fiction, film, and art. It acts as a metaphor for Black movement and dance (the Underground Railroad in the nineteenth century; Soul Train in the twentieth). It enabled the rise of the blues in the American South as well as its dissemination throughout the country; on top of that historical role, it also shows up in the lyrics of countless blues songs. Sometimes the train was an antagonist, as in the folk stories around John Henry, the African American "steel-driving man"; sometimes it was the setting of racial injustice, as in the infamous case of the Scottsboro Boys who were wrongly accused of raping two white woman while hoboing in 1931. For thousands of Pullman porters, the train offered a path toward financial stability at a time in the early twentieth century when economic opportunities for African American men were scarce. Hundreds of thousands of southern Blacks rode the train north and west during the Great Migration of the early twentieth century. As this sampling of moments makes clear, the railroad has served as a source of artistic expression, a vehicle for new opportunities, a setting of racial terror, and a path to economic security for almost two centuries.

While all these examples need to be examined, researched, and written about, this chapter focuses on the experiences of African American train passengers in the era of Jim Crow. The first and most extensive part of this chapter examines literary narratives of Jim Crow ridership: W. E. B. Du Bois's short essay "The Superior Race" (1923), James Weldon Johnson's novel *The Autobiography of an Ex-Colored Man* (1912), Anna Julia Cooper's essay collection *A Voice from the South* (1892), and Ralph Ellison's short story "Boy on a Train" (ca. 1937). Although the focus is on domestic representations of Jim Crow in the late nineteenth and early twentieth centuries, the chapter also incorporates moments from Frantz Fanon's *Black Skin, White Masks* (1952) and as well as accounts of slaves seeking freedom in Frederick Douglass's autobiography *The Life and Times of Frederick Douglass* (1881), George and Ellen Craft's memoir *Running a Thousand Miles for Freedom* (1860), and Harriet Jacobs's *Incidents in the Life of a Slave Girl* (1861). These narratives reveal how Jim Crow despatializes Black subjects and how Black passengers then negotiate the effect of that despatialization on their subjectivity and humanity. Black passengers negotiate and resist the spatial and temporal logics, laws, and conventions that govern their bodies and movements within that space. My approach in this particular chapter takes its cue from the evocative narratives of African American writers themselves, whose experiences riding "Jim Crow" on the train speak to the particular history of anti-Black racism in the United States that renders Black bodies an "absent presence" and disavows the discursive and physical violence that is often perpetrated against those bodies. William Gleason argues that the "built environment is always shaped in some way by race whether such shaping is explicitly acknowledged or understood."[3] In the case of this chapter, that built environment is the railroad, and it is the train's Black passengers who understand the extent to which race and racial violence have shaped not only how they are treated on the train but also how they experience the train itself. If, as Katherine McKittrick claims, "black matters are spatial matters," then the railroad is one of the spaces that matter most to African Americans.[4]

Black narratives of the Jim Crow train car emphasize the irreconcilable fact that while the Black body is often constitutive of the spatial in the US, it is also almost always hidden, ignored, and denied access to any space. Barbara Welke argues that one of the defining characteristics of Jim Crow is the complete resistance of whites "to the very idea of yielding space to blacks."[5] Welke cites as an example an incident that took place in Mississippi on the Illinois Central Railroad in which white passengers defied a train conductor who ordered them to move to another car because he needed the car in which they were seated to accommodate Black passengers. Even though this request bolstered the logic of Jim Crow and white supremacy, the white travelers told the conductor, "We [don't] want to give up our seats to a lot of negroes." It is this kind of radical despatialization that African Americans confronted very time they boarded a train. The railroad as represented in these texts reveal the spatial dimensions of anti-Black racism and African American responses to it. It reveals the impossibilities that Black passengers confront when they ride the train, specifically, the impossibility of a Black space that is not marked by violence against Black bodies and erasure from public view. Even as the authors use the train to reveal how Blackness defines the spatial logics of the nation, they seek out alternative forms of being in space that make visible their "absented presence."[6]

Antebellum Jim Crow

African American literature and letters is filled with train travel.[7] John C. Inscoe calls train travel "a central and traumatic aspect of southern Black life for much of the nineteenth and twentieth centuries"—central, of course, because it was an integral part of the southern landscape, but also traumatic because for many African American writers, the railroad was the setting for their first or most lasting encounters with racism.[8] These scenes of racial subjugation would not have occurred had it not been for the tremendous growth of the railroad in the South in the postbellum era. While railroads had been present in the South as early as the 1820s, it was not until 1880 that the region experienced a "railroad revival."[9] Between 1880 and 1889, the southern railroad network grew from 14,778 miles to 29,263 miles. Henry Grady, the American journalist who supported the industrialization of the New South after Reconstruction, called the southern railroads a "system grand and harmonious."[10]

Inscoe's periodization of Black narratives about train travel from the late nineteenth and early twentieth centuries dovetails with the decades of Jim Crow. However, an examination of antebellum African American letters, particularly slave narratives, reveals that slaves were grappling with the nascent forms of Jim Crow long before they were codified as the law of the land in 1896 with *Plessy v. Ferguson*, a court case that originated on a train car in Louisiana. In including antebellum depictions of segregated train travel in a discussion of Jim Crow spatializing practices, I follow the lead of Gene Andrew Jarrett, who argues for a more expansive understanding of Jim Crow. Jarrett maintains that a "narrow periodization" of Jim Crow to the first half of the twentieth century "overstates the role that constitutional or juridical events have played in race relations, while restricting the political awareness and activities of African American writers to discourses of de jure racial segregation."[11] Considering Jim Crow's reach before its enshrinement into law in 1896 makes it possible to read relatively rarer antebellum accounts of African American railroad travel in conversation with more numerous postbellum narratives.

The nature of Jim Crow segregation—whether de facto or de jure—meant that railroads "often served as testing grounds, even battle grounds, between black passengers and white" conductors or passengers.[12] The Jim Crow train is a space that is riven with seemingly oppositional and contradictory dynamics. On the one hand, it represents an attempt to control the movement of Black bodies and limit their access to any kind of space. This despatialization was frequently couched in the language of biological essentialism, which promulgated terms such as *racial instincts* or *natural affinities* (to borrow the language of Justice Henry Billings Brown in *Plessy*) to justify segregation. Despite the nation's and court's insistence that separation actually signaled equality, segregation was in effect an attempt to "despatialize [African American] sense of place."[13]

Laws and customs meant to police and control the movement of Black bodies cannot be enforced at all times. Subjects will breach barriers and move in and out of spaces, whether deliberately or not. So even though the Jim Crow train car attempted to lock down and lock out Black passengers, many still found a way to circumvent some of these restrictions. That is why in addition to being a highly disciplined space for Black bodies, the Jim Crow train car is also a space of compulsory sociability, that is, a space in which it is expected that one will interact with those of different class, racial, ethnic, or cultural backgrounds.[14] It is in these types of spaces—that seem to be governed by a rigid set of rules but operate in much more dynamic and unpredictable fashion—that conceptions of racial identity can emerge, shift, or change. Inscoe writes that for many African American writers, the railroad was "often . . . the first venue in which [racial] innocence was lost, as young people were forced to confront their blackness as defined by the larger society in which they lived."[15] These moments on the train "led to revelatory moments . . . either at the time or imposed by memory and hindsight—in which [the Black passenger's] status came into sharp focus, sometimes quite suddenly, and served as catalysts through which other, more internalized truths surfaced as well."[16] A few moments riding on the train, in other words, could lead to an acute realization and a lifelong grappling of what it means to be a racialized subject in the United States.

Inscoe's characterization as the railroad as a catalyst for "revelatory moments" for African American passengers should be read along with Grady's description of the railroad as a "system." The railroad as system is evocative, for it suggests the extent to which African American passengers had to negotiate a variety of racial, economic, and class politics while riding the train and provides insight into why trains are depicted in such a "striking number of [Black] autobiographical accounts."[17] The extent to which African American passengers must negotiate the space of the railroad as part of a total system is particularly evident in slave narratives of the antebellum era. Two examples stand out: Frederick Douglass's detailed account of his escape from slavery in his last autobiography, *The Life and Times of Frederick Douglass,* and William and Ellen's Craft's memoir, *Running a Thousand Miles for Freedom: Or the Escape of William and Ellen Craft from Slavery.* Both slave narratives recount highly charged confrontation scenes on trains, in which the runaways fear that their bodily performances of freedmen (Douglass and the Crafts were all in disguise) are about to be exposed. In the case of Douglass, he borrows the kit and paperwork of a friend who is a freedman and a sailor. Boarding a train in Baltimore at the last minute, Douglass is confronted by an initially harsh conductor, whose demeanor changes upon seeing Douglass's seafaring clothes. As he converses respectfully with the conductor, Douglass is painfully aware of his own performance as a sailor, monitoring his facial expressions and hand movements even as he keeps a discrete eye on the conductor's face to gauge the conductor's response. Despite the terror that Douglass feels at this moment, which he calls the "critical moment in the drama," Douglass remains "externally at least . . . calm and self-possessed."[18] He relies on his "skill" in playing a sailor, his "knowledge of ships and sailor's talk," and his ability to "talk sailor like an 'old salt.'"[19] He understands not only the character he is required to play but the setting in which the drama must unfold; he chooses to board the train as it departs Baltimore and buy his ticket from a conductor rather than at the station because he knows that the "jostle of the train," "the natural haste of the conductor," and the crowds of passengers will give him a better chance of freedom. Douglass calls this moment "one of the most anxious I [have] ever experienced."[20] But even at the conclusion of the interaction—with the conductor accepting Douglass's identity and moving on to the next passenger—Douglass understands that he is still in great danger, for "I was still in Maryland and subject to arrest at any moment."[21] Riding the train as a slave expands Douglass's experience of time and space, as he recognizes that the train is speeding along but nevertheless feels that it is crawling at a snail's pace. The terror of slavery and the potential consequences that Douglass faces should he be caught complicate the train's standing as an instrument of modernity that destroys space and time. The "between" spaces that the train creates in Schivelbusch's account of the railroad all continue to matter when one is a runaway slave from Maryland trying to get to Pennsylvania.

The Crafts' escape from Georgia required much more prolonged performances, involving several steamboat and railroad rides. Theirs is perhaps one of the best-known slave narratives because of the unusual route the couple took to escape. Ellen Craft—who could pass for white—dressed as an upper-class white man to avoid detection, while her husband, George, who was dark-skinned, acted as her valet. Unlike most runaway slaves, the Crafts were able to afford Ellen's clothes and the train tickets for travel because George earned a living working as a carpenter in Macon, Georgia; although his master pocketed most of George's earnings for himself, he allowed George to keep a small amount for his own use. The Crafts pinned their hopes of escape on Ellen's ability to perform white masculinity. To mask her illiteracy—which would have been highly suspicious in a wealthy white man at the time period—Ellen traveled with her right arm in a sling so as to avoid having to write anything. To hide her lack of facial hair, she kept her lower face and neck muffled as if she were ill. Unlike Douglass's narrative, in which the train is the setting for a dramatic potential showdown between conductor and runaway, *Running* portrays the train as the site where the banality of racism and white supremacy can be fully observed. While riding a first-class train car, the Crafts encounter a fellow passenger, a "stout, elderly lady," who initially insists that George must be her runaway slave, Ned. Having finally been convinced that George Craft is not the "ungrateful" Ned, this wealthy, self-professed Christian woman launches into a speech on the benefits of slavery and the ingratitude of slaves. She speaks of her intense devotion to Christ as she relays stories of her casual cruelty to her slaves. She tells her fellow passengers that she prays for a devoted maid whom she sold when the woman became too ill to work; she acknowledges that she and her son (a minister) conspired to overturn her recently deceased husband's will because in it, he had manumitted the family's slaves, an act that she feels would have been "cruel" to the slaves. Once the woman disembarks from the train, the other passengers—southerners all—call her a "hypocrite" and a "humbug" for the cruelty she shows.

The Crafts cannot participate in this conversation because they are worried that a wrong word or gesture will lead to their discovery. Their silence should not be read as acquiescence but rather as an example of the strategies Black passengers used in their attempts to go about their lives without threat of violence. We will see echoes of the Crafts' experience on the train later in this chapter in the discussion of James Weldon Johnson's *The Autobiography of an Ex-Colored Man*, but for now, I will highlight how each of these texts represents the myriad forms that Black despatialization can take. Douglass portrays the train in *The Life and Times* as a space that is always on the verge of interracial confrontation, while *Running* shows us how codes of civility and sociability are also effective in terrorizing Black slaves and passengers. These scenes of misrecognitions, near recognitions, and silent recognitions point to the multiplicitous ways that slaves such as Douglass and the Crafts must operate when occupying spaces like the train.

"The Black Man Rides Jim Crow in Georgia"

The dynamic and contradictory qualities of the passenger train heavily influence Douglass's and the Crafts' performances of freedom. One would expect that the end of slavery would radically alter the experience of Jim Crow in the postbellum era. While the laws around enslavement changed, the despatialization of Black bodies did not. It is the confrontation between compulsory sociability and the seemingly strict dictates of racial segregation that make the train an ideal space for dramatizing tensions and conflicts within and between Black and other passengers. No other system of social categorization reveals the extent to which conceptions of race are tied to ideas about space as Jim Crow does.[22] We catch a glimpse of how deeply imbricated space and race can be in a short essay titled "The Superior Race" by W. E. B. Du Bois. Although the essay is primarily "a critique of white supremacy," Du Bois makes the case that the train car is the exemplary space for forming, reinforcing, and naturalizing racial identities. Du Bois offers a description of the process by which Jim Crow interpellates subjects into state-sanctioned racial identities via the spaces they are forced to occupy.[23] "The Superior Race" consists of an imagined dialogue between Du Bois and an unnamed "white friend" who nonetheless fervently believes that "Negroes are inferior" and that Du Bois represents an exception to that general rule.[24] The two have a debate, in which the white friend recites familiar racist canards regarding white superiority and Black inferiority. Du Bois patiently elucidates the flaws in his friend's logic, winding down his defense of Blackness by pointing out that racial purity is a powerful fiction that obscures how hybridic putative white and Black bodies really are.[25] The racist interlocutor then asks Du Bois how he distinguishes white men from Black men given how intermingled the two races are; he also wonders what it means to be Black when, as Du Bois suggests, all humans contain a "mix" of different races. Du Bois ends the essay with a terse response: "The black man is a person who must ride 'Jim Crow' in Georgia."[26]

In Du Bois's final and somewhat fatalistic statement that he can "recognize" Blackness via the lens of Jim Crow on the railroad, he claims that the segregation of the Jim Crow South does not reflect racial identity or reality; rather, Blackness is created and perpetuated by a state intent on policing its citizens and occupants. Du Bois argues that Blackness is defined by the "person riding 'Jim Crow' in Georgia" because that is the space in which the "social" and the "historical" merge; it is, according to him, the *only* way an African American man can be described. It highlights the extent to which race is constructed via spaces

or practices that we tend to think of as apolitical or lacking any kind of
racial subtext. We might tend to think of Jim Crow as reflecting in spatial terms the hierarchization of racially differentiated bodies, but what
Du Bois suggests is that space does not reflect racial orders and identities so much as constitute them. Blackness is not defined by anything
essential or natural, like biology, skin color, or phenotype; it is not tied to
intelligence, beauty, or sociability. Instead, Du Bois argues, it is defined
by the spaces that certain bodies are required to inhabit. Blackness is not
the cause of segregation but rather its most visible sign. Riding Jim Crow
is what makes a Black man recognizably one. It is a category of identity
that is recognizable because the state has deemed it so; it is imposed by
the hundreds if not thousands of laws, rules, and conventions governing
American life. In Du Bois's formulation, Blackness is defined by riding
Jim Crow as much as Jim Crow is defined by Blackness.

Du Bois's use of the train to assert that social structures fix Blackness
calls to mind the moment in Frantz Fanon's *Black Skin, White Masks*
(1952) when a white child points to Fanon and blurts out, "Look! A
Negro!"[27] This exchange occurs on a train, and while this fact does not
usually attract attention or comment, it is an important aspect of Fanon's
representation of the impact of race on the Black subject. Just as Du Bois
uses the train to highlight racial identity as a process, so too does Fanon
transform the compulsory sociability of the train into an exploration of
how this declaration is elemental to the formation of Blackness, locking
in place Black subjectivity at the moment of its articulation. As George
Yancy argues, this moment is not an "inaugural event: it is an instantia-
tion of a long and continuous history of antiblack white racism . . . this
process of denigrating/assaulting the black body is historically iterative.
It neither ends nor does it begin with the visual and discursive assault
on Fanon's Black body or other Black bodies."[28] As Fanon reels in anger
and distress at these words, which are uttered and experienced as a slur,
he becomes aware of his own body in space:

> As a result, the body schema, attacked in several places, collapsed, giving
> way to an epidermal racial schema. In the train, it was a question of being
> aware of my body, no longer in the third person but in triple. In the train,
> instead of one seat, they left me two or three. I was no longer enjoying
> myself. I was unable to discover the feverish coordinates of the world. I

existed in triple. I was taking up room. I approached the Other . . . and the Other, evasive, hostile, but not opaque, transparent and absent, vanished. Nausea.[29]

Like Wideman and Du Bois, Fanon is made aware of the fact that he "tak[es] up room." The cry of "Look! A Negro!" effectively despatializes his body, erasing it from the train, even as it words make Fanon hypervisible to others and hyper-conscious of himself. Fanon apprehends the crisis that the cry of "Look! A Negro!" precipitates spatially (his "triple" position within the car, his movement toward the "evanescent other") as well as temporally (his realization that a "epidermal racial schema" has followed the "body schema"). Fanon's tripleness—his fractured subjectivity—which comes into existence at this moment, is something entirely different from the double-consciousness about which Du Bois wrote so elegantly; it is not merely that he sees himself through white eyes ("no longer the third person"); it is that his identity has been riven at the moment of its entrance into the world. Although Fanon's geographical location is very different from Du Bois's—the former is in the French colony of Martinique, while the latter is in the Jim Crow American South—Black identity only solidifies in those spaces that are characterized by compulsory sociability and a high degree of social regimentation, namely, the train. And although Du Bois and Fanon diverge in the alternatives they imagine for resisting the hostility of the white gaze, the train as a space enables them to conceptualize their constructions of Blackness.

The Pullman Porter's Closet

Like "The Seat Not Taken," *The Autobiography of an Ex-Colored Man* represents the vexed relationship between Black subjects and public spaces, and how each is defined by the other. It also presages Wideman's representation of the train as a spatialization of the history of African American experience. The unnamed narrator—the titular Ex-Colored Man—is a frequent passenger on trains as he moves through his life. As a young boy, the narrator rides on the train with his mother from Georgia, where he was born, to a small town in Connecticut, where his white father has paid for him and his mother to relocate; he rides south after his mother's death to attend university in Atlanta. Having been robbed of his college tuition money, he accepts an offer of a ride from a Pullman porter whose route runs between Atlanta and Jacksonville, Florida. Unable to afford the fare, he accepts the porter's invitation to ride for free in a laundry closet. After a sojourn in New York City (where he hears ragtime for the first time), the narrator travels to Europe with a wealthy benefactor who hires him for his musical ability. Dissatisfied with his indolent but privileged life, the narrator returns to the United States in an attempt to "take ragtime and [make] it classic."[30] He once again heads south on the train, in stages, before ending up Georgia. It is while on this research trip that the narrator witnesses the lynching of a Black man in a small town. This incident prompts his decision to "forsake [his] own race," and he hastily gets a train to return to New York, where he begins a new life as an "ex-colored" man.[31]

The Autobiography is a novel that is filled with trains and train journeys up and down the country, making its protagonist perhaps one of the best-traveled characters in early twentieth-century African American literature. The train not only drives the plot, it is also the space within which the narrator constructs his identity, first as a Black man, and then as an ex-Black man. The train, in other words, highlights the notion that Black identity and space are mutually constitutive. The first time we see this relationship represented in the novel is during the narrator's trip to the South as a young man, when he accepts an offer to travel to Jacksonville from an acquaintance who works as a Pullman porter. Knowing that the Ex-Colored Man doesn't have money for the fare, the porter lets him ride in the "closet" of the Pullman coach, which is where porters store clean linen and laundry for their passengers. While all train cars traverse the divisions between public and private, Pullman coaches particularly capture that tension between two different kinds of spaces. As Eric Arnesen notes in *Brotherhoods of Color* (2001), the Pullman porter was introduced along with the sleeping and dining cars in 1867 by the Pullman Car Company to bolster the company's claims to ultimate luxury travel. George Mortimer Pullman, the company's founder "established a veritable cast of black servants" to serve meals and act as servants to customers.[32] For much of the late nineteenth and early twentieth centuries, the Pullman company was the largest employer of African American labor in the United States, employing over six thousand in 1914 and double that number in the 1930s. Barbara Welke calls the Pullman car a "little house on wheels," with the berths being "beds" and the porters presented as domestic help rather than as employees of a corporation.[33] Being a Pullman porter required a tremendous amount of training and physical labor. Arnesen notes that new recruits undertook several days of training before starting their jobs and that porters were required to arrive hours prior to departure to "set up his car," which involved checking the linen, ensuring the cleanliness of the car, and carefully placing brushes and glasses in place. Once passengers arrived, the porter "would assist passengers for the trip's duration, while at night he would shine their shoes with high-quality polish he had purchased himself."[34]

It is this weight of domestic servitude that weighs on the Ex-Colored Man when he rides the train to Florida. As a young African American man with no friends and an ambivalent relationship with his family, the experience of riding in the Pullman porter's linen closet renders in spatial terms the constraints that he unconsciously feels. The Pullman porter's closet becomes a tomb where the narrator is buried alive, figuratively drowning in the materials of the porter's labor: the laundry. If the slave ship is the space of the Black Atlantic and the slave trade, then the Pullman porter's closet becomes the space of Jim Crow America: a hidden niche buried in the seemingly domestic heart of a public conveyance that is privately owned. And although the narrator appreciates that the porter has risked his own job to provide the Ex-Colored Man a free ride, he nevertheless finds the trip to be torturous precisely because he must remain immobile for so long:

> I spent twelve hours doubled up in the porter's basket for soiled linen, not being able to straighten up on account of the shelves for clean linen just over my head. The air was hot and suffocating and the smell of damp towels and used linen was sickening. At each lurch of the car over the none too smooth track I was bumped and bruised against the narrow walls of my narrow compartment. Then nausea took possession of me, and at one time I had grave doubts about reaching my destination alive.[35]

The Ex-Colored Man's immobility on the train echoes various other moments of immobility in African American slave narratives, including the escape of Henry "Box" Brown, who mailed himself to freedom, and the attic sojourn of Harriet Jacobs, who lived for seven years in the crawlspace under the eaves of her grandmother's house and about whom I will have more to say later in this chapter. This immobilization is the result of white despatialization that demands that Black bodies take up as little room as possible. The Pullman porter's closet becomes an allegory for the extreme disciplining of those bodies that is required in public spaces. The Ex-Colored Man's experience riding the train buried in the Pullman porter's closet emblematizes the ways that African Americans restrict their movements, contort their bodies, and are forced to take up the least amount of space in order to go about their lives and move through the country. The narrator's strong physical reaction to the closeness of his quarters—his nausea and inability to breathe, his sense that he will die before he reaches his destination—highlights how the physical threat that this type of spatial immobilization wreaks on bodies. It trains him about how to move his body in space; it inures him to the physical pain he must endure in order to move through the spaces of the nation; and it disciplines his sense of self to fragments of time (only twelve more hours, and I'll be free).

Like Du Bois, the Ex-Colored Man recognizes that space defines how others view him racially. On his trip through the South nearly the end of the novel to collect material for his songbook of spirituals and ragtime melodies, the narrator tells of his amusement "on arriving at some little railroad station to be taken for and treated as a white man, and six hours later, when it was learned that I was stopping at the house of the coloured preacher or schoolteacher to note the attitude of the whole town change."[36] The narrator himself takes advantage of this linkage between space and race, often choosing to pass for white on the railroad because he prefers the luxuries of traveling in a Pullman coach as a passenger. It is only when he enters a Black home that his identity shifts. In other words, it is the space he occupies that defines his racial identity and this positioning within space is more vital to "reading" his race than the color of his skin. Jim Crow may have been promulgated as a system that takes into account the supposedly "natural" divide between white and Black subjects, but these texts reveal that it was not a reflection of some kind of biological, essentialist destiny. Jim Crow was a furious constructing and maintaining of those binaries to justify its continuing existence.

It is not a coincidence, then, that the two most charged scenes of racism in the novel occur in a train and at a train station. The first is a conversation on a Pullman smoker between white men regarding the "Negro Problem." This key scene emblematizes the spatial dimensions of racism. It occurs behind closed doors in a private car reserved for white men that is also coded as hyper-masculine and upper class. Despite the fact that the smoker is filled with passengers, the conversation really only involves two men, an elderly Grand Army of the Republic veteran and a "raw-boned, red-faced" Texan who grows cotton for a living. Their debate falls along somewhat predictable lines; the Texan argues that the South suffered excessively during the Civil War and Reconstruction, that the emancipation of slaves was not "worth the good white blood that was spilt," and that citizenship and educational opportunities have not made the African Americans the equal of whites.[37] The GAR veteran retorts that ignorance is not a quality limited to Black voters. He goes on to note that even if the "Negro is so distinctly inferior," as the Texan argues, than "moral responsibility" requires that they still be treated equally. Regardless, the GAR veteran argues that the supposed superiority of the "Anglo-Saxon race" is an illusion based on a "matter of dates in history."[38] Despite the fact that the two men cannot convince each other to rethink their positions, the narrator describes a congenial conclusion to the conversation with the Texan passing around a flask as the occupants of the smoking car (presumably including the Ex-Colored Man himself) engage in "a general laugh and good feeling."[39]

The clubby atmosphere of the train's smoking car contributes to the narrator's sense that this is meant to be a "confidential" conversation between white men. Even the northerner who argues for Black equality believes the conversation has to be "between white men only."[40] The Ex-Colored Man initially finds the conversation to be "chilling," but he is able to rationalize away this response by arguing somewhat delusionally that the exchange is a sign of racism's weakening grip. He claims that the white southerner's response "indicates that the main difficulty of the race question does not lie so much in the actual condition of the black as it does the mental attitude of the whites; and a mental attitude, especially one not based on truth, can be changed more easily than actual conditions."[41] This conversation about the future of race relations in which Black people are not welcome to participate indicates how white supremacy spatializes its assumptions. The insistence on whites-only spaces is not about honoring the natural distinctions between the races so much as it about ensuring that Black people cannot witness the minor rifts that occasionally appear in the spaces of white supremacy. The GAR veteran's mild critique of the racism that African Americans face in this country is not only undercut by his admission that he would not want his own daughter to marry a Black man but also by his insistence on the maintenance of separate spaces. White spaces—whether they are familial or public—depend on the exclusion of Black bodies; otherwise, the privilege that whiteness confers has no meaning.

The second incident that I will focus on is perhaps the most famous in the novel: the lynching of an unnamed Black man at the railroad station of a small southern town. Whereas the scene in the smoking car between the southerner and the GAR veteran took placed behind closed doors in a segregated space, this scene takes place in front of a railroad station. The location of the lynching is significant, according to Anthony Bianculli, as railroad stations,

> especially in smaller towns and cities, [were] often . . . the hub of activity of the town. It was here that strangers arrived and news from the wider world was first received; it was from here that loved ones departed; it was through here that goods and foodstuffs were shipped and received. The townsfolk gathered at the depot to hear speeches by political candidates or to mourn beloved personages as a train bore their body to a final resting place.[42]

Bianculli's description of the railroad station as a space of public and collective ritual meshes with Johnson depiction of what happens. The narrator—who is unknown in town—"follow[s] the drift" of white people toward the railroad station. Once there, he encounters "a crowd of men, all white, [with] others were steadily arriving, seemingly from all the surrounding country." All night "the around the station continued to grow; at sunrise there were a great many women and children." The Ex-Colored Man notes the presence of "some coloured people . . . going about customary tasks."[43] But the "gathering of Negroes usually seen in such town was missing," and the Black folks who are present take care to stand at the outskirts of what is happening.[44] As the sun rises, a Black man is finally dragged into the square. A "space [is] quickly cleared" in front of the station and the victim is tied up by his neck.[45] The mob decides to burn the man alive; they chain him to a railroad tie, douse him with fuel, and light a match. The Ex-Colored Man watches in horror, "fixed to the spot," as the victim screams in agony and "before I realized that time had elapsed," the man is dead, and the smell of burned flesh fills the air.[46]

This scene in front of the station emphasizes the simultaneous centrality and peripherality of the Black body. The suffering of the man defines the space, as he occupies the center of this gathering, while the town's Black population stand on the margins, marking the boundaries of the social. All are denied the ability to move through or out of the space of the lynching. Johnson's decision to set this scene of Black terror and white terrorism in the clear space in front of the train station speaks to the ways that white spaces can quickly be transformed into something barbaric; the railroad tracks provide a stake to which the victim is tethered, the ropes that restrain him are quickly replaced with chains, and fuel is produced to accelerate and maximize his suffering. As the Ex-Colored Man watches this man being tortured and burned alive, he experiences a collapse of space and time; he remains "fixed to the spot where" he stands," and the entire episode is "over before [he] realized that time had elapsed." The narrator's inability to move through the space of Black terror and his inability to comprehend the passage of time as a man burns to death speaks to the ways that Black bodies are constituted under the violent gaze of white racism. Having witnessed this fundamental scene of national terror, he finds himself unable to locate his body in space or orient his experience in time. His discombobulation echoes that of Fanon on the train when confronted with the racist child. His body and subjectivity fractures at the moment he realizes his Blackness.

While the popular imagination tends to portray the train as a spatial microcosm for US democracy (because of its open seat configuration rather than the private cars more prevalent in Europe) and freedom (because it increased an individual's ability to travel more quickly and easily through the nation), *The Autobiography of an Ex-Colored Man* names the railroad as a space in which racial hierarchies have the power to murder without consequence. Immediately after the lynching, the narrator boards another train heading north. During this final train ride, the Ex-Colored Man makes the decision to pass as a white man in the very spaces that he has already occupied as a white man, a fact that undercuts his characterization of his decision as dramatic and transformative. He presents his decision to pass in curiously passive terms. He states that from that moment he "would neither disclaim the black race nor claim the white race," implying that that his racial identity is now in the hands of those around him, a disingenuous position given that he has passed as white in the past and knows that he can continue to do so without question.[47] The passivity of his claim is also belied by the active steps he takes; he changes his name, alters his physical appearance, cuts off all previous friends and acquaintances, and avoids certain parts of New York where he is well known. What the Ex-Colored Man presents as a moment of transformation is actually the culmination of a long slide into self-delusion. Johnson represents the narrator's decision as a betrayal and as act of cowardice, one that he refuses to acknowledge except in the famous last line when he characterizes his choice as selling his birthright for a "message of pottage."[48]

Black Women and Jim Crow

Du Bois's and the Ex-Colored Man's experiences on the train are informed by their race but also by their class and gender identifications. Their self-presentation as middle-class, well-educated men clearly informs how they see themselves as railroad passengers. But intersection of gender, sexuality, class, and race are perhaps their most fraught in the narratives of African American women who undertook train travel in the Jim Crow South. More than their male counterparts, African American women recognized the ways that gender shaped perceptions of race and vice versa and how the space of the train, in turn, impacted their own movements and interactions. This distinction is apparent even in the antebellum era in Harriet Jacobs's slave narrative *Incidents in the Life of a Slave Girl*. According to John Inscoe, *Incidents* offers the "earliest firsthand account" of segregation on a train.[49] Unlike her counterparts Douglass and the Crafts, whose narratives detail the train rides they undertook in the American South, Jacobs rides the Jim Crow car for the first time when she is already in a northern state. As she flees farther north to escape the long reach of her slave owner, Jacobs, with the help of some friends, purchases a train ticket from Philadelphia to New York City. As she arrives at the station in Philadelphia, she is told by one of her benefactors, Mr. Durham, that tickets for the first-class carriages were not available and that he fears she is in for a "disagreeable" ride. Jacobs, not fully understanding why the first-class car is barred to her, offers to provide more money to purchase the desired ticket, but she is told by Mr. Durham that no ticket "could be had for any money. They don't allow colored people to go in the first-class cars."[50] Jacobs describes her experience riding in the segregated train as being

> stowed away in a large, rough car, with windows on each side, too high for us to look out without standing up. It was crowded with people, apparently of all nations. There were plenty of beds and cradles, containing screaming and kicking babies. Every other man had a cigar or pipe in his mouth, and jugs of whiskey were handed round freely. The fumes of the whiskey and the dense tobacco smoke were sickening to my senses, and my mind was equally nauseated by the coarse jokes and ribald songs around me. It was a very disagreeable ride.[51]

This passage is striking because of the physical effect that the train ride elicits in Jacobs, a woman who has lived in slavery all her life and who has just endured seven years in the crawl space under the roof of her grandmother's house. Despite all that she has gone through, Jacobs nevertheless expresses her disgust with the traveling conditions she endures on the Jim Crow car. The lack of fresh air, the polyglot nature of her fellow passengers, the presence of screaming babies and alcoholically boisterous men—all these things sicken Jacobs, even though it is safe to say she has undergone much worse.

Jacobs's squeamishness about the travel conditions she endures on the Jim Crow car while fleeing slavery is meant to remind the reader of her feminine sensibilities. The narrative implies that these feelings of propriety and morality have not been dampened by slavery or by her acknowledged relationship with a white planter. As Claudia Tate writes in D mestic Allegories of Political Desire (1992), "Incidents specifically seeks a ympathetic white female audience, thus Jacobs' deliberate appropi ation of the conventions of sentimental fiction and constructions of pious womanhood, which were popular among readers."[52] Her outraged response to the train bolsters her claim to the limited protections that the cult of femininity offered to Black women. Claudia Tate writes that African American writers "subscrib[ed] to the rigid standards of Victorian ladyhood" in order to "enlarge its criteria, thereby granting their heroines access to Victorian ladyhood that served to counter the racist stereotype of black female wanton sexuality."[53] This would have been especially important to Jacobs, who was no doubt anticipating judgment on the part of her readership for entering into a sexual relationship with a white man in order to gain a measure of protection for herself.

The establishment of Jim Crow legally in the late nineteenth century made it even more difficult for Black women to claim these types of considerations. Welke argues that "following the war, access to first-class ladies' accommodations in public transit became a critical marker of respectability for Black women."[54] Black women were refused entry into first-class carriages as passengers—even when they had paid for the ticket—and they were also frequently barred from the "ladies' car" on trains, the ultimate sign of revered womanhood. Tate's assertion that Black women "dared to breech social and literary conventions" is echoed by Barbara Welke's arguement that while Black women were just as likely as Black men to be barred from first-class carriages, Black women were much more likely to sue carriers for their exclusion from these types of classed accommodation. The suits these women filed emphasized that the Black female passengers were "ladies," relying on class and gender norms to drive home the injustice of their exclusion. Most of these women were married, and most were middle-class with the material resources and time to hire lawyers, attend hearings, and testify in court.[55] Not coincidentally, the urge to link Black women with ideals of domestic gentility emerged at the same time as what Amy Richter calls "domesticated public spaces."[56] These new types of hybridized spaces—trains, department stores, hotel lobbies, urban parks, restaurants, theaters— were created with the expectation that women of a certain class and race would patronize them. They are spaces that were defined by "deference, privilege, and comfort," and reflected the emerging importance of "commercial" rather than "personal" relationships.[57] Richter elaborates that the "midcentury understanding of public life as uncertain, dangerous, and masculine was replaced with a modern ideal of 'public domesticity'—a vision of an orderly, comfortable, and safe realm that, while not feminized, was no longer solely masculine. This larger transformation is revealed in stark relief aboard the railroad."[58] If there were spaces that were specifically designed to cater to the leisure and consumer needs of white women, then the presence of Black woman called into question the ideology undergirding those domesticated public spaces.

Claiming the train as a type of space that Black women have a right to occupy by virtue of their gender, sexuality, and class affiliation is an important theme in the works of the late nineteenth century. In these texts, shifting notions of domesticity intersected with gendered racist ideologies to create highly stratified conceptions of space. Anna Julia Cooper's *A Voice from the South* (published in 1892) predates by four years the *Plessy v. Ferguson* decision that legalized segregation in public spaces. Yet Cooper's text offers a window into how middle-class Black women, traveling on their own, were consistently denied access to spaces that their class and gender by convention should have made available to them. Cooper works to intensify the indignation of her middle-class readership by painting a portrait of the idealized "black Woman of the South," who possesses a "quiet," "unobtrusive" manner, dresses simply, and behaves modestly. In Cooper's telling, designed to extract as much sympathy as possible from middle-class white society, the Black woman's dress, good manners, economic status, and cultured air should grant her the protections and privileges of a patriarchal society that trumpets the protection of womanhood as one of its cornerstones. Cooper targets in particular those "gentlemanly and efficient" railroad conductors who help passengers alight from the car when there is no raised platform for safe disembarkation.[59] She notes that these men often stand on a "narrow little stool" so that they can safely help "woman after woman from the steps to the stool, thence to the ground"; they carry the bags of white female passengers so that she can get off the train more easily.[60] But when a Black woman tries to exit, he "deliberately fold[s] [his] arms and turn[s] around." Along with the satchels that the Black woman carries is also the "unnamable burden" of "slighted womanhood," which is, according to Cooper, "unlike every other emotion of the soul."[61]

Cooper's exceptionalizing of the trauma of "slighted womanhood" is very much focused on interactions between Black women and white authority figures on the railroad. She claims not to object to the idea of segregation itself but rather to the lack of respect with which conductors and passengers speak to her and treat her. She notes that as a "loyal American citizen," she would cheerfully obey public officials in the "discharge of their duty." The problem lies in the fact that conductors and other railroad authorities seem not to have the sensibility or grace to recognize the gentility of Black women. Cooper notes that "when a great burly six feet of masculinity with sloping shoulders and unkempt beard swaggers in, and, throwing a roll of tobacco into one corner of his jaw, growls out at me over the paper I am reading, 'Here gurl,' (I am past thirty) 'you better git out 'n dis kyar 'f yer don't, I'll put yer out,'" her sardonic response is *"Here's an American citizen who has been badly trained. He is sadly lacking in both 'sweetness' and 'light.'"*[62] Later in the passage, Cooper describes seeing several "loafers" at the train station, sitting around while a "productive soil and inviting climate beckon in vain to industry" and mocks a hotelier who is whittling on a pine stick with his feed propped up on a box, whom she is certain would deny her room and board if she were dying of hunger—and states, "What a field for the missionary woman."[63] Her suggestion that these "loafing" white men represent the heathen who must be converted positions Black women in the role of civilizer rather than those who need to be civilized. The impossibility of Cooper's project to reconcile Black womanhood with the protections of domestic gentility are emblematized in the spatial dilemma she confronts in a "dilapidated station": whether to enter the waiting room marked "FOR LADIES" or the other marked "FOR COLORED PEOPLE." Which space is meant for her?

The indignities that Cooper and other middle-class Black female passengers endured are intensified in narratives depicting working-class African American women riding the train. Ralph Ellison's "Boy on a Train" (published in 1996) is stark in its depictions of what African American women faced as passengers. The story's interlocking of Jim Crow, the sexualization of Black womanhood, and memory is directly tied to the railroad. The mother in the story, modeled on Ellison's own formidable mother, is recently widowed and travels from Oklahoma back south with her two young sons, James and Lewis, to look for work to support the family. As the story opens, the boys are looking out the train window, with James, the older one, trying to teach the baby about Jack Frost and the sounds that animals make. The innocent antics of the children are juxtaposed with their mother's watchful behavior. The Jim Crow car in which the family is riding (they are evidently the only Black passengers) is unsanitary, unsafe, and uncomfortable; James's mother refers to it as "filthy." The car carries groceries and other goods for delivery; in the corner of the car sits a pine casket that is being transported for burial. Having recently lost her own husband, James's mother wonders to herself "what poor soul . . . is in there."[64] Because of the Jim Crow car's proximity to the engine, the windows cannot be opened, making the car uncomfortably hot. The mother is worried because cinders from the locomotive are still finding a way into the closed train car. She also anxiously keeps an eye out for the train's butcher, who will be returning to pick up his supplies, which are also evidently stored on the Jim Crow car. The mother's discomfort stems from the fact that the butcher had groped her when she and her sons first took their seats, and while she had spat in his face and "told him to keep his dirty hands where they belonged," the story implies that she is still wary of his potential presence. Filled with hate for the man who had no compunction about assaulting her in the presence of her young children, she wonders, "Why couldn't a Negro woman travel with her two boys without being molested?"[65]

James is unaware of the butcher's attack on his mother and wonders why the man will not give him and his younger brother a piece of candy when it is apparent that the butcher has plenty. As he takes in the sights, James is filled with excitement about traveling on the train, as well as a vague sense of mourning over his father's death. He evinces a lively interest in the people who pass through the train, even though it is clear that these passengers do not see him and that they view the Jim Crow car as a space that is not intended for human occupation—a white father and son walk through the car with their dog, and the story implies that they use the Jim Crow car as an appropriate place for the animal to relieve himself. James's childlike desire to take in his surroundings and his innocence about why the train's occupants do not look at him or treat him kindly speaks to the central invisibility that determine Black bodies on the railroad. White passengers and railroad workers know that they are entering a space marked as Jim Crow, but they do not need to acknowledge the Black people present on the train. On the Jim Crow train, the Black body occupies a contradictory position: invisible and irrelevant but at the same absolutely necessary in order to preserve white space and spatiality. That spatiality is predicated on the notion that it is endlessly expansive, even in those areas that are nominally designated as Black. In much the same way that the white father and son casually enter the Jim Crow car, the butcher casually assaults the narrator's mother. The story portrays how white society transforms the Black woman's body into a segregated train car: invisible and available.

As the newly minted "man" of the family, James feels a tender sense of protection toward his mother, whose continuing grief and anger he senses, although he cannot quite locate the source of her bitterness. He expresses a desire to be just like his father, who was "tall and kind and always joking and reading books."[66] He resolves that "when he got big," he would take his mother and his brother back to Oklahoma City to show everyone how well his mother had raised him.[67] James's pleasurable anticipation of the day when his family will return to Oklahoma to receive acclaim for their success is never quite articulated as a desire to right a past wrong, but it suggests that the family's trip back east is a defeat of some kind.[68]

The story's exploration of the railroad as a site of memory and futurity is triggered by the sight of a silo on the side of the track. James draws his mother's attention to it, and "her eyes [are] strangely distant [as] she turned her face back to him."[69] After a minute, James's mother begins an extraordinary monologue, one riven with grief and passion. She starts by mentioning the "old silo back there" and tells her son it "made me remember when years ago me and your daddy came over this same old Rock Island line on our way to Oklahoma City."[70] The couple were young, in love, and "very happy going west" because they believed that "colored people had a chance out here" as opposed to in the South.[71] James's parents were just two of the hundreds of thousands of Black people who took the train north and west to find better lives for themselves and for their loved ones. Initially, James is happy to hear his mother reminiscing about her youth and his father, but that happiness is quickly replaced by a disquieting realization that this story is "something different."[72] The story he expects to hear—about the happiness she felt, about his father's love for his mother, about the fresh start that they believe they are embarking upon—is the one that the railroad has tricked so many into believing: take the train, change your life. Instead, James perceives that in telling this story, "something in Mama's voice was vast and high, like a rainbow; yet something sad and deep, like when the organ played in church."[73] The story he expects to hear about her journey on the train so many years ago turns into something else: a lesson in the way that African Americans endure and conceive of time as both deeply connected to the losses of the past and an attentiveness to resistance in the future. James's mother repeatedly pleads with her son to remember this trip: "'Son, I want you to remember this trip . . . I *want* you to remember. You *must*, you've *got to* understand . . . You remember this, James . . . You must remember this, James.'"[74] About halfway through the speech, the exhortations to remember stop, and James's mother conveys to him a message that weaves together past, present, and future:

> "We traveled far, looking for a better world, where things wouldn't so hard like they were down South. That was fourteen years ago, James. Now your father's gone from us, and you're the man. Things are hard for us colored folks, son, and it's just as three alone and we have to stick together. Things is hard, and we have to fight . . . Oh Lord, we have to fight! . . ."[75]

This rich speech invokes history, loss, and resistance in the span of a dozen words. Mama's insistence to *remember* the family's hopes, to *remember* how they sought out a life that was not constantly under the veil of racism's traumas conveys to James that the act of remembering itself is itself a powerful act of self-preservation and defiance. The command to remember is paired with the command to fight, a linkage that suggests that one cannot do the latter without the former.

In the case of "Boy on a Train," memory is not just tied to the past; it is also an exhortation about the future. If we accept the notion that this story considers what it might mean, borrowing Soyica Diggs Colbert's formation, to "imagin[e] a future that entails black life and living," then that future entails taking seriously the mother's twinned exhortations to her sons to both "remember" the past and "fight" in the future.[76] The mother in "Boy on a Train" does not seek some future goal of middle-class comfort but rather something more akin to remembrance, in which the past and the future are linked together through Black community. Like Wideman's essay about riding the Amtrak train, Mama's speech fuses past, present, and future to create a Black temporality that contests the constant assault that is she has endured and that her children are already experiencing.

Empty Seats

I started this chapter with Wideman's essay and end with Ellison's story because both reveal the extent to which spatial matters endure well beyond the time frame that has traditionally delimited Jim Crow in the United States. What Wideman and Ellison describe is thus not a function of Jim Crow so much as it is a characteristic of public space in the United States. Wideman's "The Seat Not Taken" is not set in the Jim Crow South. He is not forced by law or convention to ride separately from the white commuters who populate the train car. Nevertheless, his experience of the empty seat next to him suggests a kind of temporal disjuncture in which his experience riding the train challenges the postracial picture that the nation prefers to promulgate. Wideman's melancholic if somewhat jagged trajectory through America's racial past and present offers us a hermeneutic for thinking about the relationship between Blackness and the railroad. His experience riding the train speaks to a particular history of anti-Black racism that renders African American bodies an "absent presence" and disavows the discursive and physical violence that is often perpetrated against those bodies. For Wideman, riding the train means moving through space *and* time. It is not so much about getting from New York to Providence as it is about traveling through a span of American history that is all about the policing of racialized bodies—Black, brown, and Muslim. Wideman juxtaposes the supposedly postracial moment of 2010 with a suddenly present civil rights and segregationist past. As Wideman presciently implies, the violence of this history is never truly past, and Wideman senses its presence, lurking under the seemingly mundane, seemingly apolitical experience of riding the rails from point A to point B in the United States.

Wideman's essay reminds us that the suppressed histories of violated and excluded Black bodies are embedded within the walls of the train car. His essay underscores the fact that the memory of anti-Black oppression pervades the putatively integrated train car in an era that is allegedly defined by equal rights and protections. As he notes, his enjoyment of the "bounty of an extra seat" is shadowed by the sadness and "danger" he feels as to why it's vacant. The train in "The Seat Not Taken" does not just contain the space that Wideman occupies in 2010; it also spatializes a history of anti-Black oppression and violence that is foundational to the state. Christina Sharpe writes that the violence against Black bodies is not "the violence that occurs between subjects at the level of conflict; it is gratuitous violence that occurs at the level of a structure that constitutes the black as the constitutive outside."[77] In her critique of Allan Sekula and Noel Burch's 2010 film *The Forgotten Space—A Film Essay Seeking to Understand the Contemporary Maritime World in Relation to the Symbolic Legacy of the Sea*, Sharpe examines the film's treatment of one of its interviewees, Aereile Jackson, a homeless woman living in Long Beach who has lost custody of her children to the state. Sharpe notes that Aereile Jackson speaks from a position "in the wake," namely from a "position of deep hurt and of deep knowledge."[78] Within the film however, she represents an "opportunity" for the filmmakers; "she appears only to be made to disappear. She is metaphor."[79] The modernity that the film attempts to represent is "sutured by the . . . slave ship hold . . . the hold of the so-called migrant ship . . . the prison . . . the womb that produces blackness." If Aereile Jackson is the "forgotten space" of Sekula and Burch's film, the train seat is another "hold" that sutures modernity.[80] What Wideman describes in "The Seat Not Taken" is exactly the type of violence that Sharpe describes, a violence that is "gratuitous" and structural.[81] Even as he sits in the heart of privilege—an Acela train that travels along a corridor of the country that contains "its most educated, affluent, sophisticated and enlightened citizens"—Wideman is subjected to this "violence at the level of structure," a violence that renders the space he occupies as the "constitutive outside."

White supremacy weaponizes the very space that Wideman must sit in and move through, even though that space is marked as "public" or "open to all." Wideman's narrative reminds us that white supremacist objections to Black bodies is often couched in terms of space. Prohibitions against the intermingling of African Americans and white Americans or that proscribe Black bodies are frequently conceived in spatial terms. These laws and conventions have historically been set up as dividing up space in "separate but equal" terms, but what they conceal is the way in which *all* space is marked as white space. In Wideman's case, he is not being asked to remove himself to another space (as in, for example, Charles Chesnutt's *The Marrow of Tradition*) or targeted for occupying a certain space. Rather, the empty seat on the train becomes a weapon of the "white spatial imaginary," propelled in the words of George Lipsitz by a "hostile privatism and defensive localism."[82] It isolates Wideman even as it shifts and dissipates any responsibility for the empty seat.

The collapsing of temporality as experienced by Black subjects is set up in the essay by a series of oppositions that cannot be reconciled by narratives of progress or an insistence on the postracial. The empty seat next to Wideman represents freedom from the bustle of modern life—a welcome respite for a busy professor—but also a disquieting danger. Wideman suggests that his essay is in keeping with the caution of the "see something, say something" campaign, but what triggers Wideman's response—or his decision to "say something"—is the fact that he sees nothing—that is, the empty space next to him. His presence structures the apportionment of bodies within the train car, but it also is rendered absent, unplottable, unplaceable. For the passengers on that train, there is simply no seat next to Wideman. Wideman calls attention to the railroad's ability to make manifest the contradictions of Black experience: that the Black body is both central and marginal, central in configuring how the rest of the bodies on the train car arrange themselves and yet marginalized, defined by the empty space that surrounds him. Wideman's experience riding the train reveals to us the particular process by which African American bodies have been absented in both public spaces and histories, even as those bodies are subject to excessive disciplining and policing by the state and its agents.

6

Riding the Blind

African American literary narratives about the railroad in the early twentieth century tend to focus on these elements: the experience of riding the train car (an unsurprising development given the institution-alization of segregation by the Supreme Court in 1896); the astronomical popularity of the train as a method of conveyance in the early twentieth century; the increasing mobility of African Americans as they left the South in search of better economic opportunities; the stark differences between riding conditions on a Jim Crow car versus a whites-only car; the emergence of a generation of African American intellectuals and writers like Cooper, Du Bois, and Johnson who were deeply involved in both African American politics and culture; and an awareness if not curiosity on the part of American readers about the "race problem."

African American literary texts represent the train via the lens of Jim Crow and its despatializing effects on Black bodies. However, it is important to note that representations of the railroad are not limited to African American literature. African American folk music of the same time period is also full of references to trains but the lyrics in these songs take a different approach. In this chapter, I shift away from literary representations of the train to musical ones. African American narratives of the Jim Crow train tend to focus on the ways that the train disciplines and erase Black subjects; if African American writers represent the train as a space that is hostile to Black mobility, then African American musicians tend to portray the train as enabling a certain kind of movement, one that works to disembed Black subjects from the social practices of racism in the United States that define them as invisible. This disembedding process is frequently but not universally couched in the language of romantic disappointment, with singers either lamenting the fact that their lover has left on the train or trying to get over their heartbreak by boarding a train themselves. In the blues, the train ride that is taken to signal the end of a romantic relationship stands as an analogue for a kind of Black mobility that does not require movement through segregated spaces. This is not to say that these songs do not recognize the costs of the racism that African Americans endure; rather, the train in these songs represent an attempt to explore different types of mobilities that do not rely on white spatializing practices. The train in African American folk songs is not tethered to Jim Crow; it simply enables a man or woman to leave town for any reason, even if—or, *precisely* if—one has jilted a lover. In other words, these songs present a vision of Black mobility that while not painless, is absolutely unapologetic. Whether the singer's lover has been unfaithful, whether the singer is sick of his/her lover, whether the singer is tired of the town in which he/she lives – these early songs suggest a way to imagine Black movement that is not under the control of segregated spaces.

This is not to say that music of this period depoliticizes Black movement or experience—far from it. As critics such as Angela Davis and Houston Baker have argued, blues performers and the songs they sing do not shy away from the injustices and indignities that African Americans have endured in a racist nation.[1] It is also important to remember than in an era only a few decades removed from slavery—where the movement of Black persons was considered suspicious and unlawful—and one in which rural and urban populations were still constrained by the afterlives of slavery, including poverty and Jim Crow, the fact that a person could hop on a train and leave—even if it caused pain to an abandoned lover—was indeed revolutionary.

The treatment of the railroad in early twentieth century African American music acts as a striking contrast to the discourse that usually surrounds the railroad in terms of its social and subjective impact. As I have already noted throughout this book, historical and theoretical discourse about the railroad often focuses on the way that the train *remakes* sociability by forging new types of connections between subjects and places. In the introduction, I discussed the train as a space of compulsory sociability, enabling the intermingling of people of different races from different parts of the country, with different class affiliations. Schivelbusch argues that the train's speed enabled passengers to create new relationships with cities and locales previously out of their reach. Erving Goffman theorizes how the rise of public spaces like the train created different kinds of bodily practices to allow people to be in close contact with so many strangers while maintaining a sense of privacy. The "new" type of sociability that is being explored in these early twentieth century songs is not quite like any of those. Blues and other folk songs of this time period are working to *unmake* the sociability that these other thinkers have theorized. The fact that the train is repeatedly blamed or named in so many blues songs as taking a lover away is not just the result of its longtime historical and geographic associations with the blues; it is also a strategy that counters the despatialization of Blackness by insisting that African American subjects are constantly on the move and are constantly on their own.

The first part of this chapter will narrate the relationship between the early twentieth century blues and the railroad. The rest of these pages will be taken up with an analysis of two blues songs that I argue exemplify some of the tropes I discuss above: "Jim Crow Blues" by Charles "Cow-Cow" Davenport and "Traveling Blues" by Gertrude "Ma" Rainey. I conclude the chapter with an analysis of an early African American folk song by Elizabeth Cotten titled "Freight Train." I should note here that my focus in this chapter is not on the technical aspects of the blues genre or the embodied performance of any individual African American singer/composer, topics that have been expertly explored by many African American music historians and cultural critics. Although I apply my argument primarily to blues songs of the early twentieth century, my inclusion of "Freight Train" speaks to the fact that concerns about African American mobility are not limited to any one genre of popular music and that singer/songwriters working in a variety of genres—from slave songs to folk, blues, and R&B—have explored this topic.

Riding the Blind

You cannot listen to the blues without hearing about a train. In his 1941 autobiography titled *Father of the Blues*, composer, musician, and impresario W. C. Handy claimed to have "discovered" the blues in 1903 while waiting in a railroad station in Tutwiler, Mississippi. By Handy's account, he was sleeping on the platform waiting for a long-delayed train when a "lean, loose-jointed Negro . . . commenced plunking a guitar beside me."[2] This man's clothes were threadbare, and his face was marked by a "sadness of the ages."[3] The music he played as he sat next to Handy was "the weirdest" Handy had ever heard. It was also unforgettable: "Goin' Where the Southern Cross the Dog."[4] Handy translates this phrase for his (presumably white) reader, explaining the tendency of African American passengers to nickname railroad lines. Thus, the Yazoo Delta Railroad was popularly known as the "Yellow Dog." The slow train between Clarksdale and Greenville was dubbed the "Peavine," while the fast train along the same line was called the "Cannon Ball." Given this nomenclature, Handy recognizes that the man is singing about his trip to the town of Moorhead, where the Southern Railroad intersects the Yazoo Delta Railroad, or where "the Southern cross[es] the Dog." Although hesitant initially about composing these "low folk forms," Handy quickly realized their popularity with audiences and began to see "the beauty of primitive music."[5] From this humble origin story, a genre was born.[6]

Handy's story notes the role of the railroad in bringing the blues to his attention, but the train was instrumental in growing the popularity of the genre and expanding its reach beyond the cotton belt of the South. David Evans traces the spread of the blues "along arteries of commerce and transportation, the Mississippi and Ohio Rivers, and the various railroad lines stretching northward and westward."[7] Many of the earliest blues singers (e.g., Henry Thomas and Charley Patton) were frequently on the road, a reflection of the desperate economic conditions that many African Americans in the South endured during the downturns of the 1880s and 1890s. These early performers relied upon the train to get around, just like the performer Handy meets in Tutwiler. As these performers rode the train to various stops in the South where "cotton was king," they encountered laborers and other migrant workers who sang their songs and passed them along as they hunted for work.[8] From these outposts in the South, the genre's popularity spread quickly via sheet music and live performances, but it was not until the 1920s that record companies began sending out producers to record artists. Given this history, it should come as no surprise, then, that travel is an important theme in blues music of this time period.

Although the train is heavily linked to the blues, the railroad specifically and travel more broadly are important and ever-present tropes in African American popular music. They find expression in antebellum spirituals like "Follow the Drinking Gourd" or "Swing Low, Sweet Chariot," as well as in later twentieth-century genres like R&B.[9] While blues is a term that could be applied to a broad swath of musical productions, it was the early twentieth century that saw the standardization of the genre's characterization: a certain type of chord progression, the inclusion of the "blues note" on a scale, and, perhaps most importantly of all, an emphasis on performance that spotlighted the thoughts, feelings, and expressions of the singer rather than the song's composition process.[10] It is the genre's privileging of the singer's personal experiences of loss and sadness that make the train so central to its emotional power. There is no symbol like a train pulling out of a station to express the pain of lovers separated, spurned, or betrayed.

In Handy's story, the railroad station is the setting for his musical discovery; in history, the railroad facilitated the movement of blues performers to different parts of the country, increasing the genre's popularity. But the train is more important to the blues than as just a setting or a vehicle; it also appears frequently as a major trope in blues songs particularly from the early twentieth century. I am certainly not the first critic to note this connection; Handy himself commented on it in his autobiography. Sterling Brown notes the prominence of the railroad—the "favored symbol of escape . . . and separation"—in the blues:[11] "The Santa Fe, the Southern, the Yellow Dog, the C. C. and St. Louis, the Coast Line, and N. & W., the L. & N., the C. & O., the Rock Island, the Illinois Central Railroad lines and the Cannon Ball, the Dixie Flyer"—all are invoked in blues lyrics. The prominence of the train in blues songs stems in part from the fact that the blues emerged simultaneously as the loosening of prohibitions against Black travel. During the Great Migration, hundreds of thousands of African Americans took "trains head[ed] northward to St. Louis, Chicago, [and] Kansas City," cities with large African American populations that represented a potential fresh start from the poverty and racial hierarchies of the American South.[12] John Lovell writes that African American songs about trains are a "minor miracle."[13] Trains did not reach the South until the 1840s, and even then, there were very few opportunities for slaves to examine them let alone ride on them. And yet by the 1860s, the train was already an important part of spirituals, beloved for its "seductive sounds, speed and power, its recurring schedules, its ability to carry large numbers of passengers at cheap rates, its implicit democracy."[14] Harry Elam Jr. states that "virtually from their inception, the blues have been intertwined with the railways, articulating the triumphs, trails, and tribulations of movement and migration."[15]

The railroad in these songs enables a conception of African American movement that is not tied to Jim Crow or racist regimes of space. Charles "Cow Cow" Davenport's song "Jim Crow Blues" (1927) exemplifies how the blues disembeds Black movement from white spatial practices without ignoring the realities of the racism that African Americans faced. The lyrics explicitly focus on the difficulties of life in the Jim Crow South. Davenport sings, "I'm tired of being Jim Crowed, gonna leave this Jim Crow town." The singer expresses a wish to travel to Chicago where "money grows on trees." His desire to leave this "Jim Crow town" is also attributable to a romance gone wrong, as he declares that he won't "need no baby" in Chicago and hopes that his departure "will be sad news" for his girl. The singer's optimism that a fresh start is available to him in Chicago does not seem to be sincere; by the last lines of the song, Davenport mourns:

> Lord but if I get up there, weather don't suit, I don't find no job
> Go and tell that boss man of mine,
> Lord I'm ready to come back to my Jim Crow town.

The repetition of "Lord" in the last stanza suggests the singer's renunciation of an earthly hope for freedom, both from his girl but also from the economic instability that the "boss man" represents. Before he even leaves, the singer anticipates having to return to ask his boss for his job back. The song recognizes that the train is not a solution to any of the singer's problems; it only enables him to change the scene of struggle. Movement, of course, is not the same thing as freedom, and "Jim Crow Blues" does not equate the train with any kind of liberation. But the train does enable a focus on Black subjects and the way they move through space that is independent from white spatialization. The boss man and his town may force the singer to negotiate his identity white spatial regimes, but the train, for the space of one song, is not a part of that negotiation.

Even when the train is personified and castigated for taking a lover away, the focus is on how the train *unfixes* Black subjects from social spaces. In "Chickasaw Train Blues" (1934), Memphis Minnie cries over "what that Chickasaw has done . . . She done stole my man away." In "Mean Old Frisco Blues" (1942), Arthur "Big Boy" Crudup has a similar lament: "Well that mean old, old Frisco / And that low down Santa Fe / Mean old Frisco; low down Santa Fe / Done took my babe away." Lucille Bogan sings, "I hate that train called the M & O" (1934) because "It took my baby away, and he ain't coming back to me no more." In "C & A Blues," the train is carrying away not a lover but rather the singer himself; Big Bill Broonzy sings that he's going to take a "little train" "call[ed] the C and A" to go away because his "baby got unruly, she left home." The train in these songs is decried because it enabled an ex-lover to move away—it made possible a kind of social disarticulation. Whereas the Jim Crow train in African American literature intensifies the stakes and contradictions of Black despatialization, in the blues the train enables the unknitting of the singer from the social.

"Please Don't Tell What Train I'm On"

The stakes for this type of social unfixing are clearly higher for a woman than a man, precisely because Black female mobility was constrained by gender as well as by race. While African American men were expected to travel to seek out work, travel for African American women was much more circumscribed. Angela Davis notes that the while "the traveling blues man is a familiar image . . . the traveling blues woman is not."[16] Davis's study of the blues emphasizes how female blues singers like Ma Rainey and Bessie Smith were able to claim their sexuality by singing freely about their travel on the train. Davis argues that traveling is "frequently associated with the exercise of autonomy in their sexual lives."[17] She cites in particular Ma Rainey's "Traveling Blues" (1928) as a "powerful refutation of the blues cliché that 'when a man gets the blues, he hops on a train and rides, [but] when a woman gets the blues she lays down and dies.'"[18] Hazel Carby also argues that "the women's blues of the twenties and early thirties allows us to see an alternative form of representation . . . that explicitly addresses the contradictions of feminism, sexuality, and power."[19]

Davis and Carby emphasize Ma Rainey's refusal in "Traveling Blues" to conform to gendered dynamics of heterosexual romance. The singer has been replaced in the song by another woman, but rather than simply sitting in town with her humiliation, she decides to take the train somewhere. I too find this song important, not only for the reasons enumerated by Carby and Davis but also because "Traveling Blues" presents African American women's movement through space as resistant to the spatializing conventions of both white society and Black society. The song begins with the singer noting that the "train's at the station." She has bought her ticket but disavows any knowledge of where she is heading ("I don't know where I'll go"). The ticket agent callously tells her, "Woman, don't sit and cry," before discouraging her from getting on the train because "she keeps on passing by." His brief line within the song suggests that he is the voice of conventional society, shaming her for her public display of sadness and urging her to stay home instead of riding the train.

The ticket agent's response is part of a tradition within blues songs of railroad employees—conductors, brakemen, and ticket agents—discouraging or forbidding Black riders from riding the train in illegal ways. They are there to enforce the rules, and the songs often represent that authority as working to maintain a spatial order. The singers beg these figures to allow them to "ride the blind," that is, to ride between train cars. This spot would be the covered walkway between cars on a passenger train; on a freight train, riders might cling to a ladder running up to the roof of the car. Hobos often rode the blind to avoid being seen by the police or train crew; For example, Son House in "Empire State Express" begs the depot agent to "let me ride the blind," to which the agent replies, "I wouldn't mind son, / But this Empire State ain't mine." A similar refrain can be heard in "Freight Train Blues," sung by Clara Smith in 1924. Smith proclaims her desire to ride the freight train "cause my man is so unkind," but when she pleads with the brakeman to "let me ride the blind," the brakeman says, "Clara, you know this train ain't mine." In Blind Willie McTell's "Travelin' Blues," the singer pleads with the engineer to let a "poor man ride the blind"; when the engineer gives the stock response ("You know this train ain't mine"), the narrator calls the engineer "cruel" and "lowdown."

The depot agent's response to the singer in "Traveling Blues" suggests that the spatial laws that govern Black bodies are never far away, just as the rules governing Black female sexuality cannot be fully shaken off. Nevertheless, Rainey answers both of those challenges to her personhood with typical defiance and a hint of a threat in the song's final stanza, which is undoubtedly its most famous:

> I'm dangerous and blue, can't stay here no more
> I'm dangerous and blue, can't stay here no more
> Here come my train folks, and I've got to go.

The song implies that the singer is "dangerous" for a number of reasons: she has nothing left to lose, she is in emotional distress, she feels alone and unsupported. Dangerous to whom, though? The conventional answer might be that the singer is a danger to her unfaithful lover; she might be a danger to the townspeople (as embodied by the station agent) who seem to be ignoring or minimizing the pain she feels. She might be seen as posing a danger to norms related to the intersection of race, gender, and sexuality, all of which limit and proscribe African American women's bodies, words, and experiences. And yet I interpreted these words in their broadest possible terms: a Black woman on the move, on a train, without an idea of where she is heading, is dangerous not to a single person, town, or community but to an entire system of spatiality that depends on controlling and despatializing those bodies. The juxtaposition between "Here come my train, folks" and "I've got to go" in the last line is particularly evocative. "Folks" implies familiarity with a particular community, but the line that follows ("I've got to go") is the singer's final word. As she finishes the song, the townspeople and the listeners don't know where she is going or when she will be back, an openness that is both exhilarating and disquieting.

I want to conclude this chapter by drawing comparisons between Rainey's "Traveling Blues" and Elizabeth Cotten's song "Freight Train" (ca. 1906–12). Strictly speaking, "Freight Train" is not the blues but a folk song; nevertheless, I believe that it shares with Raine's "Traveling Blues" a sense of the potentialities of Black female movement on the railroad. In making this type of comparison, I am focusing on the lyrics themselves and not on the distinctions between the blues and folk genres or differences in the embodied performances of Cotten and Rainey, who although only seven years apart in age, led as different lives as one could imagine for two Black women in the early twentieth century.[20] Both songs look to the train to express Black female mobility in ways that adamantly refuse sociability. Like "Traveling Blues," "Freight Train" captures the notion of the train as enabling a kind of movement, particularly for African American women, that is outside of the regimes of white spatiality. The singer in "Freight Train" expresses two desires: first, to ride on a local freight train that "run[s] so fast," and second, to make sure that no one will "know what route I'm going." It expresses the singer's wish to be entirely mobile and simultaneously entirely unfindable. This desire for movement without any locability is echoed in the three following stanzas, which share similar lines. The singer asks that when she dies, "tell them all I've gone to sleep." She wishes to be buried "deep / Down at the end of old Chestnut Street" so that she can "hear old Number Nine / As she comes rolling by." The song ends with a repeat of the first stanza: "Please don't tell what train I'm on / They won't know what route I'm going." Hazel Carby argues that the blues, especially those sung by female singers, "embodied the social relations and contradictions of black displacement: of rural migration and urban flux."[21] I would concur with this assessment with one caveat. The "contradictions of black displacement" that are being explored in this song are not centered around "rural migration and urban flux," as Carby suggests. Rather, the contradiction of Black displacement that Cotten is exploring in her lyrics revolves around movement that is profoundly at a remove from the social. Note that Cotten does not invoke a passenger train, which is much more common in blues songs, but a freight train. Passengers do not ride the freight train; hobos do. The desire to move or to roam seems relatively straightforward until one realizes the histories and practices of racism that make Black mobility anything but simple. Cotten expresses a desire to move without carrying the spatial practices of a nation that does not see Blacks as deserving of *any* space. Her exhortation to her listeners to keep her route secret from the unnamed "them" and her order "tell them all I've gone to sleep" when she has died asks the Black community for space rather than trying to wrest it or negotiate it from the Jim Crow train.

The railroad enables Black performers to claim a discursive space for themselves in the nation's racist geography. And while that movement is almost always contingent, forbidden, filled with heartache, or portending death, it is nevertheless defiantly taken. Ralph Ellison's evocative definition of the blues as an "impulse to keep the painful details and episodes of a brutal experience alive in one's aching consciousness, to finger its jagged grain, and to transcend it, not by the consolation of philosophy but by squeezing from it a near-tragic, near-comic lyricism" drives the argument I am making here.[22] Ellison writes that "as a form, the blues is an autobiographical chronicle of personal catastrophe expressed lyrically."[23] The blues *textualize* the experiences and histories of the Black singers and communities for whom they perform. This textualization draws in the audience, so that the "I" of the blues song" is often understand as "we." The blues in Ellison's telling is not a fantasy or romance; it is the history of the collective travails of a community. In a parallel move, the train spatializes those same experiences and histories. Hazel Carby's claim that the blues embodies "social relations and contradictions of black displacement" is also, not coincidentally, an apt description of the work of the railroad in Black life.[24] The blues transforms experience into narrative and history, while the train transforms experience into space. Both train and blues transform Black experience into something mobile that does not have to move through spaces that deny them their humanity.

7

Speculative Trains

Colson Whitehead's The Underground Railroad

"Most people think it's a figure of speech," he said. "The underground. I always knew better. The secret beneath us, the entire time. We'll uncover them all after tonight. Every line, every one."
—Arnold Ridgeway, from *The Underground Railroad* by Colson Whitehead

The Underground Railroad in Colson Whitehead's novel is real. It is not a metaphor for the "organized arrangements made in various sections of the country to aid fugitives from slavery" but an actual system of trains hurtling underground on a network of rails complete with unreliable timetables and uncertain routes that change at a moment's notice.[1] The first time the novel's protagonist, Cora, a runaway slave, sees the underground station and the tunnel, she is dizzy with awe. The walls soar twenty feet high and are "lined with dark and light colored stones in an alternating pattern." The care and craftsmanship that went into the construction of the station is evident in thoughtful details, like the smoothness and evenness of the steps that lead down from the surface to the underground station or the wooden bench that is arranged on the platform for weary passengers. In response to Cora's wondering question "Who built it?" the station agent, a white man named Lumbly, responds rhetorically, "Who do you think?" Hidden though it may be, the Underground Railroad is more than a network of wooden ties laid out in roughly shaped tunnels. As Royal, a conductor on the railroad, tells Cora near the end of the novel, "The underground railroad is bigger than its operators—it's all of you [passengers], too. The small spurs, the big trunk lines. We have the newest locomotives and the obsolete engines, and we have handcars like that one. It goes everywhere, to places we know and those we don't."[2] This characterization of the railroad as a space that is nowhere and everywhere, modern and obsolete, known and unknowable reflects the complexities of spatializing Black bodies and experiences in US imperial and racial geographies. The railroad materialized represents a critique of racial inequality and terror while at the same time a "demonstration of real and possible geographic alternatives."[3]

As impressive as the stand-alone rail network and tunnels are, they are nevertheless formed and shaped by the whims and cruelties of white supremacy. While the train is traditionally imagined as the straight line grounding the nation into its land and the surest path toward reaching its Manifest Destiny (a phrase that recurs throughout the novel), *The Underground Railroad* represents it otherwise. As Lumbly tells Cora and her travel companion Caesar, the trains depart at irregular intervals, and all he often knows about their destination is that they are heading "away from here."[4] Lumbly goes on to explain:

> "You understand the difficulties in communicating all the changes in the routes. Locals, expresses, what stations closed down, where they're extending the heading. The problem is that one destination may be more to your liking than the other. Stations are discovered, lines discontinued. You won't know what waits above until you pull in."[5]

Lumbly's characterization of the railroad as being a shot in the dark turns out to be terrifyingly accurate. Instead of taking Cora along an expected northerly and orderly route out of Georgia, the train halts, starts again, and meanders; as Cora realizes early on her journey, "the heading of the underground railroad was laid in the direction of the bizarre."[6] She never knows in which direction she is going, how long it will take to get there, or even if the station will be open once she arrives. Sometimes the train she rides is filled with small luxuries— upholstered seats, red velvet trim, room for dozens—and sometimes she finds herself lying flat on a wooden platform, clinging to floorboards as the locomotive roars ahead of her. So even as the novel suggests that the Underground Railroad may represent alternative geographies, it also reminds us that this alternative comes with a high potential cost for the slaves who decide to get on board.

It is because of the railroad that Cora is able to do something that very few slaves ever had the chance to do: travel around the country. Cora belongs to the Randall family, who own a huge cotton plantation in Georgia. Her mother, Mabel, escaped while Cora was a young girl; that fact combined with her defiant and antisocial personality have made her an outcast in slave society. Cora decides to flee with a fellow slave, Caesar, when the plantation changes hands and she realizes she and the rest of the slaves are about to become the property of Terrance Randall, whose sadism and violence stand out even among the slave-owning class. On their initial flight off the plantation, accompanied unexpectedly by Cora's only friend Lovey, the group is surprised by a group of white patrollers. In the struggle that ensues, Cora kills a young man in self-defense, and Lovey is captured (the reader later learns that she was tortured and murdered by Randall). Realizing that their resistance has marked them for certain death if they are captured, Cora and Caesar manage to find the first Underground Railroad and take a train to South Carolina, where they live in relative comfort for a few months. The sense of peace is short-lived. Ridgeway, a monomaniacal slavecatcher who is obsessed with Cora because Mabel is the only runaway slave whom Ridgeway never managed to capture, arrives, and Cora barely escapes his clutches. Caesar is not as lucky and is lynched by a white mob. Taking the next available train on the Underground Railroad, Cora finds herself in North Carolina, where she is sheltered for several months in the attic of Martin, a former station agent, and Ethel, his religious but deeply resentful wife. Cora is betrayed by Martin's Irish servant; Ridgeway arrives to take Cora away, while Martin and Ethel are executed by the townspeople. On their way back to Georgia, Ridgeway detours through Tennessee, where their party is attacked by freedmen who are agents for the Underground Railroad. The men free Cora and take her on the railroad to Indiana, where she is welcomed by the Valentines, a Black family who have established a communal farm of freedmen, freedwomen, and fugitive slaves. For the first time in her life, Cora thrives and feels at home. She begins to make friends, starts attending school, and falls in love with Royal, one of her rescuers. Her idyll is cruelly ended when a mob of white residents from the nearby town, angered by the prosperity of the farm, descend one night, setting fire to the buildings and shooting the residents who try to escape the flames.

Ridgeway, who has been tracking Cora even after her escape in Tennessee, manages to capture her again with the help of Homer, a ten-year-old former slave who acts as his valet and secretary. Ridgeway forces Cora to take him to the nearby disused Underground Railroad station so that he can confirm its existence. Determined not to betray the secret of the railroad, Cora tackles Ridgeway as they descend the staircase; weakened by the earlier fights, Ridgeway is mortally wounded by his fall. Cora escapes on the tracks by using a handcar. Days later, she emerges from the tunnel and is picked up in Missouri by wagon train. The kindly Black driver of one of the wagons tells her that the group is heading west. The novel ends with this scene of Cora "lighting out for the Territory."

As this plot summary makes clear, unlike the popular conception of the Underground Railroad, the railroad in Whitehead's novel never delivers Cora to safety. As she moves from state to state, Cora learns this hard lesson again and again: there is no destination north, south, or west where a Black person—slave or free—can be safe. This notion that the railroad cannot "free" anyone runs counter the usual nationalist and settler colonial claims about the train's purpose. As I have noted already, the railroad is typically depicted "as celebrating progress [and] America's Edenic landscape."[7] National narratives about the railroad have invested the train with a multitude of meanings that go far beyond its explicit utility as a vehicle for carrying goods and people. Ian Marshall offers a brief history of American literature's representation of the railroad that details the extent to which layers of meaning are superimposed onto the material object of the train itself. As the railroad established its presence in the nation in the 1830s, during the period of American romanticism, it is depicted as "despoilers of the vast landscapes, fresh from the hand of God, that provided America's sense of national identity and sanctity."[8] During the era of Manifest Destiny, the railroad becomes an extension of "the national domain" and serves the purpose of "preserving national unity."[9] During the Civil War, when the railroad was so vital to the movement of supplies and people, American literary discourse tends to characterize the railroad as the "preserver of the nation." As the country became increasingly industrialized and urban, writers transitioned again into depicting the railroad as a sign of disenfranchisement and alienation, the "octopus" of Frank Norris's imagination. With the passing of the railroad age in the mid-twentieth century, the train transformed yet

SPECULATIVE TRAINS | 179

again into a symbol of the past, an object of intensive "nostalgia rather than forward looking optimism."[10] What Marshall is describing in broad strokes is a history of the railroad's figuration, a history that did not stop once the age of railroad travel ended. Whether the train is a newcomer onto the American scene in the early 1800s, a part of everyday life in the early twentieth century, or a reminder of romanticized past, American literature has been less interested in it as a material object and more concerned with wrapping or unwrapping layers of meaning around it.

The Underground Railroad undoes much of our thinking about the railroad's meaning, precisely because it transforms the Underground Railroad from a metaphor for "illegal" Black movement into a built space that can hold and offer shelter to slaves. Most important, it imagines this newly concretized space as an explicitly Black space. In materializing the Underground Railroad—in insisting that the railroad has been designed, built, touched, and ridden by slaves—the novel reverses the signification process that Marshall describes, divesting the railroad of its nationalist links. The novel's characterization of the railroad as a Black space also diverges from early twentieth century African American textual narratives of Jim Crow, which tend to imagine the train as a white space that is generally hostile to African American riders and that must be approached strategically. Consider, for example, the threats of sexual violence that James's mother must endure on the family's train ride through Oklahoma in Ellison's "Boy on a Train," which I wrote about in chapter 5, with Cora's sense of awe and wonder boarding the Underground Railroad for the first time in Georgia. No matter how rickety, damp, or decrepit the space of the railroad is, Cora and the other characters always treat it as a space that is outside of the practices and institutions of racialized violence. It is the one space she occupies where she does not have to worry about being raped. By making the railroad a concrete space, the novel *The Underground Railroad* makes it an indisputably Black space, one that is largely outside of the control of white owners and the state. That space may by subterranean and buried, as in the case of the Underground Railroad, but its invisibility to white eyes does not make it any less real.

If the focus in chapter 6 was on how African American writers construct identities to move through spaces that are fundamentally hostile to their presence, then this chapter shifts the conversation to imagine alternative spatialities that are no less historical. This chapter argues that *The Underground Railroad* uses the train to conceive of Black spatiality differently through alternative imaginaries. By literalizing the Underground Railroad, Whitehead conceives of and claims a different kind of Black mobility and spatiality, what Katherine McKittrick calls "deep space," or how the "invisible, the unspoken, the unremembered, the impossible . . . spatially evidence blackness."[11] One of the ways that the novel reconceives deep space is through a trope of depth. Jim Crow's organization of space works along a horizontal axis, one in which Black Americans are required to move to the back of a bus or eat lunch at a separate counter. They must enter or exit buildings from back doors or sleep in hotels on the other side of town. *The Underground Railroad*, on the other hand, is part of a tradition within Black Atlantic culture that conceives of Black spatiality along a vertical axis. Of course, this vertical reimagining of space is constrained and contingent, and yet it is a trope that has been a part of Black Atlantic culture since the slave trade and the proliferation of folk tales about "flying Africans" who ascend into the sky to return home to Africa.[12] We see this imagining of Black space as vertical space in the story of Harriet Jacobs, who climbed into the crawlspace tucked under the roof of her grandmother's house and lived thus for seven years in order to escape the cruelties of her owner. We see it in Amiri Baraka's powerful assertion that "at the / bottom of the Atlantic Ocean. There's a railroad made of human bones. Black Ivory Black Ivory."[13] *The Underground Railroad* highlights the importance of these spaces to African American communities. And while the train is the novel's most spectacular and visible manifestation of Black determination for a different type of space, it is not the only example in the novel. The desire for Black spatiality explains why Cora protects so tenaciously the plot of land in the slave quarters—"all three square yards of it"—that she inherits from her mother Mabel and grandmother Ajarry, what Mabel calls "the most valuable land in all of Georgia."[14] Just as the Jim Crow train structures lived Black experience in the late nineteenth and early twentieth centuries, so too does Underground Railroad structure the notion of spatiality in the African American psyche.

In the pages that follow, I provide a brief overview of the historiography of the Underground Railroad, critiquing the romanticized way that it has been written about and conceived in American culture. Whitehead writes against the nation's persistent embrace of a certain version of the Underground Railroad that tends to emphasize white heroism in the face of Black victimhood. The rest of this chapter will be devoted to considering the various types of spaces that the novel reclaims for its characters in hypostasizing the Underground Railroad into an actual railroad. The book's use of the train clarifies the ways in which African Americans are despatialized and the strategies used by the slaves in the novel to make their own space.

The Underground Railroad Derailed

The Underground Railroad is one of the best-known narratives associated with antebellum history. As Kathryn Schulz writes in her revisionist history of the Underground Railroad, "Seldom has our national lexicon acquired a phrase so appealing to the imagination, or so open to misinterpretation."[15] While there is no doubt of the historical existence of a network of individuals and aid societies who provided material assistance to runaway slaves (about which I will have more to say in a moment), and while the phrase itself dates back to the late 1830s, what we might call the "myth" of the Underground Railroad took hold in the decades following the end of the Civil War.[16] In the postbellum telling, the Underground Railroad was an organized and extensive network of mostly white men who aided slaves in a variety of ways as they fled the South. So powerful was this idea of white heroism that by the time Wilbur Siebert wrote the most widely read study of the Underground Railroad a few decades after the end of Reconstruction, it was firmly implanted and ready to flower. According to the *New York Times*, Siebert's study *The Underground Railroad from Slavery to Freedom*, which was published in 1898, listed 3200 "agents"—almost all white men—who had constructed and worked within an "elaborate network of fixed routes, illustrated with maps that looked much like those of an ordinary railroad."[17] Former abolitionists told Siebert of literal underground tunnels in Illinois, complete with agents, conductors, and men laying down track from Quincy to Chicago. In this version of history, the Underground Railroad was, according to Larry Gara, a "humanitarian institution created to undermine slavery" that "dealt a deadly blow to the evil system."[18] This perspective continues to carry power and can be seen in Fergus Bordewich's 2007 op-ed published in the *New York Times*, which argued that the importance of the railroad "lies in the diverse history of the men and women, black and white, who made it work and in the far-reaching political and moral consequences of what they did."[19] Bordewich calls it

> the nation's first great movement of mass civil disobedience after the American Revolution, engaging thousands of citizens in the active subversion of federal law, as well as the first mass movement that asserted the principle of personal responsibility for others' human rights. It was also the nation's first interracial political movement, which from its beginning in the 1790s joined free blacks, abolitionist whites and sometimes slaves in a collaboration that shattered racial taboos.[20]

The appeal of this narrative for the nation is not difficult to understand for it is one that emphasizes interracial collaboration between slaves, freedmen, and white abolitionists, all of whom were risking punishment by helping runaways, absolving white Americans of their complicity with or passivity in the face of slavery. The Underground Railroad celebrates a form of interracial cooperation that is not part of the character of antebellum South. It is also one of the few moments in the history of slavery and this nation in which "white Americans can plausibly appear as heroes."[21]

This myth of the Underground Railroad was effectively put to rest from a scholarly perspective by historian Larry Gara, who essentially argued in a series of publications that while the Underground Railroad "had a basis in fact," it was nevertheless a "tradition" that had been "exaggerate[d] and oversimplifie[d]."[22] Gara argued that most slaves escaped on their own initiative with no outside help from white northerners or abolitionists. The limited reach of the Underground Railroad was in plain sight to anyone who cared to look. As Gara notes, participants in the Underground Railroad often advertised and publicized their activities in newspapers, a fact that seems to be borne out by Frederick Douglass's complaint in his *Autobiography* about the propensity of white abolitionists to trumpet their work on the Underground Railroad. Douglass famous and sardonically noted that it might be more accurate to rename the Underground Railroad the *upperground* railroad given the lack of secrecy surrounding a project that held slave lives in the balance. Douglass's complaint about the lack of discretion regarding the activities of the Underground Railroad also raises the issue of how effective this "secret" system of freeing slaves could be when its participants were advertising their work on it. Gara's point is not to dispute that there were brave men and women working actively to free slaves in the South, nor is it to claim that these individuals did not organize themselves in clever and secret ways to evade capture and arrest. Rather, it is to highlight the extent to which a decentralized and ad hoc system for aiding fleeing slaves has been reimagined into a symbol of white paternalism, only important insofar as white men were in its position of leadership and financial support. In a stinging rebuke to the popularity of this narrative, Kathryn Schulz has dismissed the sop of "moral comfort" that this narrative offers to the nation, reminding readers that

> most white Americans, North and South, either actively fought to maintain the institution of slavery or passively sustained and benefitted from it. Only a small fraction had the moral clarity to recognize its evils without caveat or compromise, and, before the war broke out, very few did anything to directly challenge it. Fewer still took the kind of action that later made agents of the underground railroad such widely admired figures.[23]

Schulz quotes Foner in estimating that the number of white Americans assisting slaves on the Underground Railroad numbered in the hundreds and not the thousands as Siebert claimed. From the work of these few hundred radical allies sprang a narrative of white rectitude in the face of racism that is so widespread and appealing that, as one scholar of abolition put it, "everybody in Ohio who has a potato cellar thinks it was an underground railroad site."[24]

The emphasis on white masculine control of the Underground Railroad has come at the cost of elaborating on the role of African American communities in providing practical support to escaping slaves. Starting with Gara's work, there has been an increasing recognition that African American community leaders and organizations were instrumental in providing practical and financial assistance to those who were fleeing, usually in urban centers like New York City and Philadelphia. While white men may have supported and/or financed the Underground Railroad, it seems clear now that it was community leaders like William Still and organizations like the newly founded African Methodist Episcopalian (AME) church that provided the backbone of the Underground Railroad. For example, Eric Foner notes that while the leadership of the New York Vigilance Committee was multiracial (consisting of David Ruggles, William Johnston, George R. Barker, James W. Higgins, Robert Brown, Theodore S. Wright, Samuel Cornish, and Charles Ray), the membership was overwhelming Black. What's more, Foner notes that Black women were often in charge of fundraising for the New York Vigilance Committee, launching and sustaining "one penny a week" campaigns to support the work of the committee.[25] Wilbur Siebert's *The Underground Railroad from Slavery to Freedom*, published in 1898, is often cited as the first study of the Underground Railroad, when in fact Still's *The Underground Railroad Records* was published in 1872 and chronicled the escape of 649 slaves (including George and Ellen Craft). Still's book is "unique [in the history of the Underground Railroad] in that it emphasized the courage and ingenuity of the fugitives" themselves, rather than the heroism of the agents.[26] The book was based on the meticulous records that Still kept while he was active on the railroad. Still's records left him open to prosecution, but he nevertheless maintained them "for possible use in helping to reunite relatives and slaves."[27] Despite the existence of Still's narrative and the stories of escapees like Douglass, Jacobs, the Crafts, and others—all of whom relied primarily on Black networks and their own ingenuity in order to escape the South—the Underground Railroad narrative that has had the most lasting impact on the American imagination is one that emphasizes white "moral clarity" in the face of slavery's evils.

The neo-slave narrative, into which *The Underground Railroad* can be categorized, is an ideal genre for pushing back against this narrative, precisely because of its ability to centralize the "history and the memory of slavery to our individual, racial, gender, cultural, and national identities."[28] But it is the connection between the neo-slave narrative and what Madhu Dubey has called "antirealist fiction" (which Dubey defines broadly as including science fiction, fantasy, ghost stories, and magic realism) that is particularly of note here.[29] According to Dubey, the emergence of the "speculative slave narrative" at the end of the twentieth century marks a refusal "to comprehend slavery as an occurrence that has passed into the register of history."[30] The popularity of speculative slave narratives expresses a "sharp sense of incredulity toward [a] historical narrative [that trumpets] racial emancipation" or insists that we have entered into a postracial era.[31] Most importantly for my purposes, Dubey's definition of the speculative neo-slave narrative emphasizes alternate spaces and temporalities that asks the reader "to consider history, especially histories of marginalized as partial, flawed, and filtered."[32] Metaphor is "essential to [the] counter- (rather than anti-) historical task" of the neo-slave narrative because it enables a "disrupt[ion] [of] temporality and narrativity" and a "reject[ion] [of] traditional notions of what constitutes the real."[33]

The Underground Railroad offers an interesting twist on Dubey's definition of the neo-slave narrative's reliance on metaphor in that Whitehead reverses the signification process embedded in the metaphor of the Underground Railroad. To put it another way, the novel materializes the metaphor that has become sedimented with white romanticism. By materializing the Underground Railroad, Whitehead undoes the despatialization that African Americans often have to endure. What makes this book antirealist is that it imagines Black space to which white supremacy has limited access. In other words, the novel's categorization as a speculative fiction is based on its construction of a Black spatiality that operates ever so slightly out of the frame of white supremacy, which is itself a devastating critique of any claim that the US has achieved some kind of postraciality in its public spaces. If speculative fiction is, as Aimee Bahng suggests, "a genre of inventing other possibilities (alternate realities, upside-down hierarchies, and supernatural inventions)," then *The Underground Railroad* highlights the fact that for African Americans, the seemingly every day and ordinary acts of building and claiming their own space outside of white society belongs in the realm of "supernatural invention."

The Underground Nation

As I noted at the start of chapter 5, John Edgar Wideman's ride on Amtrak collapses the linearity and progress that usually marks historical narrative. Although that work is firmly grounded in a realist perspective, Wideman's compression of historical events and timelines into a train ride means that his narrative bears some of the marks of the speculative. In the same way that Wideman's train ride bends history to question the "pastness" of racial bigotry and hatred, *The Underground Railroad* makes use of a wide array of temporal disjunctions to highlight how racism is always constructed as "past" to hide the fact that it permeates the present and future. The materialization of the train is, of course, the most spectacular and visible aspect of the novel's project to critique the spatiality of the nation vis-à-vis its Black residents, but others also exist. Although the novel is ostensibly set in 1850—the year of the passage of the Fugitive Slave Act—it includes descriptions of elevators, skyscrapers, and assembly lines. It depicts the forced sterilization of Black women and the injection of syphilis into Black men, a direct reference to the Tuskegee syphilis experiments of a century later. The novel evokes images of the Ku Klux Klan (in Indiana) and of the Nazi genocide of the Jews (in North Carolina). Yogita Goyal astutely notes that the novel portrays "1850 as the endless present of America," a rejoinder to any kind of contemporary notion that the nation has done with the afterlives of slavery.[34] Goyal argues that the novel's "logic of time" is "endlessly flexible and endlessly manipulated" in contrast to the more straightforwardly "linear" conception of time, which is characterized by Cora's single-minded focus on running and Ridgeway's equally single-minded focus on catching her.[35] These two times finally join at the moment that Ridgeway apprehends Cora for the last time in Indiana. This manipulation of timelines and historical events is not ahistorical or anti-historical but rather counter-historical, to borrow Schalk's term. In other words, *The Underground Railroad* bends the arc of racist history, but it is important to note that it is "rearrang[ing] history, [not] invent[ing] or exaggerat[ing]" it.[36]

Goyal's argument that "1850 [is] the endless present" of our nation is grounded in historical specificity as well as a long trajectory of anti-Black racism. The novel's conception of the nation's space is no less complex, indexing the diversity of local forms that US racism can take while simultaneously painting a national narrative of anti-Blackness. Lumbly, the first station agent that Cora encounters, acts like a choric figure, parceling out advice to the heroine as she embarks on her journey. When Lumbly tells Cora and Caesar that "if you want to see what this nation is all about [. . .] you have to ride the rails," he sounds like an advertisement for the railroad industry. Such rhetoric is used to

highlight the distinctive qualities attached to a particular tourist destination; Lumbly's appropriation of this rhetoric suggests that what distinguishes the nation is not its cities or resorts or natural wonders but
the forms of anti-Black racism that it practices. His spin on a familiar
travel theme also emphasizes Cora and Caesar's ability to assess and
evaluate these spaces, suggesting that they occupy a position that enables them to better "see what this nation is all about." His message to
the departing slaves suggests that they can learn something about the
nation that they don't already know; it holds out the hope that there is
some kind of intrinsic value to what they will be studying or in the task
he sets of trying to understand the nation.

Cora quickly learns that Lumbly's words are not prophetic or pedagogical but simply wrong. He exhorts Caesar and Cora to "look outside as you speed through and you'll find the true face of America,"
only when Cora heeds his advice, all she sees is "darkness, mile after
mile."[37] Later, when she rides the railroad for the final time from Tennessee to Indiana, she realizes Lumbly's words were "a joke . . . from
the start. There was only darkness outside the windows on her journeys
and only ever would be darkness."[38] For Cora and Caesar, the "true face
of America" is utter darkness, one that completely opposes the popular
conception of the United States as the city on the hill or as the home of
"a thousand points of light." The only accurate words that Lumbly utters
has to do with each state in the union representing "a state of possibility,
with its own customs and way of doing things. Moving through them
you'll see the breadth of the country before you reach your final stop."[39]
Only rather than seeing local features based on unique geographical features, important cultural institutions, or historical landmarks, Cora and
Caesar, and then Cora alone, experience each state as a different state of
racial terror.

The diversity of the nation lies in the varieties of racial regimes it
contains. Georgia, where Cora is born and from whence she flees, is
defined by the "ornate" and sadistic imagination of her owner Terrance
Randall.[40] South Carolina represents a "new system" of "negro uplift"
that seems to focus on vocational education but actually enacts medical
experiments on Black men and women in the name of "science" and
"progress." As Caesar's murder at the hands of angry mob lays bare,
this more liberal approach toward the management of African Ameri-

can lives, espoused by the "decent people of South Carolina with their schools and Sunday credit," masks a never-ending demand for Black death and suffering.[41] Racial terror has reached its purest form in North Carolina, where Cora hides for months in an attic, a space that is meant to evoke Harriet Jacobs's sojourn. North Carolina has made racial terror the centerpiece of its politics and social life, proclaiming that it has "abolished slavery" when what it has really done is "abolish niggers."[42] Race laws in the state "forbid colored men and women from setting foot on North Carolina soil."[43] Night riders and patrollers are let loose at night to ensure that the state remains a whites-only space. In an interview with NPR's Terry Gross, Whitehead calls the North Carolina of his novel a "white separatist, supremacist state, much in the way that towns in Oregon, when they were being settled, were settled on a white separatist, supremacist ideal."[44] Tennessee, on the other hand, is a "ruin" and "cursed."[45] Hundreds of miles of the state have been scorched by a massive fire started by a hapless homesteader trying to clear farmland, all while a yellow-fever epidemic rages unchecked through the state. Cora, chained to the back of Ridgeway's wagon as they move through the state, sees human remains in every burned-out town that they travel through. Tennessee is perhaps the purest form of the misery that chattel slavery has brought down not only on African Americans but on the entire nation: "If Tennessee had a temperament, it took after the dark personality of the world."[46]

Each of these states represent a different spatialization of white supremacy, but as I noted earlier, they each also contain very circumscribed possibilities of Black spatiality. Cora's small plot of earth in the slave quarters—which she calls the "field"—has been passed down from her grandmother to her mother and then to her; despite her anger toward her mother for abandoning her, the field inspires in Cora a fierce devotion.[47] Although as a slave, she cannot "own" anything" (not even herself), she considers this parcel her own. When Mabel runs away, the first thing that the devastated Cora sees is the "brown-red of the soil in her family's plot. It reawakened her to people and things, and she decided to hold on to her stake."[48] The novel notes that while "white men squabbled before judges over claims to this or that tract," the slaves "fought with equal fervor over their tiny parcels at their feet."[49] This intensive desire on the slaves' part to stake out a small piece of land tips into violence because of the nature of slavery itself. The uses to which the slaves wish to put the land—a space for a chicken coop, a resting spot for a dog, a patch to raise vegetables—are benign and even productive; the fact that they do not have the space to engage even in these basic domestic activities that do not in and of themselves require a great deal of room speaks to the impossibility of Black spaces on the plantation and beyond.

Cora's decision to abandon the field and flee the plantation is precipitated by Caesar, whom Cora describes as "like no colored man she had ever met."[50] Cora's devotion to the field has its parallel in Caesar's memories of his small family farm in Virginia. Caesar grew up in Virginia with his parents, all of whom were owned by a genteel and elderly white woman who taught Caesar how to read and who treated them relatively liberally. Prior to the widow's death and the sale of his family down south, Caesar had lived in his own cottage, painted "white with robin's egg trim," with a plot of land that he and his parents cultivated.[51] What sets Caesar apart, then, according to the novel is not so much his literacy, kindness, or bravery; it is the fact that he, like Cora, knows what it mean to hold—not own—a space of his own. The power or freedom that this space accorded him was illusory as it was lost the minute the widow passed away; nevertheless, it defines him as a person on the Randall plantation. As both of these examples make clear, spaces that are situated within white property networks are inherently illusory. Whether three yards square or a small vegetable garden or a few hundred acres (the size of the Valentine homestead in Indiana), any space that African Americans can lay claim to is always subject to white seizure and violence.

The Up-Top and the Down-Beneath

The Underground Railroad that Cora encounters and that slaves and freedmen have built is, in the words of Katherine McKittrick, "a key historical example of the complexities black geographies illuminate."[52] Unlike the states through which Cora travels, the Underground Railroad represents another space of possibility, one that does not fall under the jurisdiction of any state, although its existence is necessitated by the state. As I noted, Cora's first glimpse of the railroad is filled with wonder, but it also evokes in her a vision of the love and pride that Black labor can engender when it is not under the direct lash of white supremacy. As a result of her years of physical and sexual abuse, Cora finds the proximity of other bodies—whether white or Black—to fill her with dread, and yet the novel describes the tunnel as "pulling" at Cora both physically and mentally. She does not interpret her physical response to the tunnel as invasive or repellant but simply something she wants to learn more about. Nothing in her young life has prepared her for the sight of the railroad, the result of so much labor, sacrifice, and coordination. In her struggle to come up with a way of understanding the sacrifice and coordination of the Underground Railroad, the only comparison she can make is to the experience of slaves picking cotton, "the African bodies working as one, as fast as their strength permitted. The vast fields burst with hundreds of thousands of white bolls, strung like stars in the sky on the clearest of clear nights. When the slaves finished, they had stripped the fields of their color."[53] Cora acknowledges that cotton picking "was a magnificent operation, from seed to bale," but it elicits no feelings of pride or community from the workers themselves. Instead, the immensity of their feat has been "stolen from them. Bled from them."[54] Unlike the cotton rows, the railroad is a "marvel to be proud of." In that airy station and through the dark tunnel, Cora feels the presence of those "desperate souls who found salvation in the coordination of its stations and timetables."[55]

The railroad inspires a similar sensation of community near the novel's end, as she is forced to lead Ridgeway to the "ghost tunnel" that is the entry point for the Underground Railroad near Valentine's farm. She realizes that she

> never got Royal to tell her about the men and women who made the underground railroad. The ones who excavated a million tons of rock and dirt, toiled in the belly of the earth for the deliverance of slaves like her. Who stood with all those other souls who took runaways in their homes, fed them, carried them north on their backs, died for them. The station masters and conductors and sympathizers. Who are you after you finish something this magnificent—in constructing it you have also journeyed through it, to the other side. On one end there was who you were before you went underground, and on the other end a new person steps out into

the light. The up-top world must be so ordinary compared to the miracle beneath, the miracle you made with your sweat and blood. The secret triumph you keep in your heart. (303)

This passage—with its images suggesting depth ("the belly," excavation, "the up-top," "underground," "the miracle beneath," and what lies "beneath")—emblematizes the book's exploration of the different types of spaces and mobilities that slaves have constructed or imagined for themselves. Cora's sense of space is defined by the railroad: the ordinariness of the "up-top world" in contrast to the tunnels that house the trains, the journey from one end of the tunnel to the other. The novel is clear, for example, that in order to find any Underground Railroad station, one first has to dig and then descend. The novel's emphasis on depth might seem counterintuitive given the conventions of the slave narrative, which is definitionally about a protagonist who moves *across* the country to achieve freedom. But the emphasis on depth reminds the reader of the criminality and suspicion attached to Black movement of any kind. This was certainly the case in the antebellum era, when the sight of a Black person walking, riding, or traveling on his or her own was enough to arouse intense suspicion on the part of white residents. It is still the case today, as Black men and women are murdered because their mundane movements (walking to local convenience store, jogging through a neighborhood, driving a car) are continuously viewed as deeply threatening and suspicious. *The Underground Railroad* is filled with examples of slaves who attempt to slip through white spatial regimes by moving across the land, expeditions that inevitably fail since there is no land in the novel that is not overrun by white supremacy. As the novel progresses, it becomes clear that the safest spaces for slaves are those that are below ground.

The notion that Black spatiality can be mapped only in the "down-beneath" is highlighted during Cora's disastrous sojourn in the attic of Martin and Ethel Wells' home in North Carolina. Whitehead's portrayal of the attic space in the house stands in contrast to the most famous attic in African American letters, that of Jacobs's grandmother in *Incidents in the Life*. The attic in *Incident*, while by no means a sanctuary, at least provides a respite from the relentless fear of sexual violence to which Jacobs's owner subjects her and enables Jacobs to see her children and family in a family home. Cora's residence in the Wells' attic provides all of the terror with none of the comfort that Jacob is afforded. The station that Martin used to man has been closed for months, ever since North Carolina decreed death for any Black person found to be in the state or any white person who aids them. On Cora's trip to the Wells' home, conducted under the cover of night, she catches a glimpse of "the Freedom Trail"—a country road lined with trees from which hang the mutilated corpses of Black people, all of whom have been ritually killed during the town's "Friday Festival."[56] Fear of and hatred toward Blacks has turned North Carolina into a totalitarian state, in which the patrollers have total impunity to search homes, wagons, and property. An accusation of abolitionist sympathies is enough to get a white person hanged. This charged atmosphere means that the attic is a highly contingent haven from the violence and murder that Cora witnesses. Rather than seeing family members from her attic perch, as Jacobs does, Cora is witness only to these Friday Festivals that inevitably involve the public torture and murder of Black people who made the mistake of trying to travel through North Carolina. As Cora's experiences suggest, the attic in *Underground Railroad* is an unalloyed hell, only staving off what seems like inevitable death for Cora, Martin, and Ethel.

Although the details of how and by whom the Underground Railroad was built are left hazy in the novel, the novel is highly specific in its depiction of Cora's experience riding the railroad. The detailed descriptions of Cora's body in motion on the railroad works against a convention within slave narrative that requires the authors to silence themselves regarding their means of escape. Her first trip on the railroad, in Caesar's company, is filled with disbelief and excitement. The soaring nature of the station itself is a contrast to the creaky boxcar that they find themselves riding in. Instead of chairs, there are bales of hay stacked in the boxcar to serve as seating. Dead mice, nails, and the charred remains of firewood litter the floor of the car. On Cora's second trip on the railroad, out of South Carolina, she is fleeing a mob that knows she is a runaway. Caesar does not make it to the station—Ridgeway later informs her that he was lynched on the way there—but as she waits in the underground darkness, she realizes that the station is being burned over her head. After several days, a maintenance train happens to stop by the station, and the fifteen-year-old African American engineer reluctantly agrees to pick her up. Because he was not expecting to board any passengers, there is no proper passenger car attached to the locomotive; instead, there is a flatcar with "wooden planks . . . riveted to the undercarriage without walls or ceiling. She stepped aboard and the train jolted with the boy's preparations."[57] Unprotected from the elements and afraid of being blown off the flatcar, Cora sits in the center with a rope "wrapped . . . around her waist three times."[58] The experience of riding the flatcar is a "blustery ordeal," one that prevents her from sleeping and even breathing easily.[59] Her final trip on the railroad serves as a marked contrast to her previous two; this time, on the way from Tennessee to Indiana, accompanied by Justin, Red, and Royal, she rides in a "proper passenger car—well-appointed and comfortable like the ones she'd read about in her almanacs." Cora rides in an interior straight out of a railroad advertisement, with "seats enough for thirty, lavish and soft, and brass fixtures gleamed where the candlelight fell. The smell of fresh varnish made her feel like the inaugural passenger of a magical maiden voyage." Having lived the previous several months in a cramped attic crawlspace in North Carolina, Cora is able to stretch out and sleep "across three seats, free from chains and attic gloom for the first time in months."[60] These passages remind us that riding the train is highly physical in Cora's experience; for her, it evokes the warmth of a fellow slave's body, the physical pain of clinging to the boards of a roaring platform, and the comfort of being able to lie down fully on a soft surface. The novel's persistent emphasis on how it feels for a Black woman to ride a train on the Underground Railroad centralizes the experience of the Black body both physically and psychologically.

In highlighting Cora's bodily sensations while fleeing on the train, the novel differentiates itself from most historical slave narratives, which largely could not provide these kinds of detailed accounts precisely because such information might be used by slave owners, patrollers, and catchers interested to recapture fleeing slaves. Despite the stricture against speech in such situations, slave narratives often highlighted (rather than minimized) the extent to which they could not reveal information. Douglass, in his *Narrative of the Life of Frederick Douglass*, devotes just a few lines to his escape from Maryland, stating that the "direction I travelled and by what mode of conveyance—I must leave unexplained."[61] Douglass is far more expansive in expressing his frustrations with those who make "open declarations" about how they help slaves. By publicly "avowing their participation" in the freeing of slaves, Douglass argues, these "good men and women do nothing towards enlightening the slave, whilst they do much towards enlightening the master. They stimulate him to greater watchfulness and enhance his power to capture his slave."[62] Sharing any information about escape routes or means only endangers the lives of those slaves who are still trying to flee. Douglass exhorts those working on the railroad to keep the "merciless slaveholder profoundly ignorant of the means of flight adopted by the slave." At the same time, he imagines the white slaveholder in pursuit of the runaway slave, "surrounded by myriads of invisible tormentors," "feel[ing] his way in the dark" and worrying that "at every step he takes, he is running the frightful risk of having his hot brains dashed out by an invisible agent."[63] Douglass's fantasy remarkably parallels Whitehead's description of Ridgeway's first and final descent in the Underground Railroad, during which Cora tackles him and causes his ultimately death. Douglass's call to silence and Cora's decision to kill Ridgeway to protect the secrecy of the railroad (even if it means sacrificing herself in the attempt) brings to mind what Katherine McKittrick calls the "secret knowledge and secret knowledge sharing" that is characteristic of Black geographies.[64] The power in this knowledge holds only if it remains undiscussed and unknowable in white slave-owning circles. For Douglass, that "secret knowledge" is deeply spatial. Rather than focusing on the fear of the slave who is running away, Douglass strategically shifts the narrative, portraying instead the slaveowner moving through this Black space, terrified at what awaits him. In shifting the focus from the runaway slave to the slave owner at this crucial moment, Douglass not only spatializes Black knowledge, he also despatializes the white slave owner.

Like Douglass, Cora understands intuitively that sharing the routes out of enslavement would be tantamount to "closing the slightest avenue to black freedom."[65] Soon after she arrives at the Valentine farm, Royal takes her to a never-used station, the one that she will be forced to return to with Ridgeway at the novel's end. Here he tells her, "We're not supposed to talk about what we down here . . . And our passengers aren't supposed to talk about how the railroad operates . . . *They could talk if they wanted to, but they don't*" (emphasis mine).[66] This distinction is important. Even among others who have endured the horrors of slavery and the terrors of escaping, the knowledge that is so hard earned is not spoken of lightly. The knowledge that other lives hang in the balance outweighs any other considerations. Even Cora and Royal, who find themselves falling in love and dreaming of building a life together, are careful about how much they share with each other about Cora's escape and Royal's work, precisely because they recognize that their presence in each other's lives is not the result of individual choices but due to the collective effort of thousands of unnamed Black hands. Cora chooses not to reveal the details of her escape because she considers it "private, a secret about yourself it never occurred to you to share. Not a bad secret, but an intimacy so much a part of who you were that it could not be made separate. It would die in the sharing."[67]

This evocative notion—that the story of Black movement and spaces "die[s] in the sharing"—explains Cora's determination to prevent at any cost Ridgeway from seeing the Underground Railroad. It equally explains Ridgeway's insistence on seeing it rather than taking Cora directly back to Georgia. For Ridgeway, "the tunnel [is] all the gold in the world."[68] Exposing the lines to his gaze, allowing him to see all its routes and roots, would mean betraying the lives of not only slaves who might ride the railroad in the future but the lives of those who had built it in the first place. Cora's decision to topple with Ridgeway is as much about the past as it is about the future; it is about those enslaved above and those who worked below. The novel strongly implies that Ridgeway does not survive his fall (although it is silent about the fate of Homer, who seems determined to stay with Ridgeway no matter what). But Cora does survive, and her final trip on the Underground Railroad is not on a train but on a handcar, motored, in other words, by the power of her own arms, gliding on the track built by those unknowns who came before her.

The novel's assertion that Black spatiality must be kept "private" lest it "die in the sharing" plays out in the escape of Cora's mother, Mabel. Throughout the novel, Mabel is presented as the exception to the rules of Black mobility in white spaces; she has fled the plantation and has never been heard from since. All assume that she has escaped successfully, and Cora and Ridgeway, opponents though they are, are united in their hatred of Mabel. Ridgeway hates her because her escape "nag[s] at him . . . buzzing in the stronghold of his mind," while Cora hates her because Mabel left her behind. The reader learns near the novel's end the truth that Cora never will, namely, that Mabel had run off one night in a fit of despair, had gotten fairly far out, but then turned back to the plantation because she could not bear to be separated from her daughter. It is on the return journey, while tramping through swampy water, that Mabel is bitten by a cottonmouth snake. As the poison pounds through her body, she "stumbl[es] onto a bed of soft moss" and decides "it felt right. She said, Here, and the swamp swallowed her up."[69] The fact that the one character who was presumed to have somehow escaped actually died within a few miles of the Randall plantation seems to shatter any notion that there is a space for Black freedom away from white tyranny. But there is more to Mabel's death than just cruel fate. First of all, it points to the extent to which any form of slave mobility—particularly, it would seem, female slave mobility—disrupts the foundations of white supremacy. Consider that the unaccounted-for movement of two slave women—Mabel and Cora—is enough to drive both their owner Randall and the slavecatcher Ridgeway full tilt into self-destructive obsession. Most importantly, the fact that Mabel's body sinks into the swamp after her death—that it essentially goes under—affirms the novel's broader point that Black spatiality must be imagined along a different plane. As tragic and as haunting as Mabel's death is, it is her body's submersion into the swamp that frees her from the physical and/or discursive control of her white master. In this regard, Mabel's ultimate fate—as outside of the knowledge of Black or white society—is precisely what the singer in the blues folk song "Freight Train" wishes for: to able to move without anyone else realizing that she is gone in the first place. By sinking into the wet earth, Mabel is finally free of the violence and surveillance to which Black bodies are constantly subjected.

The cost of this knowledge seems unbearably high. The novel's conclusion is murky on whether there are spatial possibilities for African Americans in this country—on the railroad or somewhere else. As Cora makes her way through a "tunnel that no one had made, that led nowhere," she knows that eventually she will have to emerge above ground.[70] The train and the tunnel do not offer endless possibilities in other words; at some point, she will reach the end of the line. It is unclear where Cora is when she reaches tunnel's end—she even imagines for a moment that she is no longer in the United States. That stray thought is not as outlandish as one might initially think given the novel's

highly evocative conclusion, which sees Cora sitting on the side of a rut-
ted trail—injured, dirty, and starving—and approached by three wagons
traveling together. What happens next is straight out of the New Testament: the first wagon is driven by a white man and his wife who regard
her "neutrally" as they pass on. The second wagon is driven by a "red-
headed fellow" who pauses and inquires if Cora needs "something," to
which she responds with a silent shake of her head. The third wagon is
driven by an older Black man with kind eyes, whose face seems familiar
to Cora. He invites Cora aboard by offering her food, and this time, she
accepts.

The novel's leap into the biblical parable of the Good Samaritan suggests that perhaps a different type of time-space has been entered, one
that offers the hope of safety for Cora and her new companion. The final
line suggests as much with Cora wondering "where [the driver] escaped
from, how bad it was, and how far he traveled before he put it behind
him." Cora's belief that the driver has successfully "put it behind him"
suggests a hope on her part that such a place of healing exists. In leaving
the question open, the novel suggests that the Underground Railroad
was not the destination or the solution for a differently realized Black
spatiality but rather the first step to that goal. By materializing the railroad and emphasizing its positioning *underground*, the novel enables an
exploration of the possibilities and impossibilities of African American
mobilities and spaces.

8

Fugitive Trains

I stare at the darkness, trying not to fall asleep. Fighting to
stay awake so I won't have bad dreams. But fighting sleep re-
minds me of being on the train.
Everything reminds me of La Bestia.
I wonder if I will ever truly escape it.
—Jenny Torres Sanchez, *We Are Not from Here*

"La Bestia" is one of the nicknames for the network of freight trains that
approximately four hundred thousand migrants—mostly from Guatemala, Honduras, and El Salvador—ride northward through Mexico
annually to reach the southern border of the United States. The two-
thousand-mile journey usually starts at the Suchiate River, which serves
as the border between Guatemala and the Mexican state of Chiapas and
from there branches into several possible routes. Riding the trains allows
the migrants to avoid the checkpoints that are set up by Mexican authorities along highways and roads, but the decision to board the freight
trains carries its own set of horrors. "Boarding" the train entails running
alongside moving stock and grabbing onto a rail as the cars accelerate
away from a station. "Riding" the train usually means sitting on top of
the freight cars on sloped roofs that have no handholds; if space on the
roof is not available, migrants may "ride the blind," wedging their bodies in the dangerous gap between cars. Those who are perched on the
roof of a freight car must avoid low-hanging tree branches and wires;
they must endure exposure to heat, dust, wind, and rain. Sharp turns
or unexpected bumps can have deadly consequences. Migrants must
remain awake and alert no matter how long they have traveled or how
exhausted they are; failure to do so could lead to injury or death.

On top of the danger of riding the train itself lies the threat posed by
both law enforcement and criminal gangs. The police and immigration
agents are tasked by the Mexican state and Ferromex, the private rail

Figure 8.1. La Bestia, May 4, 2014. Photograph by John Moore/Getty Images.

consortium that operates the trains, with keeping migrants off the rails by any means possible. Capture by these officials means imprisonment and almost certain deportation. Migrants also face the strong likelihood that they will be assaulted, robbed, kidnapped for ransom, or raped at some point during their journey. Sometimes the perpetrators are gang members; sometimes they are police and security officials. According to Joseph Sorrentino:

> Eighty percent of migrants will be assaulted or robbed. Sixty percent of migrant women will be raped. A lucrative side business for the drug gangs (especially the Zetas) is kidnapping migrants; they can get as much as $2,500 for each victim. Between April and September 2010, Mexico's National Human Rights Commission cited 214 mass kidnappings involving 11,333 people. And those are just the reported kidnappings.[1]

Médecins san Frontières—which runs mobile units along the most popular routes in southern and central Mexico as well as a clinic for migrants in the town of Ixtepec, a central hub in the Mexican rail network—estimates that 60 percent of the patients it treats in its clinics have been the victims of some form of violence, ranging from being threatened with a gun to sexual assault to attempted kidnapping. There is no question that these numbers are low given how many of these assaults go unreported or are perpetrated by law enforcement.[2] There are no numbers regarding the number of migrants who are injured or die while making the journey to the US. It is no wonder than the other nicknames for La Bestia are "el tren de los desconocidos" (the train of the unknowns) and "el tren del muerto" (the train of death).

In 2015, the Mexican government, under pressure from the Obama administration, undertook a series of draconian measures—ostensibly for the safety of the migrants—to deter their travel.[3] Despite these attempts to push migrants off the trains, La Bestia was back in the news in 2018 and 2019 with the organization of migrant caravans by human rights' and migrants' rights groups such as Pueblos Sin Fronteras.[4] Migrant caravans have existed for years, but these groups were notable because of their unusually large size: the April 2018 caravan consisted of up to 1,500 individuals, mostly Hondurans. This caravan attracted press attention in the United States partly because it drew the opportunistic rage of Donald Trump and his administration at a time when the Republican party was in the midst of a difficult midterm election cycle.[5] While much of the journey was undertaken on foot, at one point, migrants boarded freight trains to evade police and immigration checkpoints that had been set up on the roads. The human drama of thousands of Central Americans coordinating with each other to undertake an epic journey to the US border—riding part of the way on a train nicknamed "The Beast"—made it the target for alarmist rhetoric, even from those news organizations that by and large were sympathetic to their plight. A *Guardian* article that was published on June 5, 2019, is typical. "In the wind-swept wilds of southern Mexico," it begins ominously, "a Beast is stirring." An article published by the Associated Press also transforms the train into something uncanny and terrorizing, dramatically announcing that the "train known as 'The Beast' is once again rumbling through the night loaded with people headed toward the U.S. border after a raid on a migrant caravan threatened to end the practice of massive highway marches through Mexico."[6] The tendency to sensationalize the freight train network into "The Beast" has the effect of transforming the migrants who ride the rails into something less than human.

Even more noteworthy for the purposes of this chapter is that the coverage of La Bestia reinforces a narrative of migrant mobility that depicts it as uncontrolled and uncontrollable. In these and other articles, "The Beast" describes migrant mobility through the lens of US immigration enforcement; in these cases, the movements of "illegal" immigrants are characterized as rampaging and criminal, fixated on the goal of violently breaching and/or ramming through the borders that protect and stabilize the nation. "The Beast" conjures images of a relentless horde riding on some kind of monstrous hell-train heading straight for the United States. La Bestia, on the other hand, names the state-sanctioned violence perpetrated on racialized migrant bodies by the nation's officers and its proxies. It describes an experience of mobility from the migrants' perspectives, as bodies in space, in which all movement is constrained and policed at every turn. It is an experience of mobility premised on the assumption that the "wrong move" can lead to catastrophe: the slip of a hand leads to the loss of a limb, the nod of a drowsing head leads to a devastating fall, an inability to run fast enough or hide quickly enough at a certain moment leads to violence, arrest, or death at the hands of the police. In her 2020 young adult novel, *We Are Not from Here*, Jenny Torres Sanchez describes the experiences of three teenagers—Pequeña, Pulgo, and Chico—as they flee violence in Guatemala and ride La Bestia to the United States. Pequeña describes how the speed of the train and her own precarious position on top of it forces her to lock down her body. The disciplining of her own body into such a rigid stance causes her physical pain:

> My fingers ache from holding on, my body feels pricked with needles. My head is itchy and my eyes sting from the rushing wind, from dirt and dust. La Bestia shifts slightly, winding through the night, and it screeches and howls like some kind of banshee as Chico holds on to me tight. It straightens and lulls us again with its rocking back and forth, with the rhythmic sound of the tracks.[7]

The terror motivating Pequeña's bodily immobility is justified; later in the novel, an exhausted and ill Chico is killed after falling off the train when it decelerates suddenly. Pequeña's intensive awareness of her body's reaction toward its enforced immobility stands in contrast to La

Bestia's constantly shifting but rhythmically "rocking" movement. The migrant caravan and La Bestia highlight how migrant mobility, which is often portrayed as unchecked and lawless, is in fact constituted by highly punitive regulatory practices.

La Bestia stands in stark contrast to the usual narrative of the railroad in the United States, which as I noted in my introduction tends to depict the train as a vehicle of freedom, pleasure, and American ingenuity, all of which feed into narratives of American exceptionalism. This difference is no doubt due in part to La Bestia's location outside of the United States and its association with Mexico. But it also reminds us that despite the romantic history that the nation imposes on the railroad, the train has long been a part of the penal system in this country, used in the transport of prisoners and the deportation of foreigners who have fallen afoul of US law. As Ethan Blue points out, "Deportation trains [were] integral to a politico-technical assemblage that put steel into federal exclusionary immigration and allowed the deportation state to cohere: the train's economies of scale allowed a massive deportation apparatus . . . to flourish."[8] La Bestia brings to light this obscured aspect of the railroad—that trains are not just vehicles of freedom but also moving prisons. Thus, the migrants riding on La Bestia emblematize the carceral nature and history not only of the railroad and the railway car but of the United States itself. In the case of these migrants, the train, which has long been associated with freedom, independence, and American preeminence, is a symbol and space of their imprisonment. La Bestia and the caravan unravel the myth of American mobility, revealing the "uneven mobility" that characterizes the lives of the racialized labor.

This chapter focuses on how the train makes the interplay between mobility and carcerality more visible—particularly as it relates to Black and brown migrant bodies—in the music video "Immigrants (We Get the Job Done)" (2017) directed by Tomás Whitmore with music and lyrics by Lin-Manuel Miranda, K'naan, Snow Tha Product, Riz Ahmed, and Residente. "Immigrants (We Get the Job Done)" was the first track released from Miranda's album *Hamilton Mixtape* (2016), which was in turn based on Miranda's smash Broadway hit *Hamilton: An American Musical* (2015). Miranda is not featured in the music video; instead, emcees K'naan, Snow Tha Product, Riz Ahmed, and Residente star and perform in the video. Both *Hamilton* and "Immigrants (We Get the Job

Done)" offer full-throated defenses of immigrants and the work that they do; they also provide a powerful counternarrative to the racist anti-immigration rhetoric and policies of Donald Trump. But despite the seemingly straightforward creative connection between *Hamilton* and "Immigrants (We Get the Job Done)" (hereafter shortened to "Immigrants"), the two diverge significantly in their representation of the nation and the role of the migrant worker within the nation. Whitmore chooses to emphasize the plight of migrants by setting all the action of the video on a moving train. The train plays a crucial role in articulating the critique the song and video is launching against the US, that the country's failure to live up to the promise of inclusion and freedom for all is not an anomaly but fundamental to the working of the nation. As represented in the video, there is nothing liberal or liberatory about the train, and by extension, there is nothing liberal or liberatory about the United States.

"Immigrants," *Snowpiercer*, and dozens of other examples indicate the continuing popularity of the train as a setting for narrative film. The particular spatial characteristics of the train—its linear arrangement of contiguously placed cars, the interiors of which are narrow and cramped—offers a dramatic and compelling spatial structure for the exploration of difference and conflict. Its historical role in the enforced movement of racialized communities, "criminals," and migrant laborers only heightens the video's critique of the unjust racial structures that immigrants and migrants face in their attempts to survive. The train is thus uniquely constructed and situated to highlight the links between carcerality and mobility in the migrant experience. In "Immigrants," there is no life off the train or outside of its narrow confines; the train *is* the nation, and ultimately, it is the world. Within its cramped spaces, immigrants work, sleep, and are imprisoned. The train is the setting for laborers rising at dawn to search for work; it is the setting for families fleeing war in their home; it is the setting for refugee camps. We see migrants engaging in the kind of backbreaking labor that is often derided as "menial": picking fruit, sewing clothes, constructing buildings, washing dishes, caring for children. In a nod to the migrants who risk their lives riding La Bestia, migrants who are trying to get into the country or hide from its police force are shown sitting on the roof of the train car. All of the spaces in migrant life—their workplaces, their homes, their homelands, the camps, the border crossings—are on the train. In "Immigrants," all the world is not a stage, it is a train, and for those who are riding it, survival means staying onboard even if the conditions are unbearable and unsustainable.

"Immigrants" illustrates how the fundamental condition of the migrant is a carceral mobility, which is mobility that is controlled or disciplined without the need for physical imprisonment. By insisting that no life exists outside the train, "Immigrants" proposes that no world exists outside the carceral. Any notion that freedom can be found off the train is an illusion. The freedom that we experience as our inalienable right is instead purchased on the backs of racially minoritized bodies. In other words, the railway car in "Immigrants" does not just allow for the flourishing of the deportation state; it *is* the deportation state. Thus, "Immigrants" highlights the fact that carceral mobility is the fundamental condition of American (and global) life, impacting not just the migrants who are attempting to board but all those who already count themselves "passengers." Migrants who ride on the train are not the exceptions of an otherwise liberal democratic state, they are rather the very bodies who keep the train running in the first place.

Although carcerality and mobility are often conceived of as being oppositional to each other, "Immigrants" deconstructs that binary. As Kimberley Peters and Jennifer Turner argue, the divide that seems to exist between these two states and their relation to space are often illusory. Recognizing that carceral spaces are not necessarily fixed spaces enables us to think about carcerality in a much more expansive manner. The walls of the rolling train car "creat[es] an *appearance* of immobility within carceral estates vis-à-vis an appearance of hyper-mobility beyond them."⁹ Capitalism and the nation require the creation and maintenance of an illusion in which mobility and immobility are dichotomized; workers and citizens are "free" to move to improve their quality of life. The response to those New Orleans residents who could not flee Hurricane Katrina (mostly Black, mostly poor) is instructive. Their inability to get out of the storm's path—to move their bodies essentially—was the result not of systemic inequalities (poverty, lack of affordable or convenient transit options) but rather their own laziness—that is, their propensity not to move.¹⁰ Michael Brown, the director of the Federal Emergency Management Agency (FEMA), when asked about his tendency to blame the victims of the storm for not leaving prior to its arrival, blandly proclaimed, "Now is not the time to be blaming" before doing just that: "Now is the time to recognize that whether they chose to evacuate or chose not to evacuate, the government is required to help them."[11] In the same interview, he noted, "I don't make judgments about why people chose not to leave, but you know, there was a mandatory evacuation of New Orleans." Here, the insistence that residents had a choice to leave reinforces the notion that mobility and immobility are mutually exclusive states of being and that those who are immobile are somehow lazy, criminal, or stupid. "Immigrants" upends that easy dichotomy by insisting that mobility is built into the carceral just as the carceral is foundation to mobility.

Although this interplay between the carceral and mobile can be seen in the lyrics for "Immigrants" and in the embodied performances of the four rappers, the key to understanding the song's and video's critique of carceral mobility is the "mobile framing" that the video employs. Mobile framing as defined by film scholars David Bordwell and Kristin Thompson refers to the "ability of the frame to be mobile as camera movement."[12] The mobile framing that I will be focusing on in my readings of the films relates to how the camera frames the mobility of the passengers and the train itself: the camera's positioning as it moves within and through the cars, its relationship to the performers as they traverse (whether willing or unwillingly) the train, and exterior shots showing the train in motion.

Whitmore's movement of the camera in a series of patterns within and outside the train car highlights the sometimes obscured connection between mobility and carcerality. "Immigrants" relies upon a pattern of tracking shots that emphasizes the forward and backward penetrative movement of the camera. Whitmore makes use of what I call a disembodied perspectival follow shot, a variation of the more ubiquitous follow shot.[13] A follow shot is exactly what it sounds like: the camera follows a subject as he or she moves through the space of the train. This traditional shot "functions primarily to keep [the viewer's] attention fastened on the subject of the shot, and it subordinates itself to that subject's movements"; it also serves the purpose of making the subject's face inaccessible to the viewer who can only see the subject's back.[14] A disembodied perspectival shot, on the other hand, does not follow an individual subject; rather, in these shots, the camera seems to stand in the for the "eyes" of the viewer as it moves through the train. Whitmore makes particular use of this disembodied perspectival shot in the transitions between performers when the camera strikingly moves forward and backward *between* train cars through an area that is known as a gangway connection. This type of transition through the interstitial spaces that connect the train cars to each other allows the viewer to hear snatches of brakes grinding and glimpses of the tracks and wheels below. The use of these filmic techniques points to the fundamental inability of migrants to possess a mobility that is not constrained by the carceral, that the very notion of movement is predicated on the notion that some cannot move. By visually emphasizing the movement through the train, including its interstitial spaces (vestibules, doors separating cars) but not focusing on any one subject in the camera's inexorable march forward or backward, these shots attune us to the lack of agency of the subjects that are shown briefly on screen. The shot's setting on a narrow railway car emphasizes how the immigrants' movement is both constrained and forced. The aim here is to consider these shots as a model of witnessing and representing violence against racialized bodies.

Carceral Mobilities

In *The Practice of Everyday Life*, Michel de Certeau writes that the railway car is a "traveling incarceration" where the "unchanging traveler is pigeonholed, numbered, and regulated in the grid" that the space and protocols of the train enforces.[15] The railway car, in de Certeau's reckoning, is a place that depends on an "immobility of order," in which the "law of the 'proper' rules." As a "bubble of panoptic and classifying power," the railway car produces an order, a "closed and autonomous insularity"; passengers are "placed . . . like a piece of printer's type on a page arranged in military order" and experience an "organizational system" that induces a "quietude of a certain reason."[16] As Simone Gigliotti points out, de Certeau "adds a mobile dimension to philosopher Jeremy Bentham's classification of the panoptic tendencies of modern architecture."[17] De Certeau highlights how one can be imprisoned even if one is able to move freely, or, especially if one is able to move freely. De Certeau's notion that "administered captivity" defines every aspect

of modern life—even those moments that are coded as being uncon-
strained by everyday cares—presages the ubiquity of carceral controls
in our current moment.

De Certeau's notion of "traveling incarceration" as a circumstance
of a repressive state points to and predicts the US's increasing reliance
on incarceration and imprisonment in an era of global capital. Many
scholars have persuasively argued that the late twentieth century is the
age of mass incarceration, with Hispanic Americans, Native Americans,
and, in particular, African Americans bearing the brunt of these institutional and bodily "practices of punishment."[18] The nation imprisons
African Americans and Hispanics at rates that quintuple and double
those of whites, respectively; African Americans and Hispanics make
up approximately 40 percent and 19 percent of the domestic incarcer-
ated population even though they make up 13 percent and 16 percent of
the population, respectively.[19] Michelle Alexander has linked the explo-
sion of mass incarceration to the nation's "war on drugs" (undertaken in
the 1970s and 1980s by law enforcement at a time when drug use was in
decline) and argues that "mass incarceration is . . . the New Jim Crow"
and "the most damaging manifestation of the backlash against the Civil
Rights Movement."[20] Kelly Lytle Hernández has argued that although
the "Age of Mass Incarceration" is dated to the last 40 years, incarceration as a means of controlling political and social unrest has a long
history in multiracial cities like Los Angeles.[21] The Age of Mass Incarceration also names a period that witnessed the increasing criminalization of migrants traveling over the US southern border. The aggressive
arrest and prosecution of migrants attempting to enter the country has
led to the establishment of the "largest immigrant detention system of
earth" with "Mexicans and Central Americans comprising 97 percent of
all deportees and 92 percent of all immigrants imprisoned for unlawful reentry."[22] US immigration is the most "highly racialized police and
penal system" in the country. These statistics, while horrifying, suggest
that the imprisonment of migrants only begins once they are "caught"
by US law enforcement or border control when in reality, incarcerational
regimes begin well before migrants reach the United States.

At first glance, it would seem that de Certeau's passenger, who is riding within the walls of the railcar, sitting quietly in a seat while star-
ing vacantly out the window at the landscape, has nothing to do with

the migrants riding train cars like La Bestia. Indeed, the experiences of those riding La Bestia are about as far away from the deadening tranquility that de Certeau argues is characteristic of rail travel as one can get. But I would argue that the distinction between migrant and passenger is illusory and that the experiences of both reflect the often obscured intertwining of incarceration and mobility. As Peter Merriman notes:

> The average fare-paying railway passenger experiences freedoms, choices, and comforts that are far removed from the experiences of those whose mobilities are enforced or severely constrained, whether migrants trafficked in lorries, refugees crammed on to boats, or prisoners transported in trains. And yet, one can observe parallels between the ordinary and everyday incarcerations experienced by passengers in public transport systems and discourses surrounding the ordering and incarceration of dangerous, deviant, and vulnerable bodies. Discourses of security, safety, efficiency, order, and segregation pervade discussions of the movements of both willing and unwilling, and voluntary and forced passengers.[23]

Merriman's point is not to compare or equate the experiences of passengers to prisoners in chains or migrants risking life and limb to hop on freight cars. Rather, it is to emphasize that all bodies are subject to the disciplining forces of "security, safety, efficiency, order, and segregation" whether they are on the roof of a freight car or in the seat of a passenger car. The central argument that Merriman and other scholars of mobility and carcerality make is that subjects who are in physical motion—like migrants on La Bestia—can be subject to the same types of incarcerational regimes as those who are physically imprisoned. La Bestia makes clear that questions of carcerality and mobility are intricately woven together and that "incarceration is a practice and an experience that is neither spatially bounded, nor spatially fixed."[24] The nature and constitution of that mobility and incarceration varies sharply. For example, P. Pallister-Wilkins notes that the tendency to characterize migrant movement as part of a "flow" obscures the violence migrants face on their journeys from all quarter. Pallister-Wilkins highlights

> "the uneven politics of mobility that is shaped by and made visible through a consideration of what I call geoinfrastructuring, alongside the

embodied effects of this uneven mobility. Here, in contrast to modernity's quest for faster, more convenient, more efficient modes of travel to overcome the limits of the body as it encounters and moves through space, the migrant caravan's mode(s) of travel—walking, stopping, starting, bus hopping, sitting, waiting, sleeping—bring into sharp relief the ways that for those excluded from privileged mobility regimes, the body is in intimate concert with the material world it encounters.[25]

Despite an iconography that suggests that the United States is a land of unrestrained freedom and the train is a symbol of that exuberant spirit, La Bestia, the migrant caravan, and de Certeau make clear that the train's putative mobility does not prevent it from being a prison. In much the same way, the fact that migrants can move does not make them free.

"Immigrants (We Get the Job Done)"

The dream of America as a land of freedom and opportunity for all is at the heart of Miranda's award-winning musical *Hamilton*. Miranda released the single and debuted the video for "Immigrants" on June 28, 2017.[26] It was the first track from his highly anticipated *Hamilton Mixtape*, which was inspired by songs from his smash hit musical *Hamilton: An American Musical*. "Immigrants" was directly inspired by a line in "Yorktown (The World Turned Upside Down)," a song from *Hamilton* that begins with Hamilton (played by Miranda in the original Broadway production) and the Marquis de Lafayette (played by Daveed Diggs) meeting on the field before the battle of Yorktown. Lafayette congratulates Hamilton on his new position of command, and Hamilton answers, "How you say? No sweat. / Finally, on the field. We've had quite a run." In response to this understated praise of their respective achievements, Lafayette gives a slight shrug and nonchalantly drawls out the word "Immigrants . . ." before Lafayette and Hamilton declare in unison "we get the job done." Lafayette and Hamilton exchange a restrained high-five; the audience erupts in cheers.[27] Given what was happening politically at the time of the show's arrival on Broadway (it had its premiere at the Richard Rodgers Theater in August 2015), it is not difficult to understand the charged nature of this exchange and the audience's overwhelmingly positive response. Daveed Diggs's compelling and graceful performance as Lafayette and the cool manner in which he delivers that line no doubt contribute to the audience reaction, but it is the line's use of understatement to describe the accomplishments of these two impressive men—both coded as immigrants by the musical—that makes this moment so memorable. This single line in "Yorktown (The World Turned Upside Down)" also reflects an important underlying assumption of Miranda's and the musical's politics: that it is immigrant labor—their embodiment of the nation's bootstrap ideology—that makes them worthy of inclusion and America the symbol of unfettered opportunity.

Miranda has called the musical a "counterweight" to the "xenophobia and vilification of immigrants" that characterized the Trump campaign and the 2016 presidential election cycle. But Miranda's and the musical's resistance to xenophobia rests largely on what Philip Gentry has called a "liberal politics characterized most of all by aspirational optimism tinged with nationalist fervor."[28] Donatella Galella calls this positioning "nationalist neoliberal multicultural inclusion," in which the nation "supersede[s] all other markers of difference—race, gender, class, sexuality, ability status—in the name of unity."[29] Galella argues that it is no coincidence that *Hamilton*'s rise and debut coincided roughly with the years of the Obama presidency (2009–17), for Obama,

> Miranda, and the musical occupy a centrist position that mobilizes performers of color and the myth of meritocracy in order to extol and envision the United States as a multiracial utopia where everyone has a fair chance to compete for access to "The Room Where It Happens," as the title of Aaron Burr's show-stopping number has it.[30]

The aspirational and entrepreneurial optimism that Gentry and Galella ascribe to the musical suggests a bedrock of belief in the nation's potential exceptionalism. This is perhaps most evident in Miranda's frequent pronouncements that link the politics of 1781 with the politics of 2016. For example, he posted in 2017, "Have we achieved full freedom in society? Nope. We've a ways to go. It was true in 1781 and it's true now."[31] Miranda's statement suggests that not only is "full freedom" available to all, it also represents an achievable goal. In acknowledgment of the country's full tilt toward white supremacy in the 2016 election, Miranda must temper the progressive hope of that statement by acknowledging that "we" are no closer to achieving "full freedom" in 2017 than in 1781 when *Hamilton* is set. Exceptionalism requires progress but not on a timeline.

This key belief can be heard at times in the lyrics of "Immigrants." Despite Miranda's clear influence in the creation of the song and the fact that Miranda was positioned by the media as the song and video's creator, I argue that the move from "Yorktown (The World Turned Upside Down)" in *Hamilton* to "Immigrants" the song and video is not frictionless; in fact, both the lyrics and the visual narrative of "Immigrants" belie any kind of easy correlation between the song and its source material. I would argue that the song and the video present a much more complex picture of what it means to immigrate to the United States than Miranda's politics and depiction of immigration in *Hamilton* suggest.

That complexity can be seen in the striking lyrical bifurcation between the song's first half, which is performed by K'naan and Snow Tha Product, and its second half, which is performed by Riz Ahmed and Residente.[32] K'naan and Snow Tha Product present a more familiar defense of immigrant and migrant rights, focusing on the work that immigrants do in jobs that are unglamorous and poorly paid but highly necessary. Although the performers express outrage and disappointment at the treatment of migrants in the US, their rhetoric is nonetheless couched generally in the ideals and language of US liberalism and exceptionalism. Their disappointment and anger stem from the nation's failure to live up to its own ideals regarding inclusion and freedom. This idea is clearly expressed in the video's prologue when a commentator on a radio news program states in disbelief that "it's really astonishing that in a country founded by immigrants, 'immigrant' has somehow become a bad word."[33]

This is the theme that serves as the basis for K'naan's and Snow's raps. K'naan's rap begins by emphasizing the excessive amount of labor he performs ("I got one job, two job, three when I need them"), and the rest of his verses focus on the broken promise of America as a land of opportunity. As a Somali, K'naan reminds the listener that migration to the United States doesn't necessarily entail an overland route; his rap references these oceanic circuits and the dangers that they pose to the travelers ("Don't think I didn't notice those tombstones disguised as waves"). K'naan's motif of the immigrant betrayed continues with the next performer, Snow Tha Product, who proclaims that she has been "scoping ya dudes" and knows that "y'all aint been working like I do / I'll outwork you, it hurts you / You claim I'm stealing jobs though / Peter Piper claimed he picked them, he just underpaid Pablo." Snow Tha Product's lyrics echo K'naan in depicting immigrants as hard working, but she also introduces more explicitly a critique of some very familiar anti-immigration motifs; she rebuts the notion that immigrants "steal" jobs from "real" Americans, and she highlights how migrant laborers are underpaid and often the victim of wage theft.

Nevertheless, the image that these performers conjure in the song's first half is of an immigrant who is eager to embody America's entrepreneurial spirit if only given the chance. K'naan's and Snow's lyrics by and large rehearse many of the defenses of immigration that will be familiar to most: immigrants contribute to the US via their labor and the taxes they pay, they only seek a better life for themselves and for their children, they risk their lives to come to the US and are greeted with mistreatment, poor wages, discrimination, and the threat of arrest and violence. The song's hook, "Immigrants, we get the job done," seems to reflect the notion that legal inclusion should be determined by the value of the labor that migrants contribute, unwittingly reinforcing the idea that immigration should be reserved for those who "deserve" it in a version of model minority politics. One of the refrains in "Immigrants" is "not yet"—a line uttered by George Washington in *Hamilton* in response to John Laurens's statement that "Black and white soldiers wonder alike if this really means freedom."[34] The line suggests that the US has "not yet" achieved the promise of freedom, with the implication being that it will eventually. This is in line with Miranda's own statements regarding racism in the United States—that while we have come a long way, we have not yet achieved equality.

K'naan's and Snow's familiar rebuttal of anti-immigrant rhetoric shifts in the song's second half. The second two emcees, Riz Ahmed and Residente, for the most part reject the liberalism of the US state and the exceptionalist rhetoric that undergirds it. Instead, both performers launch a critique based on histories of colonialism and empire. Ahmed's lyrics add a distinctly postcolonial framework to the issue of immigration, proclaiming at the start of his rap, "British empire strikes back" and that "Hindustan, Pakistan" have arrived in London. Ahmed reminds listeners that the pillars of British and American power ("Buckingham Palace or Capitol Hill") were built with the "blood of my ancestors," a history of exploitation and violence that is conveniently forgotten as the English and Americans dismiss their collective responsibility in colonizing and exploiting Asia, Africa, and the Americas. "The thin red lines on the flag" represent not only the lines on a map demarcating borders and boundaries, they also represent the blood of millions of colonized subjects brutalized by US and British empire. The historical amnesia of both empires is on display in Ahmed's characterization of their attitudes toward migrants: "Who these fugees, what did they do for me?" The answer, according to Ahmed, is everything.

Like Ahmed's, Residente's lyrics focus on the effect of empire, this time in Central America and Mexico. Notably, Residente performs entirely in Spanish, and the video provides no translations or subtitles. (Snow Tha Product also raps a few lines in Spanish, about which I will have more to say momentarily.) Residente raps, "La peleamos como Sandino en Nicaragua" (We're fighting like Sandino in Nicaragua), a reference to Augusto Cesar Sandino, the Nicaraguan leader who spearheaded the resistance to the US military occupation of Nicaragua in the early twentieth century. Residente claims that "la mitad de gringolandia es terreno mexicano" (half of gringoland is Mexican soil) and argues that migrants are simply seeking to reclaim "el oro que nos robaron" (the gold that they stole from us). The migrants in Residente's narrative are tricksters and revolutionaries, "somos como last plantas que crecen sin agua" (we are plants that grow without water), who have "mas trucos que la policia secreta" (more tricks than the secret police"). Ahmed's and Residente's lyrics abandon the liberalism that underlie Snow's and K'naan's. Instead, they argue that American wealth and power is built on its exploitation of colonized subjects, not on the hard work of immigrants. The hook "Immigrants—we get the job done" takes on a different meaning in the second half of the song, as Ahmed and Residente articulate critiques that take on US and Western imperialism's longstanding use of Black and brown bodies to nation and empire build. The goal is not assimilation or acceptance as in the first half of the song but something closer to armed resistance; Ahmed talks of the empire striking back, while Residente states that Central American and Mexican migrants are in the US to reclaim what has been stolen from them. The "job" suddenly does not seem straightforwardly productive or labor-related but rather suggests something more revolutionary.

In a sign of the song's complex and ambivalent explanation for the nation's mistreatment of migrant workers, the revolutionary message that Ahmed and Residente promulgate—that at this point in history, immigrants do not want assimilation and acceptance but a transformation in the nation's narrative about itself—can also be found in the first half of the song. Snow Tha Product conveys the message in a few lines of Spanish rather than in English:

> Ya se armó
> Ya se despertaron
> It's a whole awakening
> La alarma ya sonó hace rato
> Los que quieren buscan
> Pero nos apodan como vagos
>
> They're already armed
> They're already awake
> It's a whole awakening
> The alarm went off a while ago
> Those who want, go searching
> But they call us slackers[35]

These are the only lines that Snow Tha Product raps in Spanish, and like Residente's words, they are not subtitled or translated for the predominantly English-speaking listener who would probably be the *Hamilton Mixtape*'s primary audience. In Spanish, Snow Tha Product talks about armed immigrants and warns the nation that the "alarm went off a while ago." This is not the alarm that K'naan mentions in his section of the song—it is not an alarm that one sets to rise and get ready for work; it is an alarm for the rest of the nation that reckoning of some sort is coming.

So which is it? Is America simply failing to live up to its promise of equality in providing "lap dances for all" (as K'naan raps), or is the entire national enterprise built on theft, corruption, and death? Does the song suggest that anti-immigration/anti-migrant sentiment and policies are a betrayal of the nation's roots and history, or does it suggest that these racist policies are part of the nation's constitution and rise? To try to answer that question, I want to turn now to the video for "Immigrants," which adds yet another layer of meaning to the already complicated narrative of migration that Manuel started out to tell in *Hamilton*. I argue that the video's visual imagery and particularly its mobile framing serve as a counterpoint to the musical's belief in freedom as the fundamental condition of the United States. In conjunction with the lyrics, the visual narrative of the video launches a much more fundamental critique of American immigration policies and racial politics than the musical.

Transitions

I noted in the previous section that the lyrics for "Immigrants" are loosely organized in a thematic fashion with the performers presenting different if not competing visions of what immigration means in the United States. Likewise, the visuals of the video have an identifiably repeating format in terms of their mobile framing. A sequence of camera movements structures each of the four performances; each of the camera moves underlines the carceral nature of migrant mobility. Each camera sequence starts at the closed door of a train car's gangway connector; as the door opens, the camera makes a strong penetrative forward movement through the door and the railroad car. This forward camera movement happens in the first half of each rapper's performance. The second half of each rapper's performance is characterized by an equally assertive backpedaling of the camera through the same train car. The transitions between performers is marked lyrically and visually. Lyrically, the song's main hook ("Look how far I've come / Look how far I've come / Look how far I've come / Immigrants—we get the job done") cues the end of one rapper's performance and the start of another; visually, that transition is marked by train doors; at the start of a rapper's performance, the doors open as the camera glides forward, and at the conclusion of a rapper's performance, the doors are filmed slamming shut as the camera moves backward. All this is to say that despite the many moving parts—the multiple songwriters, the provenance from Broadway to album, the huge cast—the video has a visual and lyrical structure that always emphasizes dualities and binaries and the impossibility of ever resolving any of those tensions into anything like a "right" answer.

The camera movements are reinforced by the visual content of the video. As the camera makes its forward march through the train car, migrants are depicted in various types of work— sewing, cleaning, building, nursing. They work and move as if the camera is not there. On the camera's backward trek, however, the migrants step in front of the camera and stare directly at the lens as it backpedals. This binary framework is evident from the first performer, K'naan, who performs his rap from the back of a freight car that has been converted into a makeshift dormitory. A bare light bulb on the floor throws his surroundings and body into shadows. As he raps, the camera tracks forward slowly toward him. His performance is cross-cut with scenes of men and women rising before dawn to get ready for work, marching in a line as they move through the train to get to work, toiling in a sweatshop, sewing American flags. As he finishes his verse, the camera begins to track backward. This is the video's first transition; we hear the bridge as the camera tracks forward through a gangway connector and the door to the next car opens. The camera moves forward into a railway car that is occupied by Snow Tha Product. Unlike K'naan, who is in a seated position and somewhat slumped over, Snow is a commanding presence; she stands powerfully in the empty freight car in front of a lopsided American flag, gesticulating with her hands, making direct eye contact with the camera as the overhead lights sway back and forth and the train rushes along on its tracks. Shots of the camera tracking closer and closer to Snow Tha Product are intercut with close-ups of her face.

Cut to the camera moving through another gangway connector and into another railroad car, this one filled with laborers picking oranges off trees. Snow Tha Product begins to move forward as the camera dollies backward, and she is joined by workers from all sides who fall in step behind her. The camera tracks forward through scenes of laborers working in a meat locker, the commercial kitchen of a restaurant, a laundry, a construction site, a health-care clinic, a nursery; these are intercut with scenes of Snow Tha Product stepping forward as the camera tracks back, joined by an increasing number of fatigued and defiant laborers. As Snow Tha Product's rap finishes, the refrain can be heard

("Look how far I've come / Look how far I've come / Look how far I've come / Immigrants—we get the job done"), and the camera begins its backtrack through the railway car, gliding backward through the same scenes (nursery, restaurant, meat locker) that it had just rolled through, only this time, the migrants who had been working in the previous shots step into the middle of the railway car to face the camera directly as it moves back.

A similar series of mobile framings structure the next phase of the video. The camera dollies backward through the gangway door. This time, we are in a subway car. The camera tracks slowly forward to reveal Ahmed leaning on a handrail. The track forward is intercut with images of a father and a son fleeing a bombed-out building, all of which is set in a railroad car; they move through a train car that is filled with rubble and clearly represents a war scene. Once Ahmed begins rapping, the camera begins its slow trek backward with Ahmed moving forward. His performance is cut with scenes of the father and son crossing under a barbed-wire fence and arriving at what appears to be a refugee camp. Refugees are grouped in the railcar and welcome the young boy. By the end of the verse, Ahmed is surrounded by subway commuters who remove the black rectangles that covered their eyes. As Ahmed recites the refrain, the camera tracks forward quickly to a close shot of his face.

The only performer for whom this pattern is altered is Residente, who is filmed riding on top of a rolling freight car that is filled with other migrants. Unlike the other performers, whose relationship to the camera is defined by a forward/backward movement along the central axis of the train, Residente is filmed at a slight angle. His body remains still throughout his performance, and so does the camera. The movements of both are constrained by the fact that they are on the roof of the train and there is literally no room to maneuver. Residente's performance is cut with scenes of ICE agents moving aggressively and quickly through a train car; the camera retreats in their wake and then follows them as they bang through doors, flash their flashlights at sleeping laborers, and physically rough up and then arrest several individuals. As the refrain picks up again, the camera settles into an exterior vantage point orthogonal to the train, and we see through a window laborers being thrust into a prison car, their heads hung in despair. The camera pans up from the prison car to the figures huddled on the railway car roof and then pans out to reveals a globe that is completely covered in interlocking tracks with trains racing around the world.

As the above summary indicates, Whitmore relies on certain camera motifs across the four performances: the slow track forward is used to introduce each rapper who directly addresses the camera; each rapper's performance is cut with shots of the migrants going about their labor-intensive tasks. In the forward track, the migrants do not look at the camera as it dollies slowly forward through the train car—they are focused on their individual tasks. The second half of each performance consists of a much quicker track backward; shots of the headlining artists remain relatively unchanged, but as the camera dollies backward through the very space that it had previously filmed, the migrants now step in front of the camera, look directly at the lens, and begin to march forward as the camera moves back. The camera in the first half of each performance acts as a stand-in for a seemingly omniscient observer, the privileged viewer who can move through the space with impunity as laboring people go about their work because they do not have the luxury to stop and look as the viewer does. The camera's backward dolly, however, highlights migrant resistance to their own dehumanization; they stand defiantly in rows and step in unison to confront the retreating camera. Their movements are synchronized and rhythmic; for a brief moment, they are no longer subject to the whims of the work they must perform to survive.

This camera work plays a crucial role in the video's representation of migration and the work that migrant laborers do. The complex network of shots speaks to the fundamental condition of migrant experience in the United States and globally; migrant mobility is predicated on incarceration. The narrative that migrant mobility is uncontrolled and "illegal" and that "border patrol" must scramble to apprehend these criminalized figures belies the experiences of migrants themselves. From the start of their journey to the border, the bodily movements of migrants is circumscribed by disciplinary and technological regimes that are wholly outside of their control and that actively attempt to hurt, maim, or kill them. Prison walls are not introduced once the migrant is detained by ICE; they travel around the migrant wherever he or she goes.

In "Immigrants," those prison walls are represented by the train itself. Even as the migrant embarks on his or her journey to the US, they are trapped on the moving train; their work and home lives are bound by the walls of the moving freight car. The prison that many of them enter at the end of the video is really no different from the prison that they already occupied—they are still on the train, still constrained by the train itself. And as the final pan of the video indicates, the problem is not strictly an American one; dozens of trains circumnavigate the globe, all presumably carrying human passengers who are trying to escape poverty and violence in their homeland only to find those conditions in a slightly altered form in their new home. For these workers, whatever brought them to the United States—whether it was war, economic opportunity, or "freedom"—the end result is that they are all in the same boat (or on the same train, as it were): overworked, underpaid, with no future prospects, living in fear of capture, arrest, and worse. The video's portrayal of a nation and a world that exists because of the exploitation of migrant labor and the strict control of migrant mobility represents a starkly different vision of immigration and nationhood than that represented in *Hamilton*.[36] That difference is marked by the railroad, which becomes the site and symbol of the nation's and the world's profound hostility toward migrant movement and labor, despite the essential nature of the work that migrants undertake.

Phantom Rides

In using the railroad and mobile framing to highlight the mutual imbrication between mobility and carcerality, "Immigrants" is part of a long tradition within filmmaking that positions the train as a symbol of mobility and imprisonment in their many forms. In concluding, I want to focus on the phantom-ride footage that is part of the video's opening as well as its closing. As I noted in the introduction of this book, phantom rides highlight the narratological qualities of the train. They give the viewer a sense of movement through space and time that seems both fixed and undeterminable. This shared logic between narrative and the train is particularly visible via the medium of film. As Lynne Kirby notes, "Since 1895, when the Lumière brothers showed *L'Arrivée d'un train en gare de La Ciotat*—one of the very first films projected publicly—the railroad has occupied an important place in cinematic representation."[37] Christian Hayes argues similarly that the "cinema aligned itself with the railway from its beginning, whether observing the train, emulating its motion or recreating the experience of the train journey."[38] Kirby goes a step further and suggests that the mutual fascination between silent cinema and the train stems from the fact that the train is a "mechanical double for the cinema"; to name the most obvious example, the tracking shot—perhaps the most ubiquitous of filmic techniques—is directly inspired by the railroad, a fact that is reflected in the shot's name. Both technologies require that the passenger/viewer "sit still as they rush through space and time."[39] The train provided silent film with a way to frame physical movement, "juxtapos[e] different places," and explore the "annihilation of space and time."[40] Kirby believes that the railroad was a protocinematic phenomenon that conditioned subjects from passengers into viewers.[41] The film and the railroad prepare the viewer and the passenger for the destruction of time/space that characterizes modern industrialized life. The technological modernity that the train represented triggered "new defenses" in subjects that required them to "reconfigure[e] and readjust the relationship between people and the environment."[42] Walter Benjamin identifies shock as the means by which "technology . . . subject[s] the human sensorium to a complex kind of training"; Georg Simmel describes it as an "intensification of emotional life"; and Wolfgang Schivelbusch labels it a "psychic civilizing process" in which the subject "develops an organ protecting him against the threatening currents and discrepancies of his external environment which would uproot him."[43] The phantom ride was part of that subject conditioning.[44] Hayes goes so far as to say that the railroad and cinema "were fused together by the phantom ride."[45] Citing Schivelbusch, Hayes argues that a "subliminal fear of destruction was infused into the train films and phantom rides of the period."[46]

The use of the phantom ride in the prologue to the "Immigrants" video highlights this fear and introduces the link between carcerality and mobility that the video will explore. The video starts with the song title and the performers' names projected in block letters on a black screen. Contained within the margins of the block lettering is footage from a phantom ride (footage of railroad tracks taken from a camera affixed to the front of a moving train). Whereas most phantom rides feature the landscape through which the train is traveling, the phantom ride that opens "Immigrants" is tightly focused on the railroad tracks

Figure 8.2. Title card for "Immigrants (We Get the Job Done)" music video, 2017. Directed by Tomás Whitmore.

ahead; all we see are the parallel tracks embedded in gravel and rocks, spotlighted by the train's front running light. The relationship between text, film, and negative space, with the image or rolling track peeking out through the broad vertical lines of the title, evokes imprisonment. From the start, the train is associated with incarceration and confinement rather than freedom and broad vistas.

Hayes's assessment that a "subliminal fear of destruction" haunts the phantom ride is apt here although for different reasons than he was setting forth. Rather than preparing subjects for life at speed in the industrial era, the more slowly paced phantom ride in "Immigrants" prepares the viewer for a nation that has no place for him or her. The phantom ride does not induce anxiety as a way of protecting viewers from the traumas of physical or psychic injury; it induces anxiety to highlight to the viewer the highly circumscribed and carceral nature of the nation that constantly proclaims the freedom it bestows on its citizens. The link between the nation and carcerality is emphasized by the next section of the video's prologue: the camera cuts to the train's engineer move through the narrow spaces of a railway car before sitting in the locomotive and turning on a radio. The video quickly cuts again to migrants sitting in a freight car, huddled together in small groups, listening to the same radio broadcast. The freight car is cramped, filled with people, with bunks lining one wall, tarp covering the windows, and bare light bulbs strung from the ceiling. The migrants are racially diverse and represent all stages of life: young men traveling singly, children and teenagers being held by their parents, a middle-aged couple sitting side by side. All are despondent over the anti-immigration rhetoric they hear pouring from the radio. The juxtaposition of the phantom ride, which is ostensibly meant to invoke open vistas and new landscapes, with the experiences of the migrants riding in the train—living in cramped quarters, completely imprisoned despite the hundreds or thousands of miles they have traveled to arrive in the United States—destroys the idealized notion that mobility equals freedom.

Traditionally, the phantom ride is supposed to suggest "the experience of movement that is inherent to travel."[47] Yet as any film historian will tell you, the means by which phantom rides were filmed belies that notion. The camera is fixed to the front of train, a camera that cannot pan up or down or side to side but must always be fixed forward. (And in the very early days of film, it was not just the camera that was tied to the train; a cameraman was sometimes tied to the locomotive cowcatcher to be able to get the desired shot.) In the introduction to this book, I cited Nanna Verhoeff's eloquent description of the appeal of the phantom ride, that nothing could be a more "significant and beautiful" symbol of linear perspective than "the two parallel lines of a receding railway track that approach each other but never touch."[48] Verhoeff's belief that it is humankind's fascination with endless possibility that lends the phantom ride its power is inverted in "Immigrants": the train tracks represent not a future of possibility but the hardened and narrow prison that is foundational to the nation and the world.

This message is in stark contrast to the video's epilogue, the mobile framing of which is meant to evoke a phantom ride with a twist. The epilogue prominently features *Hamilton* alum Daveed Diggs, who is filmed walking and dancing on railroad tracks with a large group of young people. The camera that is filming him and his compatriots is clearly attached to the rear of a moving train, which is rolling slowly forward as they walk. The difference between how Diggs moves in the epilogue— freely, effortlessly, spontaneously—and how the migrants move on the train is striking. It is abundantly clear that Diggs's and his compatriots' movements are unscripted and unchoreographed; they raise their arms in triumph, shuffle their feet to the beat, clap their hands from time to time, and mouth the words to the song at random moments. This reverse phantom ride stands in contrast to the despair and immobility of the migrants at the video's start; the impromptu movements of the performers in the epilogue diverges from the labored and laboring migrant bodies in the video.

Diggs's presence immediately calls to mind not only *Hamilton* but, it would seem, the politics undergirding it, a fact that is supported by the change in mobile framing and the embodied performances of Diggs and those who surround him. As the only scene that occurs off the train, the epilogue is clearly meant to represent some kind of way forward, an alternative space where freedom can be found. And yet to me, it signals only the blindness of a politics of incremental progress. The epilogue is meant to represent a return to the liberal optimism of the musical and Miranda himself. Even though the video itself has presented a powerfully damning critique of the US as a space of mobility without prisons, the epilogue seems determined to insist that all is not lost. The problem is that the video presents no path for arriving at this joyous scene. It depicts no sacrifice, no loss, no reform, no revolt. The final image is of the group headed up by Diggs celebrating their freedom on the tracks as the train gains speed and pulls away from them. Bestowing this kind of freedom on a select group of individuals is supposed to suggest the possibility of liberty for all. It is supposed to be a sign of the progress that Miranda espouses. But it inadvertently heightens the divide between the privileged few who might be able to leave the train and the masses who have no choice. Any freedom for the few off the train is available only because there are many who are forced to ride the train. The train that leaves this group behind is still carrying its cargo of human laborers, migrants, and refugees, whose imprisonment is forgotten in the face of freedom for a few.

Coda

The Train Will Not Save Us

Marx says that revolutions are the locomotive of world history. But perhaps it is quite otherwise. Perhaps revolutions are an attempt by the passengers on this train—namely, the human race—to activate the emergency brake.
—Walter Benjamin, "On the Concept of History," 1940

This book has explored the ways that writers and artists have used the railroad to make sense of the meaning of race in America. They have written and sung songs about the experience of riding on the train; they have painted and photographed it; graffitied it; filmed it from within and without; imagined its presence in impossible places; and acknowledged those who have built it. As I noted in the introduction, the train's capacious ability to serve as a site of racial meaning-making has not been lessened a jot by the fact that passenger ridership in the United States has been on a steep decline for over five decades. There is arguably no other mode of transportation—perhaps no other technology—that has the ability to signify across as many cultural histories as the train. In witnessing the flight of the space shuttle *Endeavour* over her Los Angeles home en route to its permanent location at the California Science Center, Elizabeth DeLoughrey writes of the "sense of community" that those who witnessed *Endeavour*'s journey experienced. As a critic whose research focuses on the environmental legacies of the Cold War, DeLoughrey objected to this celebration of the US military-industrial complex; nevertheless, the "feeling of awe" that *Endeavour* aroused "testif[ies] to the power of identifying with a vessel imbued with narratives of technology and progress that connect one to a national community."[1] DeLoughrey's description of the collective appeal of the space shuttle gives us a sense of why the train is so important to the very communities that have often been exploited and violated by it. Like the shuttle, the train is "imbued with narratives of technology and progress" that enable one to feel connected to a broader national community.

As I have argued throughout this book, the seeming contrast between the train's relatively infrequent usage in quotidian life and its pervasiveness in the nation's cultural imaginary signals the railroad's continuing power to express certain types of national narratives. I want to conclude *The Racial Railroad* by returning to this topic although from a slightly different angle. Setting aside for a moment the book's focus on cultural production, I want to consider how stories about the train continue to shape our attitudes in the realm of public policy, particularly environmental policy. In *Railroaded: The Transcontinentals and the Making of Modern America*, historian Richard White wryly notes that the "kind of hyperbole recently lavished on the Internet was once the mark of railroad talk."[2] White does not elaborate on the implications of this comparison, but I think it is worth pursuing a bit further. White's formulation suggests that what the internet and the railroad have in common is the ability to elicit fantasies of greater freedom for their passengers/users. I would suggest that the root of that fantasy lies in the fact that both internet and railroad are technologies that seem to prove "mankind's mastery" over "time and space," to quote Latham Cole, the gentlemanly and genocidal railroad magnate who serves as the villain in the Verbinski-directed film *The Lone Ranger*. In other words, the railroad and internet are the subject of intense interest not because they create new ways for individuals and communities to relate to each other (a quality that was frequently extolled in the early days of both) but rather because they prove the nation's ability to use technology to reset our lived experience of time and space. In addition, the railroad of the nineteenth century and the internet of the twentieth century both created new economic growth systems that could produce new ways of "extract[ing], produc[ing], and consum[ing]."[3] And despite the utopian rhetoric that characterized the discourse of both technologies, the internet and the railroad engendered entirely new avenues for the accrual of enormous wealth by a few individuals and entities as well as spawning new ways of exploiting the labor of migrants, racialized groups, and those who were already precariously positioned by previous systems of growth.

The comparison to the internet notwithstanding, in the twenty-first century, the train has once again emerged as a potential solution to a national problem. Whereas in the nineteenth and early twentieth centuries, the nation looked to the train to pacify, control, and shift its Indigenous and racialized populations—by settling the nation's claims of sovereignty over unceded lands, by controlling the movement and wages of racialized laborers, by despatializing the bodies and histories of Black people—in the twenty-first century, we envisage the train as part of the effort to combat climate catastrophe. And although this shift in signification seems like a massive shift in thinking, I would argue that they are rooted in a similar logic, namely a seemingly unshakable belief that technology, progress, and growth are homologous terms, and that combined thusly, they are the only metrics that matter in determining the state of our society and the value of its inhabitants. The train was the first technology that led us as a nation to believe that more growth, more production, and more consumption were the keys to prosperity and happiness. It helped cement a notion that the policy solution to any social, political, or economic problem involved more tightly merging technology with conceptions of progress and growth.

This notion—now globalized—has led us to the precipice of ecological catastrophe on a planetary scale. And yet the "solutions" that are often bandied about seem only to double-down on our financial and emotional investment in technology as offering us a way forward. Instead of finding ways to reconsider the pace and scale of extraction, production, and consumption of goods and services, political leaders, industry, and the socioeconomic elite have intensified efforts to find more complex technologies to provide a long-term solution for our ills. Rather than formulating policy that makes it more difficult for people to buy, travel, and consume and that conceives of a more localized way of living, we instead pursue the possibilities that the train and its twenty-first century cognates—electric cars, carbon-neutral airplanes, nuclear power as "clean" energy, space "exploration," geoengineering, nanotechnology, the list goes on—offer precisely because they do not ask us to consider that which we cannot face: that technology, growth, and progress will eventually make the planet uninhabitable for humans and the billions of organisms that are stuck on Earth with us.

The discourse about the environmental benefits of the train is concentrated particularly on the possibilities offered by high-speed rail (HSR). Although there is no standard definition for "high speed" railroad travel, the International Union of Railways defines HSR as a transport system, with specialized rolling stock and dedicated tracks, that is designed for speeds of up to 250 km/h.[4] While the topic of HSR in the United States is controversial, it has attracted support from many—mostly but not exclusively on the left of the political spectrum—because it does not pollute the atmosphere to the same extent as automobiles and especially airplanes. The nonpartisan Congressional Research Service, in a report titled "High Speed Rail (HSR) in the United States," started the list of HSR's purported benefits with a focus on its "potential [to] alleviat[e] highway and airport congestion" and "reduc[e] pollution and energy use in the transportation sector."[5] Journalist and author Michael Grunwald also emphasized the environmental benefits of HSR to the nation, arguing that the rail would "eas[e] road and air congestion, reduc[e] fuel consumption, and jump-[start] a domestic train-making industry." In Grunwald's telling, Rahm Emmanuel, chief of staff to President Obama, insisted on including HSR funding in the administration's 2009 stimulus package because everyone, from Obama to moderate Republications, was "horny" for HSR, a sexualized characterization that echoes Whitman's homoerotic fusing of masculinity, land, and technology in "Passage to India."[6]

Supporters of HSR like Grunwald tend to portray opponents of the railroad as motivated by an uncritical NIMBY-ism. In his book *The New Deal: The Hidden Story of Change of the Obama Era*, Grunwald mocks the residents of California's Central Valley, for example, who are opposed to the state's high-speed rail system; while this part of the state is sparsely populated, it is heavily Republican in its politics. California had first proposed an HSR line in 2008 to connect the northern and southern parts of the state. Voters approved an initial allocation of $10 billion to start the project with more funds coming from the Obama administration, which had made HSR a centerpiece of its 2009 stimulus bill (whether California state officials were as "horny" for HSR as members of the administration is not known). The state broke ground on the project in 2015 but was beset by a series of funding and construction delays as well as lawsuits from local residents. As costs ballooned, the

California High Speed Rail Authority (CHSRA) abandoned its original plan for a line between San Francisco and Los Angeles and instead set a much more modest goal of linking Bakersfield to Merced. The project is not scheduled to be finished until 2023 at the earliest.

Grunwald suggests that the Central Valley's resistance to the train is rooted in fear, ignorance, or idiocy (in describing a heated town hall meeting in the Central Valley town of Hanford, Grunwald calls out one particularly angry townsperson by noting that he rhymes "Ponzi" with "bonsai").[7] Whether or not Grunwald's characterization of these residents is ultimately accurate, he does not seem to consider why members of a struggling rural community might object to having a massive infrastructure project costing billions of dollars bisect their town when they never asked for it and will most likely never benefit from it. Michael Minn's point is germane here; in an article examining the political and economic impact of the HSR in the United States, Minn argues that despite the attempts to market HSR as reflecting the "social and ecological values [associated with] mass transit . . . HSR may in fact represent something quite different: an expensive public amenity that will operate to the benefit of a select, privileged minority."[8]

Arguments that the HSR would be less environmentally harmful than automobile and airplane travel are not as straightforward as one might think. As Elizabeth Deakin and Blas Luis Pérez Henríquez point out,

> HSR is hardly a panacea for environmental effects. Its energy efficiency and GHG emissions status depend on the electric power it sources, as well as on the number of seats it fills . . . Construction impacts are substantial . . . In addition, routing and operations of a high-speed rail system create environmental and social impacts that can be substantial; while they also can be mitigated doing so tends to increase construction costs.[9]

I want to emphasize here that this critique of HSR should not be read as a defense of the automobile, airline, or any other transportation industry, all of which need to be curbed and heavily regulated to reduce their carbon footprint. I also want to point out that my critique of the HSR is not based on its supposed financial unviability, which is often endlessly flogged by Republican opponents who present themselves as protecting taxpayer dollars in the name "fiscal responsibility." Nevertheless, it is important to point out that the ability of the HSR to mitigate green-house gas emissions depends to a large degree on the system's ability to convince millions of passengers to abandon their cars and commercial flights in favor of the train. Policy scholars have expressed skepticism about the rosy ridership numbers that are often used to buttress claims of the environmentally beneficial nature of HSR. For example, econo-mists Daniel Albalate and Germà Bel point to a report issued by the United States Conference of Mayors on the viability of HSR in the United States. The report suggests that California is the only US site likely to "obtain the volumes of demand close to those on the most suc-cessful routes elsewhere, such as the Paris-Lyon route, which served 25 million passengers in 2008."[10] But Albalate and Gel point out the fact that the multinational corporation Siemens, which owns subsidiaries that sell rolling stock and information technologies for high-speed rail trains, was a sponsor of the report.

It is important to note here that the argument that HSR will reduce the release of greenhouse emissions into the atmosphere implicitly con-tradicts the other supposed benefit of HSR, namely that construction and running of the rails will stimulate economic growth. James Fallows, a committed proponent of the CHSR, defends its construction by writ-ing that large-scale "transport-infrastructure projects are . . . more often a good than a bad idea" because they encourage "the growth of states, regions, and whole countries."[11] But growth is the root of the current ecological crisis. As Kate Soper argues, "Green technologies and in-terventions" will only work to renew the planet if they are undertaken with a "revolution in thinking about prosperity, and the abandonment of growth-driven consumerism."[12] Importantly for this book, growth is also the justification for all kinds of exploitation. The production of surplus requires the stratification of labor. This is not to say that if the railroad had not existed, labor exploitation would not have existed or racism would have been eradicated. Quite the contrary. But the rheto-ric of freedom, prosperity, and progress that the train evokes makes it easier to exploit the labor of those who are marginalized or desperate. If anything, these longstanding narratives that portray technology, growth, and progress as working in benevolent tandem with each other mask the exploitation, marginalization, and criminalization of poor and mi-noritized communities. The railroad emblematizes how technology is often portrayed as a great equalizer but actually further drives divisions and gaps between the wealthy and poor, between white and other, between citizen and "illegal," between settler and Native. Our obsession with this narrative of technology, which the train emblematizes, has led our planet to the brink of a catastrophe that has already caused misery, forced migration, and death to untold numbers, all while a miniscule slice of the elite seek out solutions that propose to visit upon us horrors straight out of science fiction.

One of the questions I am most frequently asked when I talk about my research is my opinion on the possibility of HSR in this country: Why can't trains in the United States be as convenient and efficient as passenger trains in Europe or Asia? The question is almost always a lament, driven by a feeling that the absence of an affordable and accessible passenger rail system is a sign of American provincialism. I understand where the lament is coming from, even though I myself do not share it. I believe that to reduce our impact on the planet, we need to reconceive not only the technologies we use to get us around but our relationship to mobility more broadly. Better technology, even if it is labeled "green," is not going to make a difference at this late date. And the production, proliferation, and consumption of more and more advanced technology is not going to do anything but accelerate the pace at which we destroy the planet. A much more localized approach to life is going to do more to save us than some kind of super train.

ACKNOWLEDGMENTS

For years, I've kept a folder on my laptop, marked "Railroad." In this folder, I kept a running list of books, films, TV shows, images, advertisements, and photographs that in some way touched on the subject of the railroad and race. Every time I gave a talk, whether to the public or a roomful of my academic peers or to a classroom full of undergraduates, someone—an audience member, a co-panelist, or one of my students—would ask if I was aware of the train in X, Y, or Z. "Have you seen M. Night Shyamalan's *Unbreakable*?" "There was an episode of *Law and Order* that I think you should check out." "What do you make of that AMC show *Hell on Wheels*?" "Do you talk about the Harvey House girls in relation to the southwestern railroad?" "Professor Lee, you should watch that TV show *Underground Railroad*!" After each discussion or question, I would dutifully jot down the reference into my list, "just in case," I told myself, "I needed more sources." It soon became clear to me that the references and representations of the train in American culture were endless, and that if I didn't stop, the book would never be completed. Such is the presence of the railroad in American life, or, to be more precise, such is the *awareness* of the railroad in American life that this project could have been populated entirely by suggestions from my generous and astute students and colleagues. I am grateful for every such suggestion and moment because each was offered in a spirit of intellectual curiosity that sustained me at various slow points in the writing process; I'm only sorry that I couldn't follow up on every one.

The intellectual seeds for this project lie in the research for my first book, *Reciprocal Representations: Interracial Encounters in African- and Asian American Literatures, 1896–1937*, which contains a chapter on Charles Chesnutt's novel *The Marrow of Tradition* (1901), a fictionalized account of the 1898 Wilmington Race Riots, and Wu Tingfang's memoir *America Through the Eyes of an Oriental Diplomat* (1914) and what the experience of riding Jim Crow was like for the novel's protagonist, Dr.

William Miller, an African American professional, and Wu, an upper-class diplomat for China. But the psychological roots for the project probably go back much further. When I was very young, my father, Kee Chin Lee, a then-overworked and perennially exhausted surgical resident, dabbled in model railroading. Other than smoking a pipe, it might have been his only hobby. He would sometimes take my sister and me to a shop somewhere in Buffalo, New York, to purchase a new locomotive or boxcar. These trips in my memory always happened in the dead of night in the middle of winter, and in a sign of the times, my father left us in the warm car to wait while he hurried in to make his purchase. Then back home to the basement of our rented duplex where he would then run his train. Sometimes he allowed us to push the buttons that made the train go forward or backward. I knew nothing about trains, but I do remember feeling very happy at such moments, impressed with the scale and detail of what must have been a relatively rudimentary model train set-up. I also must have loved spending time with my father, although I wasn't conscious of feeling this way and I certainly would have never articulated such a sentiment. But whenever he said he was going to make a trip to the train shop, my sister and I always begged to come along, even though it didn't involve anything more than sitting in the car. Those trips clearly meant something to me, so much so that now in my forties, whenever I think of trains (and over the course of the past ten years, I've thought about them *a lot*), I think of my father. May the association remain in my heart and mind forever.

Over the course of this book's research and composition process, I have benefited from the words and wisdom of the following colleagues, friends, and mentors: Gordon Chang, Iyko Day, Sean Fraga, Robert Hayashi, Steve Hindle, Jennifer Ho, Tamara Ho, David Henry Hwang, Manu Karuka, George Lipsitz, David Martinez, Asha Nadkarni, Franklin Odo, A. Naomi Paik, Miriam Thaggert, Amy Richter, Jolie Sheffer, Caroline Yang, and Hannah Yang. Jane Hwang Degenhardt has been the most generous friend anyone could ask for, and I always treasure our visits together to talk shop and to shop. Andrew Berish, E. Samantha Cheng, Sylvia Chong, Jennifer Ho, Andrew Rosenblum, and Phil Tajitsu offered solutions to specific problems and questions and did so with grace and speed. My deepest gratitude to John Lee, the brother of Corky Lee, for granting me permission to use Corky's photograph in chapter 4. I thank audiences at the American Historical Association, the American Studies Association, the Association of Asian American Studies, the California Historical Society, the Chinese American Museum of Los Angeles, the Five College Asian Pacific American Studies Program, and the Society of Fellows at the Huntington Library for their enthusiasm and softball questions. Portions of chapter 2 and chapter 3 were published in *Western American Literature* and the *Journal of Asian American Studies*, respectively. My thanks to the readers at those journals for their judicious comments and suggestions for revision. This work was also supported by the Mayers Fellowship and the George and Arlene Cheng Fellowship at the Huntington Library as well as a Humanities Commons Faculty Collaborative Grant at the University of California at Irvine.

My colleagues in the Department of Asian American Studies at the University of California at Irvine have been the foundation upon which this book is built. Special thanks to Christine Balance, Julia Reinhard Lupton, Amanda Swain, Linda Vo, and Andrzej Warminski for smoothing paths and offering support. After several years of being the only Asian American literature specialist at my previous institution, I am delighted to find myself in the company of a stellar cohort of Asian Americanist literature scholars: Chris Fan, Joe Jeon, Jerry Lee, and Jim Lee. My eternal gratitude to Arielle Hinojoso-Garcia, Robert Escalante, and Jennifer Choy for always having the answers (and for following up when they occasionally don't). Their skills in dealing with faculty, students, and the machinery of the university make them the bedrock of our department.

Eric Zinner has been enthusiastic about this project from the start, and I could not be more grateful for his support. I am proud to be published by New York University Press and be in company with so many colleagues whose work I admire. Two anonymous readers provided generous praise and advice to improve the manuscript. My thanks to Furqan Sayeed for his speedy email replies and to the entire staff at New York University Press for their professionalism and care in shepherding these pages into a beautiful book.

Nearly nine years ago, I was unjustly denied tenure at my previous institution of employment. Thankfully, I was surrounded by a supportive coterie of friends and colleagues (not to mention family members and loved ones) who lifted me from those depths. This is my chance to publicly thank them for saving a career that should never have been in danger in the first place: Kandice Chuh, Elizabeth Cullingford, Neville Hoad, Madeline Hsu, George Lipsitz, Anita Mannur, and Min Hyoung Song. Jim Lee deserves a special mention for counseling me through those early days and for helping me get back to California. King-Kok Cheung is a treasure of a scholar, mentor, and human being; no advisor could do more than she has done for me. My thanks to JK Barret, Phil Barrish, Ann Cvetkovich, Rich Heyman, Madeline Hsu, Neville Hoad, Donna Kornhaber, Lisa Moore, Gretchen Murphy, Samantha Pinto, Snehal Shingavi and Jennifer Wilks for their friendship. It turns out that unjust tenure denials are a part of the fabric of Asian American scholarly life. I am grateful for every single senior colleague who fought to make things better for those of us who came afterward. I hope I can do the same for those who follow me.

For someone who once thought living in Orange County was the equivalent of living in hell, I have found that Irvine has its charms, mostly located in the friends that I've made during my time here. Jerry Lee and Sei Lee, Annie Ro and Fernando Rodriguez, Chris Fan and Amy Chen, Adrianne Di Castro and Stephen Lee. One of the true delights of moving back to Southern California has been being in closer proximity to Jessica Pressman and Brad Lupien; thank you for twenty plus years of friendship and camaraderie. My gratitude and love to my Amherst crew, who even twenty-five years after our graduation, continue to be my touchstones, whether through text chains or Zoom calls: Amanda Botticello, Callie Greenfield, Shayne Klein, Helen Kotchoubey, Megan Mayhugh, and Christine Wooley.

My deepest thanks to the wonderful young women who have cared for my children over the years and who have showered them with love and care when I was locked in my study: Lauren Nguyen, Leanne Nguyen, Alex Bragorgos, and Kayla McMenamin.

Any good thing I have done or will ever do in my life can be directly attributable to my parents, Kee Chin and Joung Hwan Lee. My mother has been the most influential person in my life; hers is the voice inside my head always urging me to do the right thing, telling me to trust in God, reminding me to clean my oven once in a while. She and my father have been married for forty-nine years, and I think they make a good team. I pray for their good health, long life, and happiness every day. I dedicate this book lovingly to them.

My thanks to my younger sisters Vivien, Amy, and Sarah for being so smart, funny, and terrifyingly capable; you each give me an ideal to live up to. I guess I can't boss you around anymore. Thank you to my brothers-in-law Paul Segerstrom and Sam Bryar for enduring our noisy family get-togethers with such grace and humor. To Keely, Peyton, Malia, Max, and all future nieces or nephews—Julie-emo loves you very much and promises to always take your side in any argument with your parents.

To Philip—lover of jokes, connoisseur of bourbon, eater of late-night snacks, builder of Legos, partner in laughter, aficionado of tea ceremonies, dream customer of salespeople everywhere ("But the sales guy said we have to get it *today* because lots of people are interested in it!")—there is no one else on earth I'd rather race through a fancy restaurant meal with. I apologize for disliking you so much when we first met and for publicly speculating at the time that your British accent was fake. I've told you this before, but the thing I love most about you is that even though you have endured more than your fair share of difficulties and traumas, you still have a trusting and generous heart. Thank you for taking me to Berlin only to refuse to show me the Brandenburg Gate because "only tourists go there." Thank you for loving gravy to the point of derangement. When I went on a quick work trip to England and asked you if there was anything I should avoid, thank you for telling me "the people." Thank you for your winning smile, which I see now in our children's faces. I unfairly and continually berate you for cheating at cards because I love hearing you laugh, even when you are laughing at me. Let's make it our goal to continue our deep and meaningful conversations about what we would do if we won the lottery through the time we collect social security. Deal?

As for Eleanor and Silas—my sunshine, moonlight, starry sky, and green earth—yes, umma can play with you now.

NOTES

INTRODUCTION

1 See Albro, *Railroads Triumphant*, 123.

2 Despite the fact that the United States has the largest railroad network in the world, its ridership numbers cannot compare to those of other developed nations. Railroad ridership in the US stands at 17.2 billion passenger-kilometers, which sounds impressive until you realize that a passage-kilometer represents one passenger traveling one kilometer. That number is dwarfed by rail ridership in the EU, which logged 400 billion passenger-kilometers. And when you translate ridership into a per capita number, the disparity is even more striking: per capita, Americans traveled eighty passenger-kilometers in 2011. For comparison, the Japanese, Swiss, Danes, Russians, Ukrainians, and Belgians all logged over one thousand passenger-kilometers per capita in that same time frame. See N.B., "Why Don't Americans Ride Trains," *Economist*, August 30, 2013, https://www.economist.com.

3 Amy Richter notes that African American women were the most scrutinized figures on the Jim Crow railroad car. As Richter notes, "No matter their standing in their communities, black women in the heterogeneous public of the cars had to demand recognition [given the fact that] the very idea of a black lady confounded whites' racist expectations" (Richter, *Home on the Rails*, 100).

4 Karuka, *Empire's Tracks*, xiii.

5 Sharpe, *In the Wake*, 13.

6 I am certainly not the first critic to note the tension at the heart of the railroad's cultural signification throughout American history. Alan Trachtenberg sees the railroad as "the prime instrument of the large-scale industrialization which recreated American nature into natural resources for commodity production." At the same time, it was also depicted as a "chariot winging Americans on an aesthetic journey through [their] new empire" (*The Incorporation of America*, 19). Trachtenberg famously called the railroad "the most conspicuous machine of the age" and a symbol of the nation's "republican values, diffusing civic virtue and enlightenment along with material wealth" (Ibid., 57, 42).

7 Miller, "Narrative," 68.

8 The train accident that the novel depicts occurred in real life. On October 20, 1961, the Ranchi Express derailed about 120 miles from Kolkata, killing forty-seven and injuring scores more.

9 Lahiri, *The Namesake*, 17.

10 Ibid., 21.

11 Daly, "Railway Novels," 466.

12 Ibid., 463.

13 de Certeau, *The Practice of Everyday Life*, 115.

14 Ibid., 111.

15 Ibid.

16 Cammaer, "Phantom Rides," 149.

17 Verhoeff, *The West in Early Cinema*, 282.

18 Miller, "Narrative," 72.

19 Jarrett, "Train Tracks," 31.

20 Adam Ditzler, "From Phantom Rides to GoPro Videos: Exploring the Magic of Moving Image," *Medium*, February 4, 2019, https://medium.com/.

21 Pease, "American Exceptionalism."

22 Ibid.

23 Thoreau, *Walden*. Writers such as Nathaniel Hawthorne, Herman Melville, and Henry Adams wrote suspiciously about the train, with Melville labeling it "that iron fiend" (in his short story "Cock-A-Doodle-Doo!" [1853]) and Hawthorne associating it with "all unquietness" (quoted in Marx, *The Machine in the Garden*, 13).

24 Whitman, "Passage to India."

25 Wilwhite, "His Mind Was Full of Absences," 921.

26 Smith, "Walt Whitman and Manifest Destiny," 377.

27 Ibid.

28 "Empire of liberty" is a phrase used by Thomas Jefferson in letters to George Rogers Clark in 1780 and James Madison in 1809; see www.monticello.org. "A shining city on a hill" is a scriptural phrase that appears in Jesus's Sermon on the Mount in the Book of Matthew and then was repurposed by John Winthrop for his sermon "A Model of Christian Charity" (1630); the phrase is most commonly associated with Ronald Reagan, who used it repeatedly throughout his presidency, including in his election eve address in 1980 and his farewell speech in 1989. "The last best hope of Earth" appeared in Abraham Lincoln's annual message to Congress, December 1, 1862; www.nps.gov/. "The indispensable nation" was a phrase used by Madeleine Albright in an interview with the NBC *Today Show* on February 19, 1998, as a justification for using military force when diplomacy has failed: "But if we have to use force, it is because we are America; we are the indispensable nation. We stand tall and we see further than other countries into the future, and we see the danger here to all of us. I know that the American men and women in uniform are always prepared to sacrifice for freedom, democracy and the American way of life." For a transcript of the interview, see https://1997-2001.state.gov/statements/1998/980219a.html.

29 Karuka, *Empire's Tracks*, xiii.

30 Ibid.

31 White, *Railroaded*, xxii.
32 Whitman, "To the Locomotive in Winter," https://whitmanarchive.org.
33 Wilson, "President Wilson's Personal Appeal," 145.
34 Ward, *Railroads and the Character of America*, 18.
35 Wolfe, "Dark in the Forest, Strange as Time," 175.
36 White, *Railroaded*, xxv.
37 Ibid.
38 Karuka, *Empire's Tracks*, 40.
39 Berte, "Geography by Destination," 189.
40 Gordon, *Passage to Union*, 4.
41 Ibid., 126.
42 Ibid., 4.
43 Quoted in Martin, "Temporality and Literary Theory."
44 Ibid.
45 Bauman, *Modernity and the Holocaust*, 61–62.
46 Vartija, "Racism and Modernity, 6.
47 Giddens, *The Consequences of Modernity*, 53.
48 Ibid.; Beaumont and Freeman, "Introduction: Tracks to Modernity," 13.
49 Welke, *Recasting American Liberty*, 4.
50 Daly, "Railway Novels," 470.
51 Ibid., 475.
52 Schivelbusch, *Railway Journey*, 130.
53 Harvey, *The Condition of Postmodernity*, 240.
54 Kirby, *Parallel Tracks*, 2.
55 Goodman, *Shifting the Blame*, 134.
56 Goodman's argument points to how quantum physics acts as an often invisible pillar of Western hegemony. Quantum physics' dominant influence on our notions of time and space is practically invisible, so widely and completely is it accepted as a universal truth. Derek Lee makes this explicit argument in his article "Postquantum: *A Tale for the Time Being*, *Atomik Aztek*, and Hacking Modern Space-Time," writing that the "dominance of Western physics across modernity has helped perpetuate the belief that Eurocentric conceptions of space-time are universal and uncontested—'true' for all periods, societies, and literatures around the globe" (3).
57 Schivelbusch, *Railway Journey*, 37.
58 Ibid., 13.
59 Ibid., 33.
60 Kirby, *Parallel Tracks*, 12.
61 Aguiar, "Making Modernity," 68.
62 Vartija, "Racism and Modernity," 2.
63 Schivelbush, *Railway Journey*, 37.
64 de Certeau, *The Practice of Everyday Life*, 111.
65 Bakhtin, "Forms of Time," 84–85.

66 Grosz, *Space, Time, and Perversion*, 96.
67 Ibid., 98.
68 Lye, *America's Asia*, 4.
69 R. Lee, *The Exquisite Corpse of Asian America*, 25.
70 Ibid.

1. TRACKS ACROSS THE LAND

1 Despite the similar names, the Union Pacific Railroad Eastern Division was not affiliated with the Union Pacific Railroad. In 1869, the company changed its name from UPRED to the less-confusing Kansas Pacific.
2 Palmer, *Report of Surveys across the Continent*, 191.
3 Ibid.
4 Ibid.
5 Ibid.
6 Cresswell, *In Place/Out of Place*, 16.
7 Romero, "The Politics of the Camera," 5.
8 Nye, "Technology, Nature, and American Origin Stories," 9.
9 Ibid., 8.
10 Schivelbusch, *Railway Journey*, 37.
11 Hsu, *Geography and the Production of Space*, 4.
12 Aikin, "Paintings of Manifest Destiny," 78, 80.
13 Mitchell, "Imperial Landscape," 5–34, 10.
14 Mitchell, Introduction to *Landscape and Power*, 1.
15 Aikin, "Paintings of Manifest Destiny," 80.
16 The Chief ran from Los Angeles to Chicago between 1926 and 1937 before being replaced by the all-diesel Super Chief. It was frequently called "The Train of the Stars" because of the large number of celebrities it carried cross-country and because of its luxurious appointments.
17 Barnd, *Native Space*, 2.
18 Wright, "Land Tenure," 88.
19 Brady, "'Full of Empty,'" 253.
20 Ibid.
21 Ibid.
22 Ibid.
23 Hernández, *City of Inmates*, 7.
24 Hobart, "At Home on the Mauna," 31.
25 Denevan, "The Pristine Myth," 369.
26 Johnston, *Narrating the Landscape*, 5.
27 Horwitz, *By the Law of Nature*, 55.
28 Johnston, *Narrating the Landscape*, 29.
29 Marx, *The Machine in the Garden*, 159.
30 Mitchell, "Imperial Landscape," 13.
31 Ibid.

32 Wilson, "Techno-euphoria and the Discourse of the American Sublime," 207.

33 Miller, "Everywhere and Nowhere," 208.

34 Ibid.

35 Scott and Swenson, "Introduction," 2; Aikin, "Paintings of Manifest Destiny," 86.

36 Miller, "Everywhere and Nowhere," 208.

37 Ibid.

38 Danly, Introduction to *The Railroad in American Art*, 13.

39 Aikin, "Paintings of Manifest Destiny," 86.

40 Schley, "A Natural History of the Early American Railroad," 443.

41 Schivelbusch, *Railway Journey*, 10.

42 Karuka, *Empire's Tracks*, xii.

43 Vimalassery, "Counter-sovereignty," 143.

44 Aikin, "Paintings of Manifest Destiny," 85.

45 Nathaniel Currier and James Merritt Ives were the most famous lithographers in America. For a sixty year period, between 1857 and 1907, their workshop produced lithographs on over seven thousand subjects for mass production. For more on their production, see John Gladstone, "The Romance of the Iron Horse," 14.

46 Ibid., 15.

47 Nye, "Technology, Nature, and American Origin Stories," 13.

48 Ibid.

49 Interestingly, the railroad creationism that is implicit in the JBF production logo is not echoed perfectly in the film *The Lone Ranger*. While most critics eviscerated the film for Johnny Depp's portrayal of Tonto ("the most grotesque pop culture representation of Native Americans" according to Ryan Syrek of the *Omaha Reader*), its running time (Peter Bradshaw in the *Guardian* complained that "The South American landmass peeled off from the western seaboard of African quicker than this"), or as the latest sign of the decline of the western as a popular film genre (Wesley Morris in *Grantland* opines that this "isn't the complete disaster of *Wild Wild West*, but that's only because none of the $250 million was spent to turn Kenneth Branagh into a mechanical spider"), a small but critical cadre of critics, writing mostly in more specialized venues, gave the film credit for its playful if chaotic attempts to reimagine the racism of the western. On the level of plot, the film offers a revisionist history of the West, one that centralizes the story of Tonto and depicts a US Cavalry eagerly massacring Comanche tribes at the bidding of railway magnates who are indistinguishable from the violent criminals and gangs terrorizing American frontiersmen. Director Gore Verbinski and the film's star, Johnny Depp, "explicitly and repeatedly expressed their intention to redeem the role of Native Americans with this movie by using humor and offering Tonto more agency" (Heim, "Neoliberal Violence," 1434). Verbinski's strategy involved mixing elements of the revisionist western—the "massacres and the psychosis and politicized rage"—with slapstick. As Andrew O'Heir notes in *Salon*, the film "never lets you forget that the Manifest Destiny that drove Anglo-American society across out continent was a thin veneer pasted across a series of genocidal

crimes." Matt Zoller Seitz, writing for Rogerebert.com, admired the film's deliberate inversion of "old western signifiers" so that a rendition of "Stars and Stripes
Forever" is "as chilling as the German National anthem in a World War II flick."
In this vein, the film's comic portrayal of John Reid/the Ranger as a dangerously
naïve bordering on moronic lawyer who lovingly cradles John Locke's *Second
Treatise of Government*, one of the pillars of Enlightenment thinking and of our
own Republic, is the *only* reputable way to retell this story.

50 Aikin, "Paintings of Manifest Destiny," 80.

51 Ibid., 82.

52 Ibid., 83.

53 Based on a French graphic novel *Le Transperceneige*, *Snowpiercer* introduced
Bong Joon-ho to a global audience. Already a respected auteur in Korea thanks
to previous films like *The Host* (2000) and *The Mother* (2009), Bong made his
English-language directorial debut with *Snowpiercer*, helming an international
cast that included Chris Evans (Curtis), Jamie Bell (Edgar), Song Kang-ho (Namgoong Minsoo), John Hurt (Gilliam), Octavia Spencer (Tanya), Tilda Swinton
(Mason), and Ed Harris (Wilford).

54 Bong's exacting detail even extended to mapping out the train itself, a sketch of
which he shared at MTV.com. The train encompasses sixty cars, each car measures twenty-five meters, which means that Snowpiercer is about 1.5 kilometers
long. The tail section makes up the last twenty cars of the train, while the "rich
people" zone makes up fifteen cars. The closer one gets to the locomotive, the
more luxurious the train cars become; the last several cars before the locomotive
consist of a beauty salon, a swimming pool, a sauna, a nightclub, and an opium
den. Bong's hand-drawn diagram can be viewed at www.mtv.com/news/1838603/
snowpiercer-train-diagram-bong-joon-ho/.

55 Simon Abrams, "Director Bong Joon-ho Breaks Down *Snowpiercer*'s Ending,"
Vulture, June 29, 2014, www.vulture.com.

56 Aikin, "Paintings of Manifest Destiny," 81.

57 According to Bong: "[Yona's mother] was confident that she could endure the cold-
ness. However, she went out too early. Her attempt to overthrow the system—or to
escape it—was too early. It was right after she had Yona; the revolution of the Frozen
Seven was fifteen years ago, so Yona must have been about one or two years old.
Minsu couldn't follow her but instead took care of the baby. If the seven members
go out first and build some sort of community, he was to meet them when the train
comes back to the same place a year later. However, when he looked outside the next
year with hopes in his heart, he only saw their bodies, frozen to death right on the
spot and failed even to climb over the hill." This quotation appeared in a Korean-
language article and was translated and posted by soysoya onto a tumblr dedicated to
Snowpiercer. I could not find any mention of Yona's backstory in any English language
interviews that Bong participated in. See https://fyeahsnowpiercer.tumblr.com/.

58 See Fragua's website, www.mobilsavage.com.

59 Zega and Gruber, *Travel by Train*, 23.

60 Ibid., 24.

61 The railroads were instrumental in the establishment of the nation's first national park at Yellowstone. "As John Muir himself admitted to the Sierra Club at its annual meeting in 1895: 'Even the soulless Southern Pacific R.R. Co., never counted on for anything good, helped nobly in pushing the bill for this park through Congress.'" See Runte, "Promoting the Golden West," 63.

62 Ibid., 65.

63 Lummis, "The Artists' Paradise," 451.

64 Born in Los Angeles in 1881 to parents who were artists, Villa was formally trained at the Los Angeles School of Art and Design and traveled to England and Germany to further hone his skills. He is best known for this long association with the ATSF, which used his paintings of the Chief in advertisements for the railroad for decades. For more information about Villa, see "Hernando Villa Paints Indians" at https://streamlinermemories.info/?p=2742. More biographical information can be found at the Los Angeles County Museum of Art (LACMA) website, https://collections.lacma.org.

65 Zega and Gruber, *Travel by Train*, 23.

66 Moreau and Alderman, "Graffiti Hurts,"108.

67 Ibid., 110.

68 For an interview of Fragua after the incident, see John Townsend, "This Native American Artist's Street Art Reminds L.A. Residents Who Was There First," *Fast Company*, August 24, 2016, www.fastcompany.com. An image of the wall art is also available on Fragua's website at www.mobilsavage.com.

69 Belfer, Ford, and Maillet note that the journalistic pieces on the impact of climate change on Indigenous communities tend to invoke sovereignty when the "responsibility for climate impacts is assigned to Indigenous communities" ("Representation of Indigenous Peoples in Climate Change Reporting," 67). This approach tends to overlook the long histories of settler colonialism and political marginalization that these nations have endured.

70 Interview by Soul Center for the Arts of Jaque Fragua, available at https://www.soulcenter.art.

71 Estes, "Fighting for Our Lives," 120.

72 Streeby, *Imagining the Future of Climate Change*, 44.

73 Chmielewska, "Framing [Con]text: Graffiti and Place," 149.

74 "Jaque Fragua and Brad Kahlhamer," *Bomb Magazine*, January 16, 2019, https://bombmagazine.org.

75 Ibid.

76 Interview by Soul Center for the Arts of Jaque Fragua, available at https://www.soulcenter.art.

2. THE CHINAMAN'S CRIME

1 Cather, *Willa Cather's Short Fiction*, 341, 342. This volume is the only one that contains all three of Cather's Chinese short stories. All the page numbers are taken from this edition.

2 Ibid., 342.
3 Ibid.
4 Riis, *How the Other Half Lives.*
5 Lye, *America's Asia*, 3.
6 Palumbo-Liu, *Asian/American*, 18.
7 Lee, *Orientals: Asian Americans in Popular Culture*, 90.
8 Lye, *America's Asia*, 11.
9 Cather, *Willa Cather's Short Fiction*, 343.
10 Ibid.
11 Ibid., 342.
12 A young girl later tells Rodgers that she overheard O'Toole having a conversation with a man whose face she never glimpsed but who had "red lips." While this is enough to damn him in the story, it would hardly stand up in a court of law.
13 Cather, *Willa Cather's Short Fiction*, 342, 348.
14 Ibid., 339.
15 Bhabha argues that Fanon "uses the fact of blackness, of belatedness, to destroy the binary structure of power and identity" ("Race, Time, and the Revision of Modernity," 237). This notion of temporality is important to both Fanon and Bhabha, who recognize the central role that history plays in the articulation of the relationship between whiteness and Blackness. Bhabha goes on to state that "[Fanon] too speaks from the signifying time-lag of cultural difference that I have been attempting to develop as a structure for the representation of subaltern and postcolonial agency" (Ibid.). This "time-lag of cultural difference" constitutes a moment of potential resistance for Bhabha, one that is worth stopping over and considering. Bhabha goes on to note explicitly that Fanon "rejects the 'belated-ness' of the black man because it is only the opposite of the framing of the white man as universal, normative—*the white sky all around me*: the black man refuses to occupy the past of which the white man is the future" (237–38).
16 Miller, *The Unwelcome Immigrant*, vii.
17 Gyory, *Closing the Gate*, 3–4.
18 For further analysis of this poem, see Lee, *Interracial Encounters*, 36–37.
19 Of course, other discourses proved potent in rationalizing Asian exclusion. The accusation of Chinese paganism was particularly effective in a nation that fervently imagined itself as Christian (and continues to do so to this day). African Americans residing in California worked to distance themselves from the Chinese in a state that was experiencing more anxiety about Chinese emigration than Black migration from the South. Philip Alexander Bell, editor of the Black San Francisco newspaper the *Elevator*, echoed the sentiments of many white nativists when he wrote that the Chinese are "unacquainted with our system of government, adhering to their own habits and customs, and of heathen idolatrous faith." The negro, on the other hand, is a "native American, loyal to the government and a lover of his country and her institutions—American in all his ideas; a Christian by education and a believer of the truth

of Christianity" (quoted in Johnsen, "Equal Rights and the 'Heathen Chinee,'" 57–68, 61.

20 Cather, *Willa Cather's Short Fiction*, 342.

21 Ibid., 341, 342. Although I do not have the space to explore the issue in the detail it deserves, the connection that the story draws between Jews and the Chinese demands some analysis. Freymark's attempt to pass is obviously governed by the belief that the age of Jewish and Chinese cultures has blended the phenotypical features of their citizens to such an extent as to make them indistinguishable. Given the shift in the characters' treatment of Freymark after they learn of his Chinese ancestry, it seems clear that the story considers Jewish blood preferable to Chinese, but what is striking about the comparison is that it seems to equate Jewishness with passing. That the story compares the two groups to each other is an indicator of the extent to which racial identities are intersectional. While the formation of their identities within the United States have operated along very different paths and been influenced by a distinct set of historical, geopolitical, and social factors, Asians and Jews in America are often compared because both groups have functioned as "model minorities" (whose success "proves" the ultimate justness of American democratic principles) and/or economic "middlemen," who open businesses and serve other racially marginalized communities. The relative cultural propinquity of Jewish immigrants to the "Near East" made inevitable the link between Jewish bodies and the "Orient." Freymark's use of a Jewish name and background to explain his "Oriental features" thus makes sense given how the two groups were often imagined as exotic, sexually deviant, polluting, and intrinsically foreign to American life. For more information, see Freedman, "Transgressions of a Model Minority."

22 Cather, *Willa Cather's Short Fiction*, 342.

23 Ibid., 343.

24 The supposed threat that Chinese men pose to US womanhood is a vital part of anti-Chinese discourse. There was a widely held perception that Chinatowns and other ethnic ghettos were places of danger for white women; exposure to these neighborhoods, it was thought, would lead to their corruption. The idea that Chinatowns in particular were exemplary sites of vice and immorality "reinforced and reproduced Euro-American notions of racial and cultural superiority against an immoral and vice-ridden Chinese immigrant community" (Lui, *The Chinatown Trunk Mystery*, 5.

25 Lucenti, "Willa Cather's *My Ántonia*, 194. As Lucenti states, memory in Cather's stories "mak[es] us profoundly aware of how deeply we are inscribed by the past that we have *forgotten*, as well as by the one we sometimes tenuously remember" (193).

26 Lye, *America's Asia*, 3.

27 Cather, *Willa Cather's Short Fiction*, 341.

28 Mufti, *Enlightenment in the Colony*, 106.

29 Cather, *Willa Cather's Short Fiction*, 328.

30 Ibid., 329.

31 Ibid., 523–24.

32 Ibid., 526. The question of why the United States passed the Chinese Exclusion Act in 1882 is one that does not have an easy answer. There have been two widely accepted theories to explain the act's passage. The California thesis, first proposed by Mary Robert Coolidge in 1909 and persuasively argued by Alexander Saxton in *The Indispensable Enemy: Labor and the Anti-Chinese Movement in California* (1971), suggested that organized labor and politicians in California and on the West Coast were largely responsible for Chinese exclusion. The second theory, of which Stuart Creighton Miller's *The Unwelcome Immigrant: The American Image of the Chinese, 1785–1882* is representative, argues that Chinese exclusion has its roots in national anti-Chinese sentiment and racism, which had been pervasive since the founding of the republic. Both theories rely heavily on the notion that labor movements on the local and national levels were universal in their opposition to Chinese immigration and instrumental in the passage of the Exclusion Acts. Andrew Gyory challenges the ascendency of these theories (as well as pointing out the class prejudices that underpin some of their articulations) by arguing that "national politicians of both parties . . . seized, transformed, and manipulated the issue of Chinese immigration in the quest for votes" (15).

33 Cather, *Willa Cather's Short Fiction*, 526.

34 Ibid., 527.

35 In her essay "The Novel Démeublé," Cather makes the case that writing a novel requires a process of "simplification. The novelist must learn to write, and then he must unlearn it; just as the modern painter learns to draw, and then learns when utterly to disregard his accomplishment, when to subordinate it to a higher and truer effect" (6). Cather's ideal was prose that had been stripped of "meaningless reiterations . . . [and] tiresome old patterns," and she scoffs at realist writers' obsession with "cataloging a great number of material objects" as if such detailed descriptions were "imaginative art" as opposed to a "brilliant form of journalism." In this sense, "A Son of the Celestial," with its mystical descriptions of the origins of Yung's carvings ("the mulberry and apricot and chestnut and juniper that grew about the sacred mountain; the bamboo and camphor tree, and the rich Indian bean, and the odorous camellias and japonicas that grew far to the south on the low banks of the Yang-Tse-Kiang" [524]), violates Cather's own code of artistic excellence.

36 Cather, "The Novel Démeublé," 6.

37 Cather, *Willa Cather's Short Fiction*, 350.

38 Ibid.

39 Ibid., 352.

40 Lauro and Embry, "A Zombie Manifesto," 85–108.

41 McGurl, "Zombie Renaissance."

42 Cather, *Willa Cather's Short Fiction*, 344.

43 Musset, "Rappelle-toi," 111.

44 The verb in the original French is conjugated in the imperative form ("Rappelle-toi").
45 Lowe, *Immigrant Acts*, 27.
46 Ibid., 6.
47 Cather, *Willa Cather's Short Fiction*, 339.

3. TELLING STORIES

1 See the "Chinese Railroad Workers in North America" website, codirected by Gordon Chang, at http://web.stanford.edu/group/chineserailroad/cgi-bin/word-press/. See also Sucheng Chan's *Asian Americans: An Interpretive History* (New York: Twayne, 1991); Gordon Chang's *The Chinese in America: A Narrative History* (New York: Penguin, 2003); Gary Okihiro's *The Columbia Guide to Asian American History* (New York: Columbia University Press, 2001); and Ronald Takaki's *Strangers from a Different Shore* (New York: Little, Brown, 1989).
2 Of the three, Chin is perhaps more closely associated with the railroad because he himself labored on the Southern Pacific, an experience that he imparts to his autobiographical narrators and protagonists in works such as *Donald Duk* (1991), "Railroad Standard Time" (from the collection *The Chinaman Pacific and Frisco R.R. Co.*), as well as "Riding the Rails." But the railroad plays an important part in Kingston's writings as well, appearing in two works: the autobiographical *China Men* and the postmodern novel *Tripmaster Monkey: His Fake Book* (1989), the latter of which has a protagonist inspired by Chin. The relative lack of association between the train and Kingston may have something to do with the fact that it does not appear in the work for which she is most famous, *The Woman Warrior*.
3 Spicer, "The Author Is Dead," 387.
4 De Man, "Autobiography as De-facement," 920.
5 See Steinberg, "Writing Literary Memoir," 142–47; and Eakin, "Breaking Rules," 113–27.
6 The US travel industry presents a romanticized view of cross-country train travel that feeds directly off of a lingering sense that the railroad offers a tourist a more authentic or unique vision of the country. The America by Rail company (which is no longer in business) touted railroad travel as the "best way to see America" and offered membership to customers through its "Golden Spike rewards program." Passengers on Amtrak's California Zephyr, which travels from Chicago to Emeryville, California, "will experience America," from the "waving wheat fields of the Great Plains to the craggy peaks of the Rocky Mountains, and the open desert landscapes of Utah and Nevada (see http://book.amtrakvacations.com).
7 Trachtenberg, *The Incorporation of America*, 57.
8 Ibid., 58.
9 White, *Railroaded*, xxii.
10 Wong, *Reading Asian American Literature*, 13.
11 What most people understand to be the Transcontinental Railroad is actually a slight misnomer. Although the name implies that one could hop on a train on

the Eastern Seaboard of the United States and ride without interruption to the West Coast, the truth is a little bit more complicated. The railroad that was laid down by the Union and Central Pacific Railroads had its western terminus in San Francisco and its eastern terminus in Council Bluffs, Iowa. Passengers wanting to ride coast to coast therefore had to switch trains in Council Bluffs. The completion of the railroad nevertheless dramatically cut travel time across the country, from four to six months (depending on if one went overland or by sea) to a little less than a week.

12 Carson, "Chinese Sojourn Labor and the Transcontinental Railroad," 84.

13 Swartout, "Kwantung to Big Sky," 370.

14 Saxton, "The Army of Canton in the High Sierra," 33. Saxton notes that unskilled labor, which is how the Chinese were categorized, earned about a dollar a day in 1865. However, much of the work the Chinese undertook should have counted as skilled labor, for which the going rate would have been three to five dollars a day.

15 Chang, *Chinese in America*, 63–64. Chang also notes that more than twenty thousand pounds of bones were shipped back to China for burial.

16 James Strobridge, the superintendent of the Central Pacific, was one of the Big Four who financed and managed the completion of the Transcontinental. Once the railroad was completed, according to newspaper accounts, Strobridge invited a group of Chinamen to his private boarding car where they were "cheered . . . as the chosen representatives of the race which have greatly helped to build the road—a tribute they well deserved, and which evidently gave them much pleasure." The *Sacramento Daily Bee* of May 12, 1869, also reported that Strobridge invited his Chinese foreman to take a seat at the celebratory dinner, whereupon the assembled guests cheered and then "crowded around Strobridge to congratulate [him] and assure him of [their] sympathy." For more information on the Chinese role in the completion of the Transcontinental Railroad, see the Central Pacific Railroad Photographic History Museum site at http://cprr.org/Museum/Chinese.html.

17 Okihiro, *Margins and Mainstreams*, 150.

18 Chang, *Chinese in America*, 156.

19 Okihiro, *Margins and Mainstreams*, 150.

20 Chin and Chan, "Racist Love," 65.

21 Day, *Alien Capital*, 43.

22 Eng, *Racial Castration*, 36.

23 It is important to distinguish how Eng treats the railroad in his work versus the approach I take here. Eng is interested in how Kingston and Chin rework the technology of photographic visualization with the train serving a more passive role as the object being photographed and looked at. I, however, explore how these authors' representation of the train itself reflects and confronts the problem of Chinese American marginalization.

24 Eng, *Racial Castration*, 37.

25 Ibid.

26 Day, *Alien Capital*, 41.

27 Ibid., 42.

28 Ibid., 44.

29 Ibid., 43.

30 Ibid., 46.

31 Lee, *The Theatre of David Henry Hwang*, 21.

32 Ibid.

33 Ibid., 10.

34 A word about the play's reception is useful here. In exploring these themes of erasure and absence, *The Dance and the Railroad* has been subjected to a very common critical move in the mainstream media in which the text by a writer of color is accused of failing to provide historical depth, specificity, or complexity, when in fact, the work is grappling with the erasures and exclusions that the state has inflicted on the racialized community in question. For example, in his 2013 review of an off-Broadway revival of *The Dance and the Railroad* directed by May Adrales and starring Ruy Iskandar and Yuekun Wu, *New York Times* theater critic Christopher Isherwood strikingly and repeatedly calls attention to what he believes to be the play's "thin texture." His characterization of *The Dance and the Railroad* as "thin" ascribes to the play the conditions that characterized the state's approach to the experiences of the Chinese railroad workers. Instead of naming the conditions and responsibilities of the state, the railroad companies, and/or the culture of nineteenth-century America that viewed Chinese lives as disposable and their stories as unworthy of memorialization, Isherwood blames the play for not offering a more in-depth picture of Chinese railroad workers.

35 For more information on the role of performers Tzi Ma and John Lone in the composition of the play, see Lee, *The Theatre of David Henry Hwang*, 20–21.

36 Hwang, *The Dance and the Railroad*, 79.

37 Ibid., 67.

38 Ibid., 87.

39 Ibid., 70.

40 Ibid, 61.

41 Ibid.

42 Ibid., 79.

43 Ibid., 74.

44 Oishi, "The Asian American Fakeness Canon, 1972–2002," 198.

45 Goshert, "'Frank Chin Is Not a Part of This Class!'"

46 Nguyen, "The Remasculinization of Chinese America," 135.

47 For summaries of Chin's antiracist politics, particularly as they intersect with gender, sexuality, and interracial alliances, see Cheung, "The Woman Warrior versus the Chinaman Pacific," 234–51; Kim, *Writing Manhood in Black and Yellow*; Maeda, "Black Panthers, Red Guards, and Chinamen; Wong and Santa Ana, "Gender and Sexuality in Asian American Literature."

48 Kim, *Writing Manhood in Black and Yellow*, 38.

49 Chin, "Railroad Standard Time," 1. Elgin was one of the watch companies that produced timepieces considered accurate enough to be used by railway conductors and engineers in the nineteenth and early twentieth centuries. Although each company set its own standards for what could be considered a "railroad standard watch," the requirements were generally the same across the industry.

50 Ibid.

51 Ibid., 2.

52 Ibid.

53 Ibid., 5.

54 Ibid.

55 Chin, "Riding the Rails with Chickencoop Slim."

56 Ibid., 81.

57 Ibid., 83–84.

58 Ibid., 84.

59 Ibid., 86–87.

60 While *China Men* is now often viewed as a sequel of sorts to her most famous work, *The Woman Warrior*, Kingston originally conceived of the two memoirs as part of one larger work. Worry that the themes of one might detract from the other eventually led her to publish the two separately. Despite these differences, the two books share similar interests. Both destabilize the binaries (autobiography/novel, history/fiction, public/private) that underpin the exclusionary practices of both the nation and the literary canon. For more information on the relationship between *The Woman Warrior* and *China Men*, see Nishime, "Engendering Genre"; Rabine, "No Lost Paradise"; and Sabine, *Maxine Hong Kingston's Broken Book of Life*.

61 Kingston, *China Men*, 146.

62 Ibid., 125.

63 Ibid., 126.

64 Ibid.

65 Ibid.

66 Ibid.

67 Ibid., 133.

68 Ibid.

69 David Li reads this scene quite differently, arguing that Ah Goong is "virtually castrated" by US politics and the Central Pacific's total power over his life. According to Li, Ah Goong's act reveals "he has no political [or] economic mastery over the land that he help[s] to tame." See Li, "China Men," 492.

70 Kingston, *China Men*, 151.

71 Nishime, "Engendering Genre," 67.

72 Lye, "The Literary Case of Wen Ho Lee," 251.

73 Chin, "Come All Ye Asian American Writers of the Real and Fake," 142.

74 Ibid., 152.

75 Boelhower, "The Brave New World of Immigrant Autobiography," 6.

76 Lye, "The Literary Case of Wen Ho Lee," 252; Lowe, "Autobiography out of Empire," 102.

77 Holte, "The Representative Voice," 28.

78 De Man, "Autobiography as De-facement," 930.

79 Ibid.

80 Kingston, *China Men*, 138.

81 De Man, "Autobiography as De-facement," 920–21.

82 Ibid.

4. REMEMBRANCE AND REENACTMENT AT PROMONTORY SUMMIT

1 Heath, "A Railroad Record that Defies Defeat," 3.

2 See Scott Sommerdorf, "A 'Photographic Act of Justice' for Chinese Laborers at Golden Spike," *Salt Lake Tribune*, May 13, 2014, https://archive.sltrib.com/article.php?id=57924758&itype=CMSID.

3 The 2014 reenactment received a great deal of attention, but it is typical of the work of Asian American photojournalist Corky Lee, who spent his professional life capturing key moments in Asian American history. As noted by Vanessa Hua, Lee "first saw the famed [champagne] photograph when he was in junior high," and has since 2002 been leading with Leland Wong, a descendant of a railroad worker, a "flash mob" of Chinese Americans to "recreate the tableau at Golden Spike National historical Park" (see Vanessa Hua, "Golden Spike Redux," *National Parks Conservation Association*, 2019, https://www.npca.org. According to Hua, "Lee . . . has taken pictures of Chinese workers' descendants and other Asian American supporters in front of the locomotives and a natural formation now known as the Chinese Arch because of its location near a former Chinese work camp. He characterizes these works as acts of 'photographic justice.'"

4 Agnew, "Introduction: What Is Reenactment?" 327.

5 Hartman, "Venus in Two Acts," 2.

6 See, for example, coverage of the reenactment of the 1811 slave rebellion in Louisiana, in which five hundred people participated. Rick Rojas, "A Slave Rebellion Rises Again," *New York Times*, November 9, 2019, www.nytimes.com.

7 Best, *None Like Us*, 63, 64.

8 Ibid., 65, 64.

9 Ibid., 65.

10 Hartman, "Venus in Two Acts," 11.

11 Roach, *Cities of the Dead*, 3.

12 Ibid., 2.

13 Stephen Gapps, a historian and reenactor, enumerates the truly dizzying ranks of reenactors, from the lowly "farb" (short for "far be it for me to tell them what they're doing is wrong") who do not prioritize authentic dress, to the "mainstreamer," to the "faux-progressive," to the "progressive," to the "authentic," to the "hardcore," and then the rare "superhardcore." See "Mobile Monuments," 399–400.

14 Hartman, *Lose Your Mother*, 16.

15 Shimakawa, *National Abjection*, 3.

16 Ibid.

17 Ibid.

18 Chambers-Letson, *A Race So Different*, 4.

19 Kim, *The Racial Mundane*, 3–4.

20 Ibid., 12.

21 Ibid., 16.

22 Ibid., 12.

23 A word of clarification. The correct name for the location where the Central Pacific and Union Pacific tracks meet is Promontory Summit, but many histories and sources will list the site as Promontory Point. There is a Promontory Point in Utah, but it is located about thirty-five miles south of the railroad rendezvous location. Soon after the railroad's completion, for reasons that remain unclear, journalists and railroad officials began using Promontory Point instead of Promontory Summit to describe where the two tracks met. Hart's stereograph, published soon after the railroad's completion, bears the incorrect town name of Promontory Point. I will use the name Promontory Summit to locate the events of May 14, 1869, and May 14, 2014, but I will not correct historical material—like Hart's stereograph—that make that error.

24 The painting can be viewed on the museum website of the Central Pacific Railroad at http://cprr.org.

25 Roach, *Cities of the Dead*, 30.

26 Hartman, "Venus in Two Acts," 11–12.

27 Ibid.

28 Both novels are part of a recent mini-publishing trend that I would call "Asian American historical fiction," which looks back to the nineteenth century for narrative material. Kingston's *China Men* and David Henry Hwang's *The Dance and the Railroad* are perhaps two of the best-known examples of this subgenre, which includes earlier works such as Sky Lee's *Disappearing Moon Café* (1990), Lisa See's memoir *On Gold Mountain* (1995), Ruthanne Lum McCunn's novel *Thousand Pieces of Gold* (1981), and Lawrence Yep's young adult series Golden Mountain Chronicles (published 1975–2011), but it seems to have picked up steam more recently across multiple genres of fiction. *The Fortunes* and *How Much of These Hills* join novels or novellas like Brian Leung's *Take Me Home* (2010), Monique Truong's *The Sweetest Fruits* (2019), and Ken Liu's "All the Flavors: A Tale of Guan Yu, the Chinese God of War, in America" (2018); and young adult fiction such as Linda Sue Park's *Prairie Lotus* (2020), Stacey Lee's *Under a Painted Sky* (2015), and Renee Ahdieh's *The Beautiful* (2019). These works look to the past as a way of telling a different kind of Asian American story, one that is less invested in tropes of assimilation or the model minority and more interested in marking the erasures and gaps in the formation of an Asian American subject.

29 Davies, *The Fortunes*, 58.

30 Ibid., 48.

31 Ibid., 58.

32 Construction of the tracks at Cape Horn took almost a year; according to *National Geographic*, more than three hundred Chinese laborers died during the construction period. Carleton Emmons Watkins, a photographer and childhood friend of Leland Stanford, took a famous photograph of the train at Cape Horn in 1876; the stereograph depicts a train hugging the curving roadbed that drops precipitously to the canyon of the American River below. Watkins' famous photograph can be viewed at http://www.getty.edu.

33 Davies, *The Fortunes*, 94

34 Ibid.

35 The story of the bosun chairs is one that is often repeated on historical material about construction of the railroad at Cape Horn, including on the memorial plaque that was placed at the site in 1990. Edson T. Strobridge published an article in 2001 on the Central Pacific Railroad Museum's website effectively debunking this story. He notes that there are no mentions of the baskets in the papers of Collis P. Huntington nor in any of the archives of multiple railroad companies. Newspapers at the time provided regular and detailed updates about the progress of construction, but Strobridge can find no accounts of the baskets in articles from the time. CPRR chief engineer Samuel S. Montague does note in a November 1865 report that laborers attempted a "sidehill rock cutting" technique with men suspended from ropes. The first direct mention of bosun chairs being used by the Chinese at Cape Horn is in 1927, in an article published in the *Southern Pacific Bulletin* by Erle Heath, a member of the Southern Pacific's Public Relations Department (the Central Pacific was acquired by the Southern Pacific Railroad in 1885). While it seems highly likely that Chinese were tied to ropes to place explosives for blasting the rock, the image of Chinese workers being lowered down a cliff in baskets is almost certainly historically inaccurate. See Strobridge, "The Central Pacific Railroad and the Legend of Cape Horn."

36 Davies, *The Fortunes*, 60.

37 Ibid.

38 Ibid., 82

39 Ibid.

40 Cheng, *Ornamentalism*, 4. Cheng's discussion of the yellow woman poses some of the same issues as Saidiya Hartman poses in her discussion of the Venus, the Black woman "variously named Harriot, Phibba, Sara, Joanna, Rachel, Linda, and Sally" who is mentioned in travel journals, memoirs, ship ledgers, court proceedings, and novels. Hartman eloquently notes that "hers is the same fate as every other Black Venus: no one remembered her name or recorded the things she said or observed that she refused to say anything at all. Hers is an untimely story told by a failed witness" (Hartman, "Venus in Two Acts," 2).

41 On the other side of these discussions, the crux of Afropessimist thought—that the history of slavery marks Blackness as irreconcilable with the world—impugns

any restorative efforts. Frank Wilderson's theorization of Blackness as necessarily antagonistic to human subjectivity unveils Blackness as a lack in the symbolic order, a lack that prevents the possibility of historical recovery and is actually maintained by the archive.

42 Cheng, *Ornamentalism*, 1, 3.
43 Ibid.
44 Ibid., 18.
45 Zhang, *How Much of These Hills Is Gold*, 174.
46 Ibid.
47 **Ibid.**, 270.
48 Ibid.
49 Ibid.
50 Ibid.
51 Ibid., 267.
52 Cheng, *Ornamentalism*, 4.
53 Chang, *Ghosts of Gold Mountain*, 6.
54 Ibid.
55 Quoted in Lee, *The Theatre of David Henry Hwang*, 21.
56 Lee, "Contemporary Asian American Drama," 406.

5. THE JIM CROW TRAIN IN AFRICAN AMERICAN LITERATURE

1 Here, Wideman is referencing the Department of Homeland Security's "If You See Something, Say Something" public service campaign, which was inaugurated by Director Janet Neapolitano in 2010 to raise public awareness about potential terrorist attacks. For more information and to see the public service announcements, see http://www.dhs.gov.
2 Wright, *Physics of Blackness*, 4.
3 Gleason, *Site Unseen*, 3.
4 McKittrick, *Demonic Grounds*, xii.
5 Welke, *Recasting American Liberty*, 308. Welke goes on to argue that "Jim Crow raced space."
6 McKittrick, *Demonic Grounds*, 33.
7 Trains feature prominently in the following African American texts: Maya Angelou's memoir *I Know Why the Caged Bird Sings* (1969); Charles Chesnutt's novel *The Marrow of Tradition* (1901); Countee Cullen's poem "Incident," (1925); W. E. B. Du Bois's novel *Dark Princess* (1928); Jesse Redmond Fauset's novel *Plum Bum: A Novel without a Moral* (1928); Langston Hughes's short story "Fine Accommodations" (1963) and play *Scottsboro Limited* (1932); Zora Neale Hurston's novel *Jonah's Gourd Vine* (1934); Nella Larsen's novel *Quicksand* (1928); Nat Love's memoir *The Adventures of Nat Love, Better Known in the Cattle Country as "Deadwood Dick," by Himself* (1907); Claude McKay's short story "Truant" (1932); Jean Toomer's short story "Fern" from *Cane* (1923); and Richard Wright's essay "The Ethics of Living Jim Crow" (1940) and his short story "Big Boy Leaves Home" (1938).

8 Inscoe, *Writing the South through the Self*, 98.

9 Huffard, *Engines of Redemption*, 2. The railroad's role in the Civil War has long been debated by historians, although it falls outside the scope of this study. Railroads in the antebellum era serviced local areas, and gauges were not standardized across state lines or even between municipalities (see Huffard, *Engines of Redemption*, 2). Scott Reynolds Nelson argues that a plantation-based economy hobbled the development of railroad systems in the antebellum South (*Iron Confederacies*, 16). Confederate leaders struggled to transform the region's disparate and diffused lines into a cohesive system of transport. After the Civil War, Jefferson Davis and other southern military leaders blamed the railroads—or the lack of them in the South—for the defeat, suggesting a largely false image of the antebellum South as "precapitalist" (Nelson, *Iron Confederacies*, 19).

10 Huffard, *Engines of Redemption*, 2.

11 Jarrett, "What Is Jim Crow?" 389.

12 Inscoe, *Writing the South through the Self*, 99.

13 McKittrick, *Demonic Grounds*, xiii.

14 The compulsory nature of sociability in modern spaces like the train or railway stations lead to a new type of bodily social practice, what Erving Goffman has called "civil inattention," or "being in public but minimizing attention to others." Civil inattention is necessary in spaces like a train car but can be difficult to maintain unless one is looking in another direction. Goffman argues that novels and other reading materials offer a way to be "visibly immersed" (quoted in Urry, *Mobilities*, 106). Goffman's account of civil inattention dovetails with the rise of whole subgenres of literature that were meant to be consumed while one was traveling. Today, we call these works "airport novels," but in fact, the popularity of novels of sensation and railway novels is directly attributable to the leisure time that train and others forms of travel afforded.

15 Inscoe, *Writing the South through the Self*, 99.

16 Ibid.

17 Ibid.

18 Ibid.

19 Ibid.

20 Douglass, *The Life and Times of Frederick Douglass*, 139.

21 Ibid. This is not the only close call Douglass experiences while on this train. While still in Maryland, Douglass's train stopped at a station next to a southbound train. Directly opposite Douglass on the other train sat a Captain MacGowan. Had this man looked up for even a second, he would have seen and recognized Douglass instantly; fortunately for Douglass, "in the hurry of the moment," MacGowan's gaze never rests on the escaping slave. Later, "a German blacksmith whom [Douglass] knew very well" is a passenger on the same train as Douglass; although Douglass is certain the man has recognized him, he says nothing to any authorities: "He saw me escaping and held his peace" (*The Life and Times of Frederick Douglass*, 139).

22 Inscoe writes that by 1908, segregation had spread from the train car to "waiting rooms and other facilities in train stations"; these spaces often "became contested spaces" in Black narratives of the time period (Inscoe, *Writing the South through the Self*, 102).

23 Rabaka, "The Souls of White Folk," 7.

24 Du Bois, "The Superior Race," 470.

25 Du Bois's insistence on the racial intermixture of Blacks and whites subverts the myth of white racial purity. It also gives lie to the notion that whites were somehow not produced by the slavery and oppression of the south. Du Bois notes that he himself is "related to [whites] and they have much that belongs to me—this land, for instance, for which my fathers starved and fought" (476). Du Bois's claim to "this land" creates a complicated genealogy for African Americans, one that is bound up in blood and justified by the suffering that his "fathers" endured at the hands of white slave owners. The gesture toward racial hybridity works both ways. Du Bois points out that his interlocutor is as much a product of racial intermixture as he himself is, with "yellow blood and black" in his veins, "as the measurements of [his] head will show" (Du Bois, "The Superior Race," 477).

26 Du Bois, "The Superior Race," 477.

27 Fanon, *Black Skin, White Masks*, 91.

28 Yancey, "Black Embodied Wounds and the Traumatic Impact of the White Imaginary," 144.

29 Fanon, *Black Skin, White Masks* 92.

30 Johnson, *The Autobiography of an Ex-Colored Man*, 71.

31 Ibid., 96.

32 Arnesen, *Brotherhoods of Color*, 17.

33 Welke, *Recasting American Liberty*, 317.

34 Arnesen, *Brotherhoods of Color*, 16.

35 Johnson, *The Autobiography of an Ex-Colored Man*, 65.

36 Ibid., 87.

37 Ibid., 80.

38 Ibid., 81.

39 Ibid., 84.

40 Ibid., 86.

41 Ibid., 83.

42 Bianculli, *The American Railroad in the Nineteenth Century*, 134.

43 Johnson, *The Autobiography of an Ex-Colored Man*, 93.

44 Ibid.

45 Ibid., 94.

46 Ibid.

47 Ibid.

48 Ibid., 106.

49 Inscoe, *Writing the South through the Self*, 102.

50 Jacobs, *Incidents in the Life of a Slave Girl*, 189.

51 Ibid.
52 Tate, *Domestic Allegories of Political Desire*, 26–27.
53 Ibid., 63.
54 Welke, *Recasting American Liberty*, 283.
55 Ibid., 296.
56 Richter, *Home on the Rails*, 8.
57 Ibid.
58 Ibid.
59 Cooper, *A Voice from the South*, 90.
60 Ibid.
61 Ibid.
62 Ibid., 96.
63 Ibid.
64 Ellison, "Boy on a Train," 13.
65 Ibid., 13–14.
66 Ibid., 15.
67 Ibid.
68 Keith Byerman suggests that the father may have been lynched, a reading partially based on the fact that Ellison as a child visited Tulsa just before and in the aftermath of the massacre of the Black community of Greenwood in 1921. See Byerman, "'I Did Not Learn Their Name,'" 108.
69 Ellison, "Boy on a Train," 17.
70 Ibid.
71 Ibid.
72 Ibid.
73 Ibid.
74 Ibid., 17–18.
75 Ibid.
76 Colbert, *Black Movements*, 175.
77 Sharpe, *In the Wake*, 28.
78 Ibid., 27.
79 Ibid.
80 Ibid., 27, 29.
81 Ibid., 27.
82 Lipsitz, *How Racism Takes Place*, 13.

6. RIDING THE BLIND

1 Hazel Carby examines how female blues performers challenged conventions and taboos relating to Black women's sexuality. Houston Baker argues that the blues is characteristic of African American expression "the enabling *script* in which Afro-American cultural discourse is inscribed." Sterling Brown describes the blues as grounded in "folk-life" and argued that blues that "concentrate[d] on love" tended to be more "marketable." For Brown, "the true blues were sung by people close

to the folks"—singers like Ma Rainey; Mamie, Bessie, and Clara Smith; Victoria
Spivey; Ida Cox; Jim Jackson; Lonnie Johnson; Blind Lemon Jefferson; and Leroy
Carr. S. A. Williams calls the blues a "communal expression of Black experience
which had developed out of the call and response patterns of work songs from
the nineteenth century and have been described as a 'complex interweaving of
the general and the specific' and of individual and group experience." See Baker,
Blues, Ideology, and Afro-American Literature, 286; Carby, "It Jus Be's Dat Way
Sometime"; and Williams, "The Blue Roots of Contemporary Afro-American
Poetry," 123.

2 Handy, *Father of the Blues*, 72. Handy's famous "Yellow Dog Blues" was composed
   in remembrance of this incident, although not until several years later.

3 Ibid.

4 Ibid.

5 Ibid., 76, 77.

6 Of course, Handy's origin story radically simplifies the emergence of the blues as
   a popular music category. This is a history that is well covered by others in countless books and articles, so I will only add here that despite the prominent role of
   the train and train station in his "discovery" of the blues, Handy is surprisingly
   dismissive of the role that the railroad plays in the blues. His explanation for the
   preponderance of the train in blues songs is that "southern Negroes [sing] about
   everything. Trains, steamboats, steam whistles, sledge hammers, fast women,
   mean bosses, stubborn mules—all become subjects for their songs" (*Father of the
   Blues*, 74). Handy depicts the train as merely one of the many things that African
   Americans sing about, perhaps as a way of arguing for blues as an elevated
   cultural form as opposed to a "primitive" one (an anxiety he expresses in his autobiography).

7 Evans, "The Development of the Blues," 20.

8 Ibid.

9 Johnson, "'I'll Be with Him on the Midnight Train to Georgia,'" 1.

10 Evans, "The Development of the Blues," 21.

11 Brown, "The Blues," 289.

12 Ibid.

13 Quoted in Angela Davis, *Blues Legacies and Black Feminism*, 71.

14 Ibid.

15 Elam, "The Dialectics of August Wilson's *The Piano Lesson*," 378.

16 Davis, *Blues Legacies*, 71.

17 Davis, *Blues Legacies*, 67–68.

18 Davis, *Blues Legacies*, 74.

19 Carby, "It Jus Be's Dat Way Sometime," 474.

20 For one thing, even though Cotten composed "Freight Train" sometime in the
   early 1900s, the song did not reach audiences until the mid-twentieth century,
   when it made its way to England and was unjustly claimed (and copyrighted) by

two British songwriters. Cotten was able to reclaim the copyright and record the song herself for the first time in 1957, when she was in her sixties.

21 Carby, "It Jus Be's Dat Way Sometime," 477.

22 Ellison, "Richard Wright's Blues," 90.

23 Ibid.

24 Carby, "It Jus Be's Dat Way Sometime," 476.

7. SPECULATIVE TRAINS

1 Foner, *Gateway to Freedom*, 6.

2 Whitehead, *The Underground Railroad*, 267.

3 McKittrick, *Demonic Grounds*, 17.

4 Whitehead, *The Underground Railroad*, 67–68.

5 Ibid.

6 Whitehead, *The Underground Railroad*, 90.

7 Marshall, "Steel Wheels on Paper," 37.

8 Ibid., 38.

9 Ibid.

10 Ibid.

11 McKittrick, *Demonic Grounds*, 18–19.

12 See Sophia Nahli Allison's moving essay on this myth memory in her essay "Revisiting the Legend of the Flying Africans," *New Yorker*, March 7, 2019, www.newyorker.com.

13 These lines are taken from the Africa section of Baraka's volume *Wise, Why's, Y's*, which has never been published. Baraka recited these lines in part 1 of Bill Moyer's *Fooling with Words* program for PBS. The transcript can be found at https://billmoyers.com.

14 Whitehead, *The Underground Railroad*, 17, 294.

15 Schulz, "The Perilous Lure of the Underground Railroad."

16 While the myth of the Underground Railroad only fully emerged in the years following the end of Reconstruction, it is important to remember that if white abolitionists needed to promulgate an expansive and highly centralized view of the Underground Railroad to glorify their own courage, so too did southerners need the Underground Railroad, albeit for an entirely different set of reasons. White southerners clung to the myth of a vast network of abolitionist spies hellbent on infiltrating the South to lure away slaves who would otherwise be perfectly content to remain as property. In the case of abolitionists, the myth of the Underground Railroad enlarged their role in freeing slaves, while in the case of southerners, the myth of the Underground Railroad enabled the perpetuation of the stereotypical happy slave.

17 Jennifer Schuessler, "Words from the Past Illuminate a Station on the Way to Freedom," *New York Times*, January 14, 2015, www.nytimes.com.

18 Gara, "The Underground Railroad in Illinois," 509.

19 Fergus Bordewich, "History's Tangled Threads," *New York Times*, February 2, 2007, www.nytimes.com.

20 Ibid.

21 Schulz, "The Perilous Lure of the Underground Railroad."

22 Gara, "The Underground Railroad in Illinois," 527.

23 Schulz, "The Perilous Lure of the Underground Railroad."

24 Paul Finklelman, quoted in Jennifer Schuessler, "Words from the Past Illuminate a Station on the Way to Freedom," *New York Times*, January 14, 2015, www.nytimes. com. My thanks to Professor Timothy Yu for his help in locating this quotation.

25 Foner, *Gateway to Freedon*, 65–66, 83.

26 Gara, "William Still and the Underground Railroad," 40.

27 Ibid., 37.

28 Smith, "Neo-slave Narratives," 168. The neo-slave narrative as a genre was identified and named by Bernard W. Bell in 1987 in *The Afro-American Novel and Its Tradition*. According to Bell, the neo-slave narrative pays homage to a tradition of oral storytelling as it describes a protagonist's escape from bondage to freedom. While Margaret Walker's *Jubilee* (1966) is often identified as the first neo-slave narrative, Ashraf Rushdy argues that the genre is part of the "logical continuity in African American writing" dating back to William Wells Brown's *Clotel* (1853). Valerie Smith also notes that any discussion of the history of the neo-slave narrative should include Arna Bontemps *Black Thunder* (1936), which narrates the slave revolt led by Gabriel Prossier in 1800. For a discussion of the historical reasons for the emergence of the neo-slave narrative in the years following Walker's *Jubilee*, see Rushdy, "The Neo-Slave Narrative"; for a discussion of the genre in a transatlantic or non-Anglophone contexts, see Anim-Addo and Lima, "The Power of the Neo-Slave Narrative Genre," 3–13.

29 Dubey, "Speculative Fictions of Slavery," 779. The emergence of science and speculative fictions as genres with widespread popular and critical appeal is not limited to African American letters. Asian diasporic and Latinx writers have also taken up the genre with enthusiasm, and it has now become an established area of study within contemporary ethnic American literary scholarship. For more information on the links between speculative fiction and race, see the following selection of texts: Aimee Bahng, *Migrant Futures: Decolonizing Speculation in Financial Times* (Durham, NC: Duke University Press, 2018); Andre Carrington, *Speculative Blackness: The Future of Race in Science Fiction* (Minneapolis: University of Minnesota Press, 2016); Mark Jerng, *Racial Worldmaking: The Power of Popular Fiction* (New York: Fordham University Press, 2018); Kara Keeling, *Queer Times, Black Futures* (New York: New York University Press, 2019); Kristen Lillvis, *Posthuman Blackness and the Black Female Imagination* (Athens: University of Georgia Press, 2017); Cathryn Josefina Merla-Watson and B. V. Olguín, *Altermundos: Latin@ Speculative Literature, Film, and Popular Culture* (Los Angeles: UCLA Chicano Studies Research Center Press, 2017); Therí Alyce Pickens, *Black Madness: Mad Blackness* (Durham, NC: Duke University Press, 2019); Mark

Rifkin, *Fictions of Land and Flesh: Blackness, Indigeneity, Speculation* (Durham, NC: Duke University Press, 2019); David S. Roh, Betsy Huang, and Greta A. Niu, eds., *Techno-Orientalism: Imagining Asia in Speculative Fiction, History and Media* (New Brunswick, NJ: Rutgers University Press, 2015); Ramón Saldívar, "Historical Fantasy, Speculative Realism, and Postrace Aesthetics in Contemporary American Fiction," *American Literary History* 23, no. 3 (2011): 573–99; Stephen Hong Sohn, *Racial Assymmetries: Asian American Fictional Worlds* (New York: New York University Press, 2017); Shelley Streeby, *Imagining the Future of Climate Change: World-Making through Science Fiction and Activism* (Oakland: University of California Press, 2018).

30 Dubey, "Speculative Fictions of Slavery," 780.
31 Ibid., 793.
32 Schalk, *Bodyminds Reimagined*, 2.
33 Ibid., 37.
34 Goyal, *Runaway Genres*, 133.
35 Ibid., 134.
36 Dischinger, "States of Possibility," 83.
37 Whitehead, *The Underground Railroad*, 69, 70.
38 Ibid., 262–63.
39 Ibid., 68–69.
40 Ibid., 208.
41 Ibid., 229.
42 Ibid., 165.
43 Ibid., 165.
44 Quoted in Dischinger, "States of Possibility," 83.
45 Whitehead, *The Underground Railroad*, 211, 215.
46 Ibid., 216.
47 Ibid., 14.
48 Ibid.
49 Ibid., 13.
50 Ibid., 49.
51 Ibid.
52 McKittrick, *Demonic Grounds*, 18.
53 Whitehead, *The Underground Railroad*, 68.
54 Ibid.
55 Ibid.
56 Ibid., 156.
57 Ibid., 147.
58 Ibid.
59 Ibid.
60 Ibid., 262.
61 Douglass, *Narrative of the Life of Frederick Douglass*.
62 Douglass, *Narrative of the Life of Frederick Douglass*.

63 Ibid.
64 McKittrick, *Demonic Grounds*, 18.
65 Douglass, *Narrative of the Life of Frederick Douglass*.
66 Whitehead, *The Underground Railroad*, 266.
67 Ibid.
68 Ibid., 301.
69 Ibid.
70 Ibid., 303.

8. FUGITIVE TRAINS

1 Sorrentino, "Train of the Unknowns."
2 Morales, "The Forgotten Border in the South."
3 The policy was called Programa Frontera Sur and was a partnership between the Mexican government and Ferromex. Mexican immigration beefed up its presence at train stations and at other transit points in an effort to intimidate riders. Ferromex for its part increased train speeds across its network and installed metal poles alongside the tracks at stations to prevent people from running next to the trains as they departed and jumping onboard. Ferromex also hired private security firms to police the trains more assiduously. While these measures were effective in driving migrants off the trains, Sorrento notes that Programa Frontera Sur and other police actions have not stemmed the numbers of those journeying northward but have rather driven migrants to use even less visible—and therefore more dangerous—means and routes for travel.
4 Chávez, "Understanding Migrant Caravans," 11.
5 As *Vox* noted, if the migrant caravan had not existed, President Trump would have had to invent it. It dovetailed perfectly with right-wing fantasies of brown-skinned people breaking like a tidal wave on the pristine shores of the United States. See also Adolfo Flores, "A Huge Caravan of Central Americans Is Headed for the US, and No One in Mexico Dares to Stop Them," *Buzzfeed News*, March 31, 2018, www.buzzfeednews.com.
6 Mark Stevenson and Sonia D. Perez, "Migrant Caravan on the 'Beast' Train to Avoid Mexican Police Raids and Make It to U.S. Border," *USA Today*, April 24, 2019, www.usatoday.com.
7 Jen Sanchez, *We Are Not from Here*, 185.
8 Blue, "Strange Passages," 175.
9 Peters and Turner, "Carceral Mobilities," 2.
10 According to a study that examined the impact of Hurricane Katrina on New Orleans, a disproportionate number "of those seeking refuge at the designated shelters in New Orleans were African American, and three fourths of the 23,000 reported missing and the majority of the 668 reported dead from Louisiana were African American." See Elder et al., "African Americans' Decisions Not to Evacuate New Orleans," S124.
11 "FEMA Chief: Victims Bear Some Responsibility," September 1, 2005, www.cnn.com.

12 Bordwell and Thompson, *Film Art*, 195.

13 Although the follow shot has existed since the early days of film, it became hugely popular in contemporary film. To get a sense of its ubiquity, see Brian Carroll's highly entertaining supercut YouTube video "Keep On Walking," which splices together follow shots from dozens of movies from the 1970s onward, at https://www.youtube.com/watch?v=brZ3MnGU7UY.

14 Bordwell and Thompson, *Film Art*, 199.

15 de Certeau, *The Practice of Everyday Life*, 111.

16 Ibid.

17 Gigliotti, *The Train Journey*, 138.

18 Thompson, "Why Mass Incarceration Matters, 703.

19 Sakala, "Breaking Down Mass Incarceration."

20 Alexander, *The New Jim Crow*, 11.

21 Hernández, *City of Inmates*, 1.

22 Ibid., 2.

23 Merriman, "Afterword: Ordinary Mobilities, Ordinary Incarcerations," 250

24 Moran, Foreword to *Carceral*, xxi–xxii, xxi.

25 Pallister-Wilkins, "Walking Not Flowing."

26 The video was enthusiastically received by the media, which called it "powerful" (*Forbes*), "necessary" (*Salon*), and "replete with stark political imagery" (*New York Times*). The video won a Video Music Award from MTV in the clunkily named category of "Best Fight against the System."

27 A performance of "Yorktown (The World Turned Upside Down)" that was broadcast for the Seventieth Annual Tony Awards in January 2016 is available to view on YouTube at https://www.youtube.com/watch?v=8odeMTS-sLg.

28 Gentry, "Hamilton's Ghosts," 272.

29 Galella, "Being in 'The Room Where It Happens,'" 364.

30 Ibid.

31 Miranda, "Immigrants, We Get the Job Done," https://genius.com/10817093.

32 K'naan was born Keinan Abdi Warsame in 1978 in Mogadishu, Somalia. Along with his family, he fled the country's civil war in 1991 and ultimately landed in Canada. He learned English by listening to rap music. For more information on K'naan's musical output and his life, see Sobral, "The Survivor's Odyssey," 21–36.

Snow Tha Product is the performance name of Claudia Feliciano, a Mexican American rapper born in San Jose, CA in 1987. Her original stage name was Snow White The Product, but after Disney claimed copyright infringement, she shortened it to its present form. For more information on Snow's career, see Onita, "Translating Chicana Rap," 132–44.

Riz Ahmed, sometimes known by the stage name Riz MC, is a British-Pakistani rapper, writer, and actor. A native of Wembley in London and a graduate of Oxford University, Ahmed first gained fame as a musician for his rap "Post 9/11 Blues," released in 2006, which was banned from British radios. Although Ahmed shot to fame as a musician first, he is perhaps better known to Americans as an actor. He played the lead in Mira Nair's adaptation of Mohsin Hamid's novel *The Reluctant Fundamentalist* and appeared in Disney's *Rogue One*. He has been nominated for a Golden Globe and British Independent Film Awards; he is the first actor of Asian descent and the first Muslim to win an Emmy award in an acting category for his performance in the HBO miniseries *The Night Of*.

Residente was born René Pérez Joglar in Puerto Rico in 1978. He is a rapper, writer, and producer; he is also a founder of the rap group Calle 13. He has won twenty-five Grammy awards, the most ever awarded to a Latin artist. For more information, see his website, http://residente.com/.

33 This formulation of the nation as being "founded by immigrants," of course, conveniently and completely erases the fact that the United States is a settler state and that the "founders" were colonists.

34 The role of Laurens was originated on Broadway by Anthony Ramos.

35 The Spanish-to-English translation of these lyrics are taken from the website https://lyricstranslate.com.

36 Part of that transformation can no doubt be traced to the different genres of the two cultural forms, as well as to their intended audiences. Broadway audiences tend to be whiter, wealthier, and older; listeners of the *Hamilton Mixtape* and viewers of the video are probably younger and more politically liberal.

37 Kirby, *Parallel Tracks*, 1.

38 Hayes, "Phantom Carriages," 185.

39 Ibid.

40 Kirby, *Parallel Tracks*, 2.

41 Ibid.

42 Shih, *The Lure of the Modern*, 329.

43 Benjamin, "On Some Motifs in Baudelaire," 314–35, 328; Simmel, "The Metropolis and Mental Life," 11; Schivelbusch, *Railway Journey*, 168, 167.

44 Nicholas Daly makes a similar argument about the novel of sensation, calling the genre "an attempt to register and accommodate the newly speeded-up world of the railway age." The sensation novel performs this accommodation by invoking in the reader a feeling of nervousness. Based on the distinction between nervousness and shock made by Walter Benjamin, Daly argues that "low-level anxiety" is the "subject's *defense* mechanism against" the more traumatic experience of shock. Daly argues that the sensation genre inoculated the subject against the deleterious reaction of shock by instead producing anxiety/nervousness. See Daly, "Railway Novels," 463–64.

45 Ibid.

46 Hayes, "Phantom," 193.

47 Cammaer, "Phantom Rides," 149.

48 Verhoeff, *The West in Early Cinema*, 282.

CODA

1 DeLoughrey, "Satellite Planetarity," 258.

2 White, *Railroaded*, xxii.

3 Kallis, *Degrowth*, 1.

4 Any HSR network built in the United States would almost certainly travel much slower.

5 Peterman, Frittelli, and Mallett, "High Speed Rail (HSR) in the United States."

6 Grunwald, *The New New Deal*, 228.

7 Ibid., 411.

8 Minn, "The Political Economy of High Speed Rail in the United States," 191.

9 Deakin and Henríquez, "Conclusions," 358–59.

10 Albalate and Bel, "High Speed Rail," 337.

11 Fallows, "The California High-Speed Rail Debate."

12 Soper, *Post-Growth Living*, 1.

BIBLIOGRAPHY

Agnew, Vanessa. "Introduction: What Is Reenactment?" *Criticism* 46, no. 3 (2004): 327–39.

Aguiar, Marian. "Making Modernity inside the Technological Space of the Railway." *Cultural Critique* 68 (2008): 66–85.

Aikin, Roger Cushing. "Paintings of Manifest Destiny: Mapping the Nation," *American Art* 14, no. 3 (2000): 78–89.

Albalate, Daniel, and Germà Bel. "High Speed Rail: Lessons for Policy Makers from Experiences Abroad." *Public Administration Review* 72, no. 3 (2012): 335–49.

Albro, Martin. *Railroads Triumphant: The Growth, Rejection, and Rebirth of a Vital American Force.* New York: Oxford University Press, 1992.

Alexander, Michelle. *The New Jim Crow: Mass Incarceration in the Age of Colorblindness.* New York: New Press, 2010.

Anim-Addo, Joan, and Maria Helena Lima. "The Power of the Neo-Slave Narrative Genre." *Callaloo* 40, no. 4 (2017): 3–13.

Arnesen, Eric. *Brotherhoods of Color: Black Railroad Workers and the Struggle for Equality.* Cambridge, MA: Harvard University Press, 2001.

Bady, Aaron. "A *Snowpiercer* Thinkpiece, Not to Be Taken Too Seriously, But for Very Serious Reasons." *New Inquiry*, July 29, 2014. https://thenewinquiry.com.

Bahng, Aimee. *Migrant Futures: Decolonizing Speculation in Financial Times.* Durham, NC: Duke University Press, 2018.

Baker, Houston. *Blues, Ideology, and Afro-American Literature: A Vernacular Theory.* Chicago: University of Chicago Press, 1987.

Bakhtin, Mikhail. "Forms of Time and of the Chrontope in the Novel." In *The Dialogic Imagination*, edited by Michael Holquist, translated by Caryl Emerson and Michael Holquist, 84–258. Austin: University of Texas Press, 1982.

Barnd, Natchee Blu. *Native Space: Geographic Strategies to Unsettle Settler Colonialism.* Corvallis: Oregon State University Press, 2017.

Bauman, Zygmunt. *Modernity and the Holocaust.* Cambridge, UK: Polity, 1989.

Beaumont, Matthew, and Michael Freeman. "Introduction: Tracks to Modernity." In *The Railway and Modernity: Time, Space, and the Machine Ensemble*, edited by Matthew Beaumont, 13–44. Oxford: Peter Lang, 2007.

Belfer, Ella, James D. Ford, and Michelle Maillet. "Representation of Indigenous Peoples in Climate Change Reporting." *Climactic Change* 145 (2017): 57–70.

Benjamin, Walter. "On Some Motifs in Baudelaire." In *Selected Writings. Vol. 4, 1938–1940*, edited by Howard Eiland and Michael W. Jennings, translated by

Edmund Jephcott et al., 314–55. Cambridge, MA: Belknap Press of Harvard University Press, 2003.

Berte, Leigh Ann Litwiller. "Geography by Destination: Rail Travel, Regional Fiction, and the Cultural Production of Geographical Essentialism." In *American Literary Geographies*, edited by Martin Bruckner and Hsuan Hsu, 171–90. Newark: University of Delaware Press, 2007.

Best, Stephen. *None Like Us: Blackness, Belonging, Aesthetic Life*. Durham, NC: Duke University Press, 2018.

Bhabha, Homi K. "'Race,' Time and the Revision of Modernity." *Oxford Literary Review* 13, no. 1–2 (1991): 193–219.

Bianculli, Anthony J. *The American Railroad in the Nineteenth Century. Vol. 3, Track and Structures*. Newark: University of Delaware Press, 2003.

Blue, Ethan. "Strange Passages: Carceral Mobility and the Liminal in the Catastrophic History of American Deportation." *National Identities* 17, no. 2 (2015): 175–94.

Boelhower, William. "The Brave New World of Immigrant Autobiography." *MELUS* 9, no. 2 (1982): 5–23.

Bong Joon-ho, dir. *Snowpiercer*. New York: The Weinstein Company, 2013. Amazon.com.

Bordwell, David, and Kristin Thompson. *Film Art: An Introduction*. 8th ed. Boston: McGraw Hill, 2008.

Brady, Mary Pat. "'Full of Empty': Creating the Southwest as 'Terra Incognita.'" In *Nineteenth Century Geographies: The Transformation of Space from the Victorian Age to the American Century*, edited by Helena Michie and Ronald R. Thomas, 251–64. New Brunswick, NJ: Rutgers University Press, 2003.

Brown, Sterling. "The Blues." *Phylon* 13, no. 4 (1952): 286–92.

Byerman, Keith "'I Did Not Learn Their Name': Female Characters in the Short Fiction of Ralph Ellison." *American Studies* 54, no. 3 (2015): 101–14.

Cammaer, Gerda. "Phantom Rides as Images of the World Unfolding." In *Critical Distance in Documentary Media*, edited by Gerda Cammaer, Blake Fitzpatrick, and Bruno Lessard, 149–67. Cham: Palgrave Macmillan, 2018.

Canavan, Gerry. "'If the Engine Ever Stops, We'd All Die': *Snowpiercer* and Necrofuturism." *Paradoxa* 26 (2014): 1–26.

Carby, Hazel. "It Jus Be's Dat Way Sometime: The Sexual Politics of Women's Blues." In *The Jazz Cadence of American Culture*, edited by Robert G. O'Meally, 469–82. New York: Columbia University Press, 1998.

Carrington, Andre. *Speculative Blackness: The Future of Race in Science Fiction*. Minneapolis: University of Minnesota Press, 2016.

Carson, Scott Alan "Chinese Sojourn Labor and the Transcontinental Railroad," *Journal of Institutional and Theoretical Economics* 161, no. 1 (2005): 80–102.

Cather, Willa. "The Novel Démeublé." *New Republic* 30 (1922): 5–6.

———. *Willa Cather's Short Fiction, 1892–1912*. Edited by Virginia Faulkner. Lincoln: University of Nebraska Press, 1965.

de Certeau, Michel. *The Practice of Everyday Life*. Translated by Steven Rendell. Berkeley: University of California Press, 1988.

Chambers-Letson, Joshua. *A Race So Different: Performance and Law in Asian America*. New York: New York University Press, 2013.

Chang, Gordon. *Ghosts of Gold Mountain: The Epic Story of the Chinese Who Built the Transcontinental Railroad*. New York: Houghton Mifflin, 2019.

Chang, Iris. *Chinese in America*. New York: Penguin, 2004.

Chávez, Karma. "Understanding Migrant Caravans from the Place of Place Privilege." *Departures in Critical Qualitative Research* 8, no. 1 (2009): 9–16.

Cheng, Anne Anlin. *Ornamentalism*. New York: Oxford University Press, 2019.

Cheung, King-Kok. "The Woman Warrior versus the Chinaman Pacific: Must a Chinese American Critic Choose between Feminism and Heroism?" In *Conflicts in Feminism*, edited by Marianne Hirsch and Evelyn Fox Keller, 234–51. New York: Routledge, 1990.

Chin, Frank. "Come All Ye Asian American Writers of the Real and Fake." In *A Companion to Asian American Studies*, edited by Kent Ono, 133–45. New York: Wiley-Blackwell, 2007.

Chin, Frank, and Jeffery Paul Chan. "Racist Love." In *Seeing Through Shuck*, edited by Richard Kostelantz, 65–79. New York: Ballantine, 1972.

———. "Railroad Standard Time." In *The Chinaman Pacific and the Frisco R.R. Co.*, 1–7. Minneapolis: Coffee House Press, 1988.

———. "Riding the Rails with Chickencoop Slim." *Greenfield Review* 6, no. 1–2 (1977): 80–89.

Chmielewska, Ella. "Framing [Con]text: Graffiti and Place." *Space and Culture* 10, no. 2 (2007): 145–69.

Cooper, Anna Julia. *A Voice from the South*. 1892. New York: Oxford University Press, 1998.

Cresswell, Tim. *In Place/Out of Place: Geography, Ideology, and Transgression*. Minneapolis: University of Minnesota Press, 1996.

Daly, Nicholas. "Railway Novels: Sensation Fiction and the Modernization of the Senses." *ELH* 66, no. 2 (1999): 461–87.

Danly, Susan. Introduction to *The Railroad in American Art: Representations of Technological Change*, edited by Susan Danly and Leo Marx, 1–50. Cambridge, MA: MIT Press, 1988.

Davies, Peter Ho. *The Fortunes*. Boston: Houghton Mifflin, 2016.

Davis, Angela. *Blues Legacies and Black Feminism: Gertrude "Ma" Rainey, Bessie Smith, and Billie Holiday*. New York: Vintage, 1998.

Day, Iyko. *Alien Capital: Asian Racialization and the Logic of Settler Colonial Capitalism*. Durham, NC: Duke University Press, 2016.

De Man, Paul. "Autobiography as De-facement." *MLN* 94, no. 5 (1979): 919–30.

Deakin, Elizabeth, and Blas Luis Pérez Henríquez. "Conclusions: High-speed Rail and Sustainability." In *High Speed Rail and Sustainability: Decision-Making and the Political Economy of Investment*, 354–65. New York: Routledge, 2017.

DeLoughrey, Elizabeth. "Satellite Planetarity and the Ends of the Earth." *Public Culture* 26, no. 2 (2014): 257–80.

Denevan, William. "The Pristine Myth: The Landscape of the Americas in 1492," *Annals of the Association of American Geographers* 82, no. 3 (1992): 369–85.

Diggs Colbert, Soyica. *Black Movements: Performance and Cultural Politics*. New Brunswick, NJ: Rutgers University Press, 2017.

Dischinger, Matthew. "States of Possibility in Colson Whitehead's *The Underground Railroad*." *Global South* 11, no 1 (2017): 82–99.

Douglass, Frederick. *Narrative of the Life of Frederick Douglass, an American Slave, Written by Himself*. Boston: Anti-Slavery Office, 1845. https://docsouth.unc.edu/.

———. *The Life and Times of Frederick Douglass: Written by Himself*, 1892. Mineola, MN: Dover, 2003.

Dubey, Madhu. "Speculative Fictions of Slavery." *American Literature* 82, no. 4 (2010), 779–805.

Du Bois, W. E. B. "The Superior Race." In *W. E. B. Du Bois: A Reader*, edited by David Levering Lewis, 470–77. New York: Henry Holt, 1995.

Eakin, Paul John. "Breaking Rules: The Consequences of Self-Narration." *Biography* 24, no. 1 (2001): 113–27.

Elam, Harry, Jr. "The Dialectics of August Wilson's *The Piano Lesson*." *Theatre Journal* 52, no. 3 (2000): 361–79.

Elder, Keith, Sudha Xirasagar, Nancy Miller, Shelly Ann Bowen, Saundra Glover, and Crystal Piper. "African Americans' Decisions Not to Evacuate New Orleans before Hurricane Katrina: A Qualitative Study." *American Journal of Public Health Supplement 1* 97, no. S1 (2007): S124-S129.

Ellison, Ralph. "Boy on a Train." In *Flying Home*, edited by John F. Callahan, 12–21. New York: Vintage International, 1998.

———. "Richard Wright's Blues." In *Shadow and Act*, 77–94. New York: New American Library, 1964.

Eng, David. *Racial Castration: Managing Masculinity in Asian America*. Durham, NC: Duke University Press, 2001.

Estes, Nick. "Fighting for Our Lives: #NoDAPL in Historical Context," *Wicazo Sa Review* 32, no. 2 (2017): 115–122.

Evans, David. "The Development of the Blues." In *The Cambridge Companion to Blues and Gospel*, edited by Allan Moore, 20–43. Cambridge, UK: Cambridge University Press, 2011.

Fallows, James. "The California High-Speed Rail Debate—Kicking Things Off." *Atlantic*, July 9, 2014. www.theatlantic.com.

Fanon, Frantz. *Black Skin, White Masks*. Translated by Richard Philcox. New York: Grove, 1967.

Fisher, Mark. *Capitalist Realism: Is There No Alternative?* Hampshire: Zero Books, 2009.

Foner, Eric. *Gateway to Freedom: The Hidden History of the Underground Railroad*. New York: Doubleday, 2015.

Freedman, Jonathan. "Transgressions of a Model Minority." *Shafar: An Interdisciplinary Journal of Jewish Studies* 23, no. 4 (2005): 69–97.

Galella, Donatella. "Being in 'The Room Where It Happens': *Hamilton*, Obama, and Nationalist Neoliberal Multicultural Inclusion." *Theatre Survey* 59, no. 3 (2018): 363–85.

Gapps, Stephen. "Mobile Monuments: A View of Historical Reenactment and Authenticity from Inside the Costume Cupboard of History." *Rethinking History* 13, no. 3 (2009): 395–409.

Gara, Larry. "The Underground Railroad in Illinois." *Journal of the Illinois State Historical Society* 56, no. 3 (1963): 508–28.

———. "William Still and the Underground Railroad." *Pennsylvania History: A Journal of Mid-Atlantic Studies* 28, no. 1 (1961): 33–44.

Gentry, Philip. "Hamilton's Ghosts: Review Essay," *American Music* 35, no. 2 (2017): 271–80.

Giddens, Anthony. *The Consequences of Modernity*. New York: Polity, 1990.

Gigliotti, Simone. *The Train Journey: Transit, Captivity, and Witnessing in the Holocaust*. New York: Berghahn, 2009.

Gladstone, John. "The Romance of the Iron Horse." *Journal of Decorative and Propaganda Arts* 15 (1990): 6–37.

Gleason, William. *Site Unseen: Architecture, Race, and American Literature*. New York: New York University Press, 2011.

Goodman, Nan. *Shifting the Blame: Literature, Law, and the Theory of Accidents in Nineteenth-Century America*. Princeton, NJ: Princeton University Press, 1998.

Gordon, Sarah. *Passage to Union: How the Railroads Transformed American Life, 1829–1929*. Chicago: Ivan R. Dee, 1996.

Goshert, John. "'Frank Chin Is Not a Part of This Class!' Thinking at the Limits of Asian American Literature." *Jouvert: A Journal of Postcolonial Studies* 4, no. 2 (2000). http://english.chass.ncsu.edu.

Gossett, Thomas. *Race: The History of an Idea in America*. New York: Oxford University Press, 1963. Reprinted 1997.

Goyal, Yogita. *Runaway Genres: The Global Afterlives of Slavery*. New York: New York University Press, 2019.

Grosz, Elizabeth. *Space, Time, and Perversion: Essays on the Politics of Bodies*. New York: Routledge, 1995.

Grunwald, Michael. *The New New Deal: The Hidden Story of Change in the Obama Era*. New York: Simon and Schuster, 2012.

Gyory, Andrew. *Closing the Gate: Race, Politics and the Chinese Exclusion Act*. Chapel Hill: University of North Carolina Press, 1998.

Handy, W. C. *Father of the Blues: An Autobiography*. New York: Macmillan, 1944.

Hartman, Saidiya. *Lose Your Mother: A Journey along the Atlantic Slave Route*. New York: Farrar, Straus and Giroux, 2008.

———. "Venus in Two Acts." *Small Axe* 26, no. 2 (2008): 1–14.

Harvey, David. *The Condition of Postmodernity: An Enquiry into the Origins of Cultural Change*. 1990. Reprint, Malden, MA: Blackwell, 2000.

Hayes, Christian "Phantom Carriages: Reconstructing Hale's Tours and the Virtual Travel Experience." *Early Popular Visual Culture* 7, no. 2 (2009): 185–98.

Heath, Erle. "A Railroad Record That Defies Defeat." *Southern Pacific Bulletin* 16, no. 5 (1928): 3–5. http://cprr.org.

Heim, Cecile. "Neoliberal Violence: Colonial Legacies and Imperialist Strategies of the Contemporary Western Adventure," *Journal of Popular Culture* 51, no. 6 (2018): 1434–52.

Hernández, Kelly Lytle. *City of Inmates: Conquest, Rebellion, and the Rise of Human Caging in Los Angeles, 1771–1965*. Chapel Hill: University of North Carolina Press, 2017.

Hobart, Hi'ilei Julia. "At Home on the Mauna: Ecological Violence and Fantasies of Terra Nullius on Maunakea's Summit." *Native American and Indigenous Studies* 6, no 2 (2019): 30–50.

Holte, James Craig. "The Representative Voice: Autobiography and Ethnic Experience." *MELUS* 9, no. 2 (1982): 33–35.

Horwitz, Howard. *By the Law of Nature: Form and Value in Nineteenth-Century America*. New York: Oxford University Press, 1991.

Hsu, Hsuan. *Geography and the Production of Space in Nineteenth-Century American Literature*. Cambridge, UK: Cambridge University Press, 2010.

Huffard, R. Scott, Jr. *Engines of Redemption: Railroads and the Reconstruction of Capitalism in the New South*. Chapel Hill: University of North Carolina Press, 2019.

Hwang, David Henry. *The Dance and the Railroad*. In *Trying to Find Chinatown: The Selected Plays of David Henry Hwang*, 53–88. New York: Theatre Communications Group, 2000.

Inscoe, John C. *Writing the South through the Self: Explorations in Southern Autobiography*. Athens: University of Georgia Press, 2011.

Jacobs, Harriet. *Incidents in the Life of a Slave Girl: An Autobiographical Account of an Escaped Slave and Abolitionist*, 1861. New York: Simon and Brown, 2018.

Jarrett, Gene Andrew. "What Is Jim Crow?" *PMLA* 128, no. 2 (2013): 388–390.

Jarrett, Michael. "Train Tracks: How the Railroad Rerouted Our Ears." *Strategies* 14, no. 1 (2000): 27–45.

Jerng, Mark. *Racial Worldmaking: The Power of Popular Fiction*. New York: Fordham University Press, 2018.

Johnson, James Weldon. *The Autobiography of an Ex-Colored Man*. New York: Vintage, 1989. First published anonymously in 1912 by Sherman, French (Boston).

Johnsen, Leigh Dana. "Equal Rights and the 'Heathen Chinee': Black Activism in San Francisco, 1865–1875." *Western Historical Quarterly* 11, no. (1980): 57–68.

Johnson, Lindsay. "'I'll Be with Him on the Midnight Train to Georgia': The Traveling Woman in 1920s Blues and 1970s R&B." *American Music Review* 42, no. 2 (2014): 1–6.

Johnston, Matthew N. *Narrating the Landscape: Print Culture and American Expansion in the Nineteenth Century*. Norman: University of Oklahoma Press, 2016.

Kallis, Giorgos. *Degrowth*. Newcastle-upon-Tyne: Agenda, 2018.

Karuka, Manu. *Empire's Tracks: Indigenous Nations, Chinese Workers, and the Transcontinental Railroad*. Berkeley: University of California Press, 2019.

Keeling, Kara. *Queer Times, Black Futures*. New York: New York University Press, 2019.

Kim, Daniel. *Writing Manhood in Black and Yellow: Ralph Ellison, Frank Chin, and the Literary Politics of Identity*. Stanford: Stanford University Press, 2005.

Kim, Juyon. *The Racial Mundane: Asian American Performance and the Embodied Everyday*. New York: New York University Press, 2015.

Lauro, Sarah Juliet, and Karen Embry. "A Zombie Manifesto: The Nonhuman Condition in the Era of Advanced Capitalism." *boundary 2* 35, no. 1 (2008): 85–108.

Kingston, Maxine Hong. *China Men*. 1980. New York: Vintage, 1989.

Kirby, Lynne. *Parallel Tracks: The Railroad and Silent Cinema*. Durham: Duke University Press, 1997.

Lahiri, Jhumpa. *The Namesake*. New York: Mariner Books, 2003.

Lee, Derek. "Postquantum: *A Tale for the Time Being, Atomik Aztek*, and Hacking Modern Space-Time." *MELUS: The Society for the Study of the Multi-ethnic Literature of the United States* 45, no. 1 (2020), 1–26.

Lee, Esther Kim. "Contemporary Asian American Drama." In *The Cambridge History of Asian American Literature*, edited Rajini Shrikanth and Min Hyoung Song, 406–42. London: Cambridge University Press, 2016.

———. *The Theatre of David Henry Hwang*. London: Bloomsbury Methuen Drama, 2015.

Lee, Julia H. *Interracial Encounters: Reciprocal Representations in African and Asian American Literatures, 1896–1937*. New York: New York University Press, 2011.

Lee, Rachel. *The Exquisite Corpse of Asian America: Biopolitics, Biosociality, and Posthuman Ecologies*. New York: New York University Press, 2014.

Lee, Robert G. *Orientals: Asian Americans in Popular Culture*. Philadelphia: Temple University Press, 1999.

Li, David. "China Men: Maxine Hong Kingston and the American Canon," *American Literary History* 2, no. 3 (1990): 482–502.

Lillvis, Kristen. *Posthuman Blackness and the Black Female Imagination*. Athens: University of Georgia Press, 2017.

Lipsitz, George. *How Racism Takes Place*. Philadelphia: Temple University Press, 2011.

Lowe, Lisa. "Autobiography out of Empire." *Small Axe* 13, no. 1 (2009): 98–111.

———. *Immigrant Acts: On Asian American Cultural Politics*. Durham, NC: Duke University Press, 1996.

Lucenti, Lisa Marie. "Willa Cather's *My Ántonia*: Haunting the Houses of Memory." *Twentieth Century Literature* 46, no. 2 (2000): 193–213.

Lui, Mary. *The Chinatown Trunk Mystery: Murder, Miscegenation and Other Dangerous Encounters in Turn-of-the-Century New York*. New York: Princeton University Press, 2005.

Lummis, Charles. "The Artists' Paradise." *Out West* 28, no 6 (June 1906): 437–51.

Lye, Colleen. *America's Asia: Racial Form and American Literature, 1893–1945*. Princeton, NJ: Princeton University Press, 2005.

———. "The Literary Case of Wen Ho Lee." *Journal of Asian American Studies* 14, no. 2 (2011): 249–82.

Maeda, Daryl. "Black Panthers, Red Guards, and Chinamen: Constructing Asian American Identity through Performing Blackness, 1969–1972." *American Quarterly* 57, no. 4 (2005): 1079–1103.

Marshall, Ian. "Steel Wheels on Paper: The Railroad in American Literature." *Railroad History* 165 (1991): 37–62.

Martin, Theodore. "Temporality and Literary Theory." In *Oxford Research Encyclopedias in Literature*, edited by Paula Rabinowitz. New York: Oxford University Press, 2016. doi:10.1093/acrefore/9780190201098.013.122.

Marx, Leo. *The Machine in the Garden: Technology and the Pastoral Ideal in America.* Thirty-fifth anniversary edition. New York: Oxford University Press, 2000.

McGurl, Mark. "Zombie Renaissance: Eating Your Brains." *n+1*, April 27, 2010. http://nplusonemag.com.

Merla-Watson, Cathryn Josefina, and B. V. Olguín. *Altermundos: Latin@ Speculative Literature, Film, and Popular Culture.* Los Angeles: University of California, Los Angeles Chicano Studies Research Center Press, 2017.

Merriman, Peter. "Afterword: Ordinary Mobilities, Ordinary Incarcerations." In *Carceral Mobilities: Interrogating Movement in Incarceration*, edited by Jennifer Turner and Kimberley Peters, 250–51. London: Routledge, 2017.

McKittrick, Katherine. *Demonic Grounds: Black Women and the Cartographies of Struggle.* Minneapolis: University of Minnesota Press, 2006.

Miller, Angela. "Everywhere and Nowhere: The Making of the National Landscape." *American Literary History* 4, no. 2 (1992): 207–29.

Miller, J. Hillis. "Narrative." In *Critical Terms for Literary Study,* 2nd ed., edited by Frank Lentricchia and Thomas McLaughlin, 66–79. Chicago: University of Chicago Press, 1990.

Miller, Stuart Creighton. *The Unwelcome Immigrant: The American Image of the Chinese, 1785–1882.* Berkeley: University of California Press, 1969.

Minn, Michael. "The Political Economy of High Speed Rail in the United States." *Mobilities* 8, no. 2 (2013): 185–200.

Mitchell, W. J. T. "Imperial Landscape." In *Landscape and Power*, 2nd ed., 5–34. Chicago: University of Chicago Press, 2002.

———. Introduction to *Landscape and Power*, 2nd ed., 1–4. Chicago: University of Chicago Press, 2002.

Moran, Dominique. Foreword to *Carceral Mobilities: Interrogating Movement in Incarceration*, edited by Jennifer Turner and Kimberley Peters, xxi–xxii. London: Routledge, 2017.

Moreau, Toni, and Derek H. Alderman. "Graffiti Hurts and the Eradication of Alternative Landscape Expression." *Geographical Review* 101, no. 1 (2011), 106–24.

Mufti, Aamir. *Enlightenment in the Colony: The Jewish Question and the Crisis of Postcolonial Culture.* Princeton, NJ: Princeton University Press, 2007.

Musset, Louis Charles Alfred de. "Rappelle-toi." In *The Penguin Book of French Poetry 1920–1950*, edited and translated by W. H. Rees, 111. London: Penguin, 1992.

Nelson, Scott Reynolds. *Iron Confederacies: Southern Railways, Klan Violence, and Reconstruction*. Chapel Hill: University of North Carolina Press, 1999.

Nguyen, Viet. "The Remasculinization of Chinese America: Race, Violence, and the Novel." *American Literary History* 12, nos. 1–2 (2000): 130–57.

Nishime, Leilani. "Engendering Genre: Gender and Nationalism in *China Men* and *The Woman Warrior*." *MELUS* 20, no. 1 (1995): 67–82.

Nye, David. "Technology, Nature, and American Origin Stories." *Environmental History* 8, no. 1 (2003): 8–24.

Oishi, Eve. "The Asian American Fakeness Canon, 1972–2002." *Aztlán: A Journal of Chicano Studies* 32, no. 1 (2007): 197–204.

Okihiro, Gary. *Margins and Mainstreams: Asians in American History and Culture*. Seattle: University of Washington Press, 1994. Reprinted 2014.

Onita, Adriana. "Translating Chicana Rap: Snow Tha Product." *TranscUlturAl* 9, no. 1 (2017), 132–44.

Pallister-Wilkins, P. "Walking Not Flowing: The Migrant Caravan and the Geoinfrastructuring of Unequal Mobility." *Society+Space*, February 21, 2019. https://dare.uva.nl.

Palmer, William Jackson. *Report of Surveys across the Continent in 1867–68 on the Thirty-Fifth and Thirty-Second Parallels, for a Route Extending the Kansas Pacific Railway to the Pacific Ocean at San Francisco and San Diego*. Philadelphia: W. B. Selheimer Printer, 1869.

Palumbo-Liu, David. *Asian/American: Historical Crossings of a Racial Frontier*. Stanford: Stanford University Press, 1999.

Pease, Donald. "American Exceptionalism." In *Oxford Bibliographies in American Literature*, edited by Jackson Bryer and Richard Kopley. New York: Oxford University Press, 2018. doi:10.1093/OBO/9780199827251-0176.

Peterman, David Randall, John Fritelli, and William J. Mallett. "High Speed Rail (HSR) in the United States." *Congressional Research Service*, December 8, 2009. www.crs.gov.

Peters, Kimberley, and Jennifer Turner. "Carceral Mobilities: A Manifesto for Mobilities, an Agenda for Carceral Studies." In *Carceral Mobilities: Interrogating Movement in Incarceration*, edited by Jennifer Turner and Kimberley Peters, 1–14. New York: Routledge, 2016.

Pickens, Therí Alyce. *Black Madness: Mad Blackness*. Durham, NC: Duke University Press, 2019.

Rabaka, Reiland. "The Souls of White Folk: W. E. B. Du Bois's Critique of White Supremacy and Contributions to Critical White Studies." *Journal of African American Studies* 11 (2007): 1–15.

Rabine, Leslie. "No Lost Paradise: Social Gender and Symbolic Gender in the Writings of Maxine Hong Kingston." *Signs* 12, no. 3 (1987): 471–92.

Richter, Amy. *Home on the Rails: Women, the Railroad, and the Rise of Public Domesticity*. Chapel Hill: University of North Carolina Press, 2005.

Rifkin, Mark. *Fictions of Land and Flesh: Blackness, Indigeneity, Speculation.* Durham, NC: Duke University Press, 2019.

Riis, Jacob. *How the Other Half Lives.* New York: Charles Scribner's Sons, 1890. https://www.bartleby.com.

Roach, Joseph. *Cities of the Dead: Circum-Atlantic Performance.* New York: Columbia University Press, 1996.

Roh, David S., Betsy Huang, and Greta A. Niu, eds. *Techno-Orientalism: Imagining Asia in Speculative Fiction, History and Media.* New Brunswick, NJ: Rutgers University Press, 2015.

Romero, Channette. "The Politics of the Camera: Visual Storytelling and Sovereignty in Victor Masayesva's Itam, Hakim, Hopiit." *Studies in American Indian Literatures* 22, no. 1 (2010): 49-75.

Runte, Alfred. "Promoting the Golden West: Advertising and the American Railroad." *California History* 70, no. 1 (1991): 62–75.

Rushdy, Ashraf. "The Neo-Slave Narrative." In *The Cambridge Companion to the African American Novel,* edited by Maryemma Graham, 87–105. Cambridge, UK: Cambridge University Press, 2004.

Sabine, Maureen. *Maxine Hong Kingston's Broken Book of Life.* Honolulu: University of Hawai'i Press, 2004.

Sakala, Leah. "Breaking Down Mass Incarceration in the 2010 Census: State-by-State Incarceration Rates by Race/Ethnicity." Prison Policy Initiative, May 28, 2014. https://www.prisonpolicy.org.

Saldívar, Ramón. "Historical Fantasy, Speculative Realism, and Postrace Aesthetics in Contemporary American Fiction." *American Literary History* 23, no. 3 (2011): 573–99.

Sanchez, Jenny Torres. *We Are Not from Here.* New York: Philomel, 2020.

Saxton, Alexander. "The Army of Canton in the High Sierra." *Pacific Historical Review* 35, no. 2 (1966): 141–152.

———. *The Indispensable Enemy: Labor and the Anti-Chinese Movement in California.* Berkeley: University of California Press, 1995.

Schalk, Sami. *Bodyminds Reimagined: (Dis)ability, Race, and Gender in Black Women's Speculative Fiction.* Durham, NC: Duke University Press, 2018.

Schivelbusch, Wolfgang. *Railway Journey: The Industrialization of Time and Space in the Nineteenth Century.* Berkeley: University of California Press, 1977.

Schley, David. "A Natural History of the Early American Railroad." *Early American Studies* 13, no. 2 (2015): 443–66.

Schulz, Kathryn. "The Perilous Lure of the Underground Railroad." *New Yorker,* August 15, 2016. www.newyorker.com.

Scott, Emily Eliza, and Kirsten Swenson. "Introduction: Contemporary Art and the Politics of Land Use." In *Critical Landscapes: Art, Space, Politics,* edited by Emily Eliza Scott and Kirsten Swenson, 1–16. Oakland: University of California Press, 2015.

Sharpe, Christina. *In the Wake: On Blackness and Being.* Durham, NC: Duke University Press, 2016.

Shih, Shumei. *The Lure of the Modern: Writing Modernism in Semicolonial China, 1917–1943*. Berkeley: University of California Press, 2001.

Shimakawa, Karen. *National Abjection: The Asian American Body Onstage*. Durham, NC: Duke University Press, 2002.

Simmel, Georg. "The Metropolis and Mental Life." In *The Blackwell City Reader*, edited by Gary Bridge and Sophie Watson, 11–19. Malden, MA: Wiley-Blackwell, 2010.

Smith, Henry Nash. "Walt Whitman and Manifest Destiny." *Huntington Library Quarterly* 10, no. 4 (1947): 373–389.

Smith, Valerie. "Neo-slave Narratives." In *The Cambridge Companion to the African American Slave Narrative*, edited by Audrey A. Fisch, 168–88. Cambridge, UK: Cambridge University Press, 2007.

Sobral, Ana. "The Survivor's Odyssey: K'naan's 'The Dusty Philosopher' as a Modern Epic," *African American Review* 46, no. 1 (2013): 21–36.

Sohn, Stephen Hong. *Racial Assymmetries: Asian American Fictional Worlds*. New York: New York University Press, 2017.

Soper, Kate. *Post-Growth Living: For an Alternative Hedonism*. London: Verso, 2020.

Sorrentino, Joseph. "Train of the Unknowns." *Commonweal*, November 26, 2012. https://www.commonwealmagazine.org.

Spicer, Jakki. "The Author Is Dead, Love Live the Author: Autobiography and the Fantasy of the Individual." *Criticism* 47, no. 3 (2005): 387–403.

Steinberg, Michael. "Writing Literary Memoir: Are We Obliged to Tell the Real Truth?" *Fourth Genre: Explorations in Nonfiction* 1, no. 1 (1999): 142–47.

Streeby, Shelley. *Imagining the Future of Climate Change: World-Making through Science Fiction and Activism*. Oakland: University of California Press, 2018.

Strobridge, Edson. "The Central Pacific Railroad and the Legend of Cape Horn, 1865–1866." Central Pacific Railroad Museum. June 3, 2003. http://cprr.org.

Swartout, Robert. "Kwantung to Big Sky: The Chinese in Montana, 1864–1900." In *Chinese on the American Frontier*, edited by Arif Dirlik, 367–82. Lanham, MD: Rowman & Littlefield, 2001.

Tate, Claudia. *Domestic Allegories of Political Desire: The Black Heroine's Text at the Turn of the Century*. New York: Oxford University Press, 1992.

Thompson, Heather Ann. "Why Mass Incarceration Matters: Rethinking Crisis, Decline, and Transformation in Postwar American History" *Journal of American History* 97, no. 3 (2010): 703–34.

Thoreau, Henry David. *Walden; Or, Life in the Woods*. Boston: Ticknor and Fields, 1854. https://www.gutenberg.org.

Trachtenberg, Alan. *The Incorporation of America: Culture and Society in the Gilded Age*. New York: Hill and Wang, 1982.

Urry, John. *Mobilities*. Cambridge, UK: Polity, 2007.

Vartija, Devin. "Racism and Modernity." *International Journal for History, Culture and Modernity* 7 (2019): 1–15.

Verhoeff, Nanna. *The West in Early Cinema: After the Beginning*. Amsterdam: Amsterdam University Press, 2006.

Vimalassery, Manu. "Counter-sovereignty." *J19: The Journal of Nineteenth Century Americanists* 2, no. 1 (2014): 142–48.

Ward, James. *Railroads and the Character of America, 1820–1887*. Knoxville: University of Tennessee Press, 1986.

Welke, Barbara. *Recasting American Liberty: Gender, Race, Law, and the Railroad Revolution, 1865–1920*. Cambridge, UK: Cambridge University Press, 2001.

White, Richard. *Railroaded: The Transcontinentals and the Making of Modern America*. New York: W. W. Norton, 2011.

Whitehead, Colson. *The Underground Railroad*. New York: Doubleday, 2016.

Whitman, Walt. "Passage to India." In *Leaves of Grass*. Boston: James R. Osgood and Company, 1881. https://whitmanarchive.org.

Whitmore, Tomás. "Immigrants (We Get the Job Done)." Produced by Kimberly Stuckwisch, Melora Donoghue. YouTube, June 28, 2017. Video, 6:08. https://www.youtube.com.

Williams, Sherley A. "The Blue Roots of Contemporary Afro-American Poetry." *Massachusetts Review* 18, no. 3 (1977): 542–54.

Wilson, Rob. "Techno-euphoria and the Discourse of the American Sublime." *boundary 2* 19, no.1 (1992): 204–29.

Wilson, Terry P. "American Art and Its Images of Native Americans." In *Standing Rainbows: Railroad Promotion of Art, the West, and Its Native People. A Special Exhibition of Paintings from the Collection of the Atchison, Topeka & Santa Fe Railway*. Topeka: Kansas State Historical Society, 1981. Exhibition catalogue.

Wilson, Woodrow. "President Wilson's Personal Appeal." In *Advocate for Peace*, Vol. 79, 144–45. Washington DC: American Peace Society, 1917.

Wilwhite, Kevin. "His Mind Was Full of Absences: Whitman at the Scene of Writing." *ELH* 71, no. 4 (2004): 921–948.

Wolfe, Thomas. "Dark in the Forest, Strange as Time." In *The Complete Short Stories of Thomas Wolf*, edited by Francis E. Skipp, 167–76. New York: Simon and Schuster, 1989.

Wong, Sau-ling Cynthia. *Reading Asian American Literature: From Necessity to Extravagance*. Princeton, NJ: Princeton University Press, 1993.

Wong, Sau-ling, and Jeffrey Santa Ana. "Gender and Sexuality in Asian American Literature." *Signs* 25, no. 1 (1999): 171–226.

Wright, John B. "Land Tenure: The Spatial Musculature of the American West." In *Western Places, American Myths: How We Think about the West*, edited by Gary Hausladen, 85–110. Reno: University of Nevada Press, 2003.

Wright, Michelle M. *Physics of Blackness: Beyond the Middle Passage Epistemology*. Minneapolis: University of Minnesota Press, 2015.

Yancy, George. "Black Embodied Wounds and the Traumatic Impact of the White Imaginary." In *Trauma and Transcendence: Suffering and the Limits of Theory*, edited by Eric Boynton and Peter Capretto, 142–62. New York: Fordham University Press, 2018.

Zega, Michael E., and John E. Gruber. *Travel by Train: The American Railroad Poster, 1870–1950*. Bloomington: Indiana University Press, 2002.

Zhang, C. Pam. *How Much of These Hills Is Gold*. New York: Riverhead, 2020.

INDEX

JULIA H. LEE is Associate Professor of Asian American Studies at the University of California at Irvine. She is the author of *Interracial Encounters: Reciprocal Representations in African and Asian American Literatures, 1896–1937* (New York University Press, 2011) and *Understanding Maxine Hong Kingston* (University of South Carolina Press, 2018). She teaches courses on Asian American literature, Asian American popular culture, and race and urban space.